Against the Wind

AGAINST THE WIND

Stories by Martin A. Hansen

Translated, with an introduction, by H. Wayne Schow

Frederick Ungar Publishing Co.   New York

The stories are translated from the original Danish by arrangement with Gyldendalske Boghandel, Nordisk Forlag A.S., Copenhagen.
Source volumes are the following: *Tornebusken; Agerhønen;* and *Konkyljen.* © 1946, 1947, 1955 by Gyldendalske Boghandel, Nordisk Forlag A.S., Copenhagen
English translations
Copyright © 1979 by Frederick Ungar Publishing Co., Inc.
Printed in the United States of America
Designed by Jacqueline Schuman
Library of Congress Cataloging in Publication Data
Hansen, Martin Alfred, 1909–1955.
  Against the wind.
  CONTENTS: The partridge.—The owl.—The book.—The morning hour.
—Sacrifice.—The soldier and the girl.—The just.—The birds. [etc.]
  I. Title
PZ3.H19866Ag 1979   [PT8175.H33]   839.8′1′372
ISBN 0-8044-2342-3   78-20926

Contents

Introduction

A writer in a language infrequently understood beyond his own small country does not easily win an international reputation. A few Scandinavians—literary giants like Kierkegaard, Ibsen, and Strindberg—managed to do it because, in addition to being great artists, they were revolutionary and ahead of their time. Viewed from an international perspective, Martin A. Hansen (1909–1955) is not a towering or unique figure. But his work can justifiably be compared with that of a Knut Hamsun, a Pär Lagerkvist, or a Sigrid Undset, and he too deserves the wider recognition they have gained.

Hansen is generally acknowledged as the greatest Danish author of his generation and among the foremost Danish writers of this century. He came to artistic maturity during the war-scarred forties. In this spiritually troubled time, Hansen focused the cultural, ethical, and existential concerns of his countrymen in such a way as to appeal to sophisticated and common readers alike. His writing seemed to embody what many were searching for—a way of believing that did not deny or distort the grim realities they had recently experienced. Perhaps that is why his books sold during his lifetime in far greater numbers than is usual for works of serious literature. Two decades after Hansen's death and the passing of the immediate conditions out of which his writing grew, his broad appeal, as measured by book sales, continues. How does one explain this lasting appeal?

Part of the answer lies in the curious, even paradoxical, way that Hansen initially engages his readers, as those coming to his fiction for the first time will discover. Our initial impression is that here is an author with whom we can feel "comfortable." His language seems disarmingly simple, relaxed, unpretentious—it does not intimidate us. Its rhythms are the rhythms of oral storytelling, and its idiom and imagery those of everyday reality. Although Hansen's style varies from story to story, especially because he uses a variety of narrative voices, it consistently suggests a feet-on-the-ground, straightforward view of reality. It implies an honest, sincere presence behind it.

One important element in Hansen's expression, a rich vein of humor, is never long submerged. Often it is playful, yet even when it arises from a perception of grimly painful ironies, this humor is never sardonic. Rather it is humor characterized by tolerance and warmth and seems to originate in a kindhearted view of humanity. It is difficult not to like and trust immediately the Hansen who stands behind this humor.

The simplicity that is so engaging to a reader is also felt in the vigorous directness of Hansen's narration. He is a natural storyteller. Because of his uncanny instinct for selection, combination, and pacing, his stories engross us quickly and sustain our interest at a high level to their often startling conclusions. We are simply drawn in and held. In an age when artistic fiction has often spurned conventional storytelling in favor of subtle spatial and symbolic patterns, most readers still are grateful to encounter old fashioned narrative power.

But once caught up in the web of Hansen's engaging style, some readers discover that their initial impression of simplicity is gradually undermined. They become increasingly aware (and here is where the paradox enters) that formalistically Hansen's fictions are subtler than they had thought, that his understanding and delineation of human nature are anything but simpleminded, and that his analysis of difficult ethical questions is searching and provocative. When one pauses to contemplate Hansen's writing, this paradoxical yoking of simplicity and complexity in both vision and form may well be one of its most striking features. Certainly the tensions generated by this joining of the subtle and the seemingly naïve affect even unsophisticated readers in an unsettling way.

Hansen's origins and his subsequent spiritual odyssey shed much light on these contrasts in his work. The eldest son of religious parents who were small farmers, he grew up in Stevns, a peninsular region south of Copenhagen. There he was exposed to the last phase of the dying *almue kultur*, i.e., the culture of the rural commoners derived from the old peasant tradition. It was a blend of the simple, steady agricultural life and the values of Christianity, a conservative life style predicated on hard work and interdependence, on faith and resignation. One can scarcely overemphasize the degree to which Hansen's character and sympathies were influenced by this cultural background. Markedly calm in manner, deliberate in thought, measured in speech, he conveyed throughout his life the impression of a man possessed of balance and good common sense. At seventeen Hansen left the farming life to enter Haslev Seminary, and subsequently he became a public school teacher in Copenhagen. But just as James Joyce, living in self-chosen continental exile, wrote only about the Irish, so Hansen, living in an urban setting, chose largely to depict the milieu in which he had been formed as a youth, the farms and villages of the Danish countryside. The rural life is Hansen's *terra cognita*. One will not find in any language more vivid representation of the physical ambience, the daily tasks, and the social, economic, and religious life of country people. Hansen makes us touch the pulse of rural existence, makes us feel its privations and its satisfactions.

This rural background contributed to Hansen's love for nature. Consistently his fiction is linked to birds and seasons, fields and plants, water and weather. And his vision of man's relation to nature is strongly influenced by the values of his *almue* cultural heritage. One feels as a constant strain in his work that people ought to be in touch with nature—in touch with seasons and other natural cycles, in touch with the land, in touch with animals, in touch with other humans at a very basic level. Being in touch is partly a matter of recognizing homely correspondences between man and other facets of nature. And being in touch teaches vital lessons—appreciation of simple beauty, acceptance of vicissitude, the rewards of hard work, the value of a generous heart. It teaches humility, tolerance, contentment.

To be in harmony with nature at this fundamental level implies a reverence for natural creation. In fact, Hansen's writing rests on a certain religiosity. Partly it is Christian, for Hansen's religious background was a form of devout low-church Lutheranism, and in his own vision of Danish rural life he could never entirely remove the parish church from the physical and spiritual center of the community. But his religiosity was at least as much pagan in its essence; like a primitive theology, it was linked to crops and seasons, to light and darkness, to life and death.

Whether this natural piety is evident on the surface of Hansen's fiction, as it occasionally is, or whether it simply is there on a subtler level, most readers have responded positively to its affirmative implications. Beyond merely feeling comfortable with Hansen, they have been grateful in an uncertain world for even an indirect assurance that some things endure and give meaning to existence. Hansen thus seems to them a good man. Surely his values must be right, surely he himself must be in touch.

But was he? The answer derived from a careful reading of Hansen's fiction is by no means a confident, unqualified yes. Clearly he did not find it easy personally to establish harmony between himself and his environment, nor is his picture of rural life a simple idyl. His stories are filled with people out of touch with self and others, burdened with weakness, beset with doubt, cut off finally from universal meaning. Nor does he set up such situations merely as straw men to be knocked over by a philosophy of simplicity and natural harmony. As in the fiction of Dostoevsky or Thomas Mann, a powerful tension is developed precisely because the alternative vision is so credible. Here is the other Hansen, a man who knew ambiguity, doubt, and anguish at first hand.

Again Hansen's biography is helpful as we attempt to understand this Janus face and its influence on his art. In the heady intellectual atmosphere of Haslev Seminary, the youth espoused both Darwinism and atheism. From his father he had inherited the seeds of political radicalism, and in the early thirties when his social indignation was aroused by—among other things—the desperate hard times experienced by small farmers like his father, he became a communist sympathizer. Thus in the late 1920s and early 1930s Hansen, like many a young radical before him, repudiated —intellectually at least—his more traditional religious, social, and political roots. But with the evolution of the thirties into the forties, his own experience gradually disclosed to him the inadequacies of the rational and theoretical systems he had accepted. Into the resulting intellectual vacuum flowed nihilism with all of its terrible enticements. He was doubly vulnerable to it, first in his view of himself as a poet, second in his responses to external developments in the world around him.

Like Thomas Mann, Hansen was persuaded that from his paternal and maternal progenitors he had inherited a dual nature. His father's people had been comfortably established farmers, steady and responsible, respected among their rural neighbors. His mother—of a more artistic and passionate temperament—was the daughter of a poor woodcutter, from a family whose history was marked by excess, irrationality, and tragedy. "Two kinds of blood course in my veins," he said. To the first he attributed his feelings of social and ethical responsibility, to the second his dedication—both reluctant and willing—to the poet's calling, including its asocial and demonic dimensions.

Indeed, in the years leading up to 1946, Hansen's own experience persuaded him that the artist is one of the damned. Art was a sickness which consumed one physically and humanly, and at the same time the artist's perceptions were sharpened, not only by physical illness but by moral perversity as well:

> The pen has stunted the fellow, and ink has made him a predator and a parasite [Hansen once wrote]. This insatiable spider, the poet, must suck the blood from everything in order to fill his inkwell. Yes, there is something evil and devilish in his power to conceive and project, for he devours and destroys the living.

Like Mann's Tonio Kröger, Hansen was convinced for a time that the artist bore Cain's mark on his brow. In a fragment from this period we read:

> Cain fled and found a woman of unknown origin, a woman not created by that old, strict, and simple Creator we are told of. With her Cain founded a race cursed with the burden of artistic insight. Few of those who buy a ream of paper and rent a typewriter in order to write immortal works in three months have the slightest suspicion of this. But the old ones knew it. The poet must ride Pegasus, who is the son of Medusa the terrible, whose countenance no one can look on without turning to stone. Medusa the terrible lurks behind the veil of poetry.

This is the other side of the outwardly calm and imperturbable Hansen. This is the man with a guilty conscience who felt alienated from family and social responsibility. This is the man who was irrationally convinced that he would die young, who therefore drove himself demonically for the fourteen years of his teaching career, hunched over the typewriter night after night "until the first streetcars clattered in the distance." This is the man who, plagued with chronic headaches and, paradoxically, sleeplessness, relied increasingly on strong drugs and stimulants to enable him to continue in this costly service, undermining his health in the process and hastening the premature death he feared.

The external impetus to Hansen's nihilism was the overwhelming impact of World War II on his sensibilities. At first he was deeply ashamed of the Danish capitulation and frustrated that he and others were not called up to resist the German invaders, however futile the effort may have been. Subsequently, under the conditions of enemy occupation, he intensified his personal search for meaning, and to his horror it disclosed the lack of an all-embracing meaning in life—in a word, absurdity: "Europe's immense harvest of youthful corpses, piled in heaps, burned on ashen mounds, buried in the pits of Maidanek." Death, the ultimate negation, seemed ubiquitous at home and abroad, and it thrust itself into his writing. Drift toward death, angst in the face of death, refusal to accept death become central themes in his work during this period.

The only adequate response, he became convinced, was existential. One must begin not with preconceived formulas but

with experience. Accordingly, when the Danish resistance movement came to enlist his talent, he responded not in the name of
nationalism or democracy, but simply because an inner voice
demanded resistance and he had no right to deny that voice.

Eventually Hansen found a way out of his nihilism in what
he called ethical pessimism. If one can imagine a point of con-
vergence and overlapping in the thought of Kierkegaard, Dostoevsky, Lagerkvist, and T. S. Eliot, he will have a notion of the
position Hansen gradually defined. With these writers he agreed
that man cannot avoid responsibility, however meaningless the
world around him may seem. Like them, he was fundamentally a
religious man who repudiated institutionalized Christianity; like
them he passed through a furnace of doubt, as Dostoevsky phrased
it. Like the latter in particular, he implied in his writing that one
who feels responsibility cannot avoid suffering and sorrow. But if,
like Kierkegaard and Dostoevsky, Hansen was driven to find a
personal meaning beyond nihilism, he was convinced that the
existentially aware modern man must first pass through the abyss
of despair. In his notebooks he wrote:

> I could remain a poet of the night and damnation if I let
> myself be carried along, but I will not. . . . I have stood and
> stared into the abyss, and it tempted me. I could easily sink
> into it, and I could depict men as things and monsters; that
> would perhaps make me more interesting as a poet, but
> destructive.

And so he made a Kierkegaardian leap, a choice beyond reason to
build rather than destroy.

Gradually he turned back to Christianity, not to that of his
youth but to an existential Christianity marked by unsettling
irony, one which attacks most vigorously the self-satisfaction of
the religious establishment. However, as one critic has observed,
the Christianity in his works usually rests more on the will to believe than on confident capability. A number of his principal
characters are but dilettantes of faith in this way.

In view of these facts, we understand why it was that Hansen's
most powerful fiction was forged in the years between 1939 and
1947. For these were years of extreme personal anguish in which

the temptations of nihilism were seductively presented to him by
the madness of Europe as well as by his own inner demons. But
it was also a time in which he struggled intensely to find elements
in his *almue* cultural past that could be viable in an existential
world. It is not difficult to understand, then, that he should have
struck so responsive a chord in the hearts of his contemporary
countrymen. They sensed that he was a good man with decent
instincts, one earnestly seeking to affirm the best of their cultural
past: at the same time they saw that he was an intelligent man
who would not underestimate the difficulty of existence, an intensely honest man who would not flinch from the truth.

Paradoxically, Hansen's production of fiction diminished quan-
titatively and, with several exceptions, qualitatively after 1947. It
was as if in his intense effort to find a positive vision he triumphed
too definitely, in the process eliminating that fruitful, if terrible,
tension between nihilism and affirmation under the pressure of
which his best fiction had been formed.

In his twenty years as a writer, Hansen produced a substantial
body of work—five novels, four collections of short stories, three
volumes of travel impressions, a large and impressive work on
Denmark's cultural past, four essay collections, plus numerous essays published in periodicals. Especially notable among these are
Jonatans Rejse * (1941), a satiric picaresque tale in which a smith,
having captured the devil in a bottle, sets out to bring him to the
king; *Lykkelige Kristoffer* (1945), an episodic quest novel about an
impoverished young nobleman who leaves the provinces and
journeys to Copenhagen against the background of the religious
wars of the Reformation; *Tornebusken* (1946) and *Agerhønen*
(1947), collections of short fiction from which most of the stories
in this volume have been taken; *Løgneren* (1950), Hansen's best-
known novel, presented as the anguished journal entries of a
schoolmaster on a small Danish island; and *Orm og Tyr* (1952),
an extraordinary treatment—both literary and historical—of the
relationships of pagan and Christian elements in Nordic culture.

* For English versions of the Danish titles, see the Chronology, pp. 275-
76.

Only two of these books have been translated into English in their entirety, *Løgneren* as *The Liar* in 1954 and *Lykkelige Kristoffer* as *Lucky Kristoffer* in 1973. Now with the publication of this volume, English language readers will have convenient access to a substantial part of Hansen's impressive short fiction. In this format, the cumulative impact of his stories can be judged, and as the examples of many of the best short fiction writers demonstrate—Joyce, Lawrence, and Kafka, for example—the value of the whole exceeds the simple sum of the pieces considered individually. The stories included here have been selected not merely for their intrinsic merit but as far as possible to illustrate the versatility of the writer in range and treatment of subject matter. As a group they give the reader a broader impression of Hansen's artistic capabilities than a single novel, however excellent, could do.

A few examples will suggest the diversity of theme and setting that the reader can expect to encounter here. The wonder of youthful discovery, the mystery of youthful awakening are presented in autobiographical stories like "The Book" and "The Morning Hour." The nihilistic impact of war is the subject of two greatly dissimilar pieces, the amusing but ultimately disturbing fable called "The Soldier and the Girl," in which a young man spiritually scarred by war seeks and keeps a private appointment with death, and the intensely personal, anguished lyricism of "March Night," in which the speaker responds in the context of a loved one's death to the absurdity which has shaken Europe. The burden of isolation and resulting loneliness is felt in several of the stories, notably in "Haavn," "Daniel," and "The Soldier and the Girl." Even more pervasive is man's confrontation with evil in a world where suffering is avoidable only by the insensitive and the cowardly; two powerful stories, "Sacrifice," a study of superstition and self-interest, and "The Harvest Feast," which examines the relationship of guilt and faith, stand out especially in their treatment of these themes.

Hansen was intrigued by the paradox that strength sometimes emerges from certain kinds of weakness, an idea examined in "The Birds," a playful but at the same time intensely serious tale of an inept priest, to a lesser degree in "Daniel," the story of a consumptive young man on the verge of death. And perhaps it was inevitable that Hansen should write about the burden of the artist; he has done that in "The Just," a story in which a real artist, who must pay for his creativity with a kind of human weakness and tragic alienation, is contrasted with his dilettante son who avoids the father's extremity for the sake of goodness and bourgeois security. The shadow of Kierkegaard hovers over several stories in which protagonists must struggle to find a faith adequate in an absurd world, in "Harvest Feast" for example, in which a young priest must reject the clichéd generalities associated with his role, must plunge into the abyss of doubt before he can function in his office.

One need not be especially perceptive to observe that many of these seemingly diverse themes have a common ground in existential awareness, that repeatedly in Hansen's stories people are examining their lives within the framework of a complex and difficult existence, making choices, and paying the inevitable price that accompanies awareness and moral responsibility.

The formal variations in these stories, too numerous to catalog, provide continual pleasant surprises for the reader. Let me simply comment here on the especial vividness of Hansen's description. Repeatedly we are struck by his ability to evoke the real world of people and things, yet to describe him as a realist primarily would be misleading. It is more accurate to say that his vividness is the product of the lyric poet's special way of seeing, of the lyric poet's boldness is selection of detail, for Hansen's language is characterized by the jolting freshness of image and metaphoric description that makes poetry more arrestingly "real" than mere documentation. In fact, even when he seems most realistic, Hansen is not primarily concerned with surface description. His aim was to write about man "as though he were a myth in the universe." Like Cervantes, Melville, and Dostoevsky, whom he admired, Hansen pushes with a sure instinct beyond surface reality to discover symbols of universal import, or put another way, to focus patterns of archetypal experience. This is a valid description of his work, whether the narrative seems obviously symbolic, as does "The Soldier and the Girl," or realistic, as does "Haavn." That novella begins with very concrete description of Haavn, an aging farmer, confronting the multiple and typical betrayals of his body and his environment on a subzero winter morning. As with the protagonists of Samuel Beckett (a similarly mythic writer employing highly concrete and often amusing surface detail), we must suffer with Haavn through a painstakingly delineated series of minor events, we must experience every excruciatingly painful movement as he attempts to rise from his frozen bed, must meet with him every absurd obstacle as he begins his day in darkness. As a result we are made to feel that what we call existence is bearable only if one takes it a detail at a time and refuses to be overwhelmed with despair at the larger view. Eventually we realize that Hansen has provided us with a powerful symbolic representation of a universal condition, the individual wrestling with existence at a very basic, very challenging level. Not every reader will be consciously aware of this mythic, or archetypal, dimension in Hansen's stories, but most will feel it and respond emotionally nonetheless.

Only a few writers are gifted with an instinct for finding symbols (thus broadly understood) and charging them with meaning. The words "gifted" and "instinct" are used deliberately, for it is doubtful that mythic vision of this kind is acquired with intent. Such ability, it seems, can at best be honed if natively possessed. In any case, Hansen possesses it, and it is significant that among the greatest novelists one discovers a similar, perhaps unconscious instinct for charging a highly engaging surface with larger, mythic meaning. Cervantes did it in *Don Quixote,* Melville did it in *Moby Dick,* Dostoevsky and Tolstoy did it in their best novels, and for precisely these works and novelists Hansen reserved his greatest admiration. Their symbols emerged powerfully and organically from their realistic materials; by virtue of this fact their works force us behind or beyond the surface to contemplation of truth at the level of universals or myth.

A comment on the arrangement in this volume: The four brief stories that comprise Section I draw on materials from Hansen's own youth and may be regarded as episodes in the *Bildung* of a young man. Despite technical differences in point of view, they illustrate alike a lightly ironic disparity between youthful and adult perception. The stories of the second section are not grouped in order of their composition or publication. Rather they have been arranged to emphasize their considerable contrasts in style, mood, and setting and to create in the process a satisfying, dramatically varied reading rhythm. In the stories of this section the implications darken, the human stakes are raised. "Easter Bells" occupies the third section alone, partly by virtue of its greater length, partly because its spectrum of human types and motives, its broadly compassionate and humane vision, and its impressive artistic control sum up so effectively much of what can be perceived in the earlier stories.

H. Wayne Schow

Idaho State University
January, 1979

Part One

Part One

THE PARTRIDGE

THEY heard the wind, that homeless vagabond, outside. He was tired, or at least seemed so. Now and then he lay down on the field to rest, but before long he must be up and off again.

And once in a while the snow rose up by the window, swirled, danced, and was gone again. It's looking in at us, they thought, laughing at us, even though there isn't anything here to laugh at.

It blew, and the evening advanced. In fact, the wind increased, though sluggishly. It dragged itself through the trees in the garden. A drudging wind it was, like someone who hesitates to tell the truth but must tell it nonetheless. That was doubtless what the grownups in the room heard in the drudging wind.

The evening advanced, and outside snow fell steadily. At first the large, heavy flakes came sailing out of the dark against the panes and became great anemones. But gradually they grew smaller, denser, falling in long diagonal lines. Faster and faster they came, horizontally, drifting. And when the snow did not happen to stop, it turned in its long, white cape and peeked inside.

"Oh, but look at the snow!" said the smallest girl. "Ssh," said her sister. Ordinarily they were glad when snow came, but now it seemed they shouldn't be. And that whole evening little was said excepting what the little one had said about the snow. It was during the war, the first great war, in a remote place, in a humble house in which something was wrong.

The father sat reading the paper. He read steadily at the same article. Upon reaching the middle, he would begin again. The mother was darning stockings. She worked quickly, needle in, needle out, in and out, in and out, thread over, next hole—too quickly. The children sat close together at the corner of the table and looked at old magazines. They were unusually quiet.

With proper light, the room would have been inviting, with wall hangings and pretty knickknacks, with white table cloths and pictures. But from the ceiling there hung only a strange and lifeless thing which in turn deprived all else of life. It helped not a bit that the brass of the oil lamp was polished and shining. For there was no oil, and the lamp seemed not merely hanging but hanged.

The light came from a carbide lantern on the shelf. The father had tried to shade it, but nevertheless it gave off a stark, unpleasant light. Its temperamental flame, crooked and blue, hissed as long as its strength was constant; but when it began to dip and flutter, it was like an animal whose tail moves oddly. Not until just before it died did it seem to be a light for humans.

There stood the lantern, pointing to worn places on the furniture and to spots on the curtains, revealing every flaw, making the thin, small faces easy to read. In that harsh light everything seemed poor, even souls, which likewise lacked oil for their lamps.

And then it happened that the vagabond outside thrust a long arm down the chimney, and smoke was forced out of the stove into the room. This brought awkward, uncertain smiles to the children's faces, for finally something interesting had occurred.

There was, to be sure, a glow about the little stove; the room was not altogether without warmth. If a stranger had come, perhaps he would not have noticed anything wrong. And the parents would have done their best to put a good face on things. For in their pride, they would conceal everything until the last.

Now and then, of course, acquaintances did come to visit. Undoubtedly they had their suspicions, and some of them had eyes just as sharp as the carbide lantern. Secretly they looked into the children's ears: yes, the ears were clean, the clothes mended. On the sly they looked at the undersides of the family's wooden shoes: yes, they were decent and well-kept. On the surface things

did not look altogether bad for this family. Theirs was at least a
respectable poverty. If one really begins to sink, it is always revealed in slovenliness.

At first things had gone quite well for the family. But then the
father had been a soldier for a long time. After that came poor
work, low wages, high prices—in short, downhill. And then came
sickness. Isn't that the way it goes? When adversity has broken the
wheel, sickness comes and says, "Now it's my turn." Finally frost
and snow had stopped the father's spade, the means by which
they had been living. You can't hang by a single finger indefi-
nitely. They had hidden their difficulty in respectability for so
long that even the mice gave up and quit coming to the kitchen.

The father read the paper, the same piece over and over again.
The mother's needle jumped out and in, out and in—too briskly.
The next stocking, yarn in the needle, in and out, in and out.
This can't continue. Only a little barley porridge, day after day.
Small portions, and getting smaller. Frost and snow. Can't hide it
any longer.

What to do? There must be some alternatives for the family.
Surely they could ask someone for a little help. On the walls are
pictures of people who appear to be kind. You have only to come
and ask, the pictures say. And if it came to that, the pictures
themselves could be sold; they would enhance any wall and so
must be valuable. Then there is the brass lamp, which can't be
used anyway and just hangs there looking uncomfortable. The
mother has kept it so bright and shining that it could bring a lot
of money from someone who has oil. And then too there is the
old conch shell on the bureau. It's a valuable possession, strange
to listen to, and every time the father takes it in his hand, he
begins to tell what he has read of foreign lands. It's as if the tale
were coming directly out of the shell. Yes, the family could surely
get by for a while by selling these things, for each person in the
room knows they are worth a lot.

The father read the paper, the mother darned stockings, the
children leafed steadily in the old magazines whose pages had become soft from much turning, and none of them noticed how the
evening crept on toward bedtime.

But the wind had increased. It was no longer a vagabond but powerful, like a great general leading a procession. There were great, roaring minutes as the flying army passed, and the tails of the horses of the storm swept against the panes; then strangely dead moments when stillness lay about the house and one could hear the gale riding through the great trees of the churchyard.

During just such a hushed moment they heard a muffled blow against the outer door. Both the kitchen and the entry lay between the room and the outer door, but they heard it. The single blow.

The children looked at their mother, and she looked at them. Her eyes were large, and so were theirs, dark and full of fear. And they turned those eyes on the father, who looked steadily at the newspaper, though his eyes did not move, though he was not reading.

He didn't turn toward them, and they didn't know what his thoughts were. For he was a man, possessed of a different kind of mind than they, and in this moment of fright, when he did not turn and look at them, they knew nothing about him. But the mother and children were united. For when something unknown approached, there was fear in them. They remembered too much. There was that night when, as they lay sleeping, someone banged on the door. A man stood there outside the window. You're called up, and you must come tonight.

And there was still war.

The father lifted his head, looked at the clock which hung on the wall, and said, "All right, all right!" There was a strange glare in his expression, perhaps the secret response of his man's mind to the call of the wild and unknown. All right, I'm coming.

"What was that?" came the mother's whisper.

He turned to face the many eyes, and as he did, strength came into his own.

As his footsteps echoed through the kitchen and the entry, they sat listening, still and absent, as though he had taken their life's breath with him. They heard him open the frostbound door, heard the wind spring in. When it was quiet again, they heard him ask: "Is anyone there?"

It seemed to them a long wait. But although they had heard each of his returning footsteps, they began to tremble as he stood in the doorway, serious, wondering. He held something in his hands. One of the little girls cried out at the sight of it, and a chill ran down all of their spines, so hideous and terrible it seemed to them.

"What can it be?" whispered the mother.

"It's a partridge," answered the father, and then they could see that it was indeed a plump, small partridge, its head lying still on one of his thumbs.

"It was lying on the step," he said.

"Yes, but who . . . ," began the mother.

"There were no footprints in the snow," he answered. "It simply flew against the door."

The mother took the bird; she kissed its wing. "It's completely warm," she said. "Come and feel it." And the children came and touched the bird. Yes, it was warm under the feathers. It seemed hard to believe that a dead bird could be so burning warm under its limp wings.

"Strange," said the father, almost to himself; "it must have been blinded by the snow. But to hit the door hard enough for us to hear it . . ."

"I think the explanation is clear enough," said the mother, and while the little girls gently touched the partridge, their brother went hesitatingly to the window. He pressed his face against the black, cold pane and looked out. He knew what he would see. As he gazed, everything became more clear, and he saw a dark form, larger than a man, going away into the trees.

The partridge had fallen into the snow, and here in the warm room the starry snowflakes became clear drops on the arched feathers. Some say that the partridge is drably clad; showy it surely is not. But it wears with distinction its common apparel which has borrowed color from the brown lion, the ripe wheat, just a touch from the poppy, and several drops from the darkness of night. It is a secret of the field; and he who knows it may give it a name, but he must not reveal it.

The bird had beautiful small feet, delicate yet firm. Everything about it was softly rounded, the head with half-opened eyes, the beak from which a little blood ran.

The father sat down again with the paper, but then immediately got up and went out into the kitchen with the others. Almost all of them dropped a few tears, but of course the partridge was dead and so would have to be plucked—that was the meaning of it after all. There was not much to look at after the feathers were removed, pitifully little. Small curled intestine, liver, gizzard, and an inconceivably little, firm heart emerged; it was on the inside that the bird had its brightest colors.

The father went outside, returned in a few minutes—covered with snow—bringing a handful of fresh parsley. They put fat in the fry pan—perhaps it was the last of it—but the mother resolutely attacked the food reserves. She put potatoes into a saucepan on the fire. Nor did she scrape the bottom in despair; rather she was preparing a feast of hope. Though it was long past bedtime, she spread a white cloth on the table, beautiful even in the light of the carbide lantern. But then they carried the lantern out of the room, where it could hiss to itself, and they lit an expensive candle on the table.

Out in the darkness the wind roared. They washed themselves and ordered their hair so that they looked nice. Then they sat down to the feast table. The partridge was divided, and there was only a little for each of them. But truly, the little bird did fill them all.

THE OWL

MISERABLE DAY.

"Tup, tup, tup."

I hear him calling over there. Pay no attention to it.

"Tup, tup, tup."

Yes, a miserable day. Ruined. Black fingers on the sky.

"Tup, tup, tup!"

Can still hear it. Him over there. Have other things to think about. Scratched face. Was on the bottom. Didn't give up. Even if I die, I don't give up. Twisted my nose. Ha, couldn't make it bleed.

Have other things to think of. Sauntering along the highway. Toward home. Wading with bare feet in the warm dust along the road. A nose so fat and big you'd have to stretch your hand a long way out there to touch the tip of it. That's how it seems. Nose could shade the whole town. Doesn't matter, just so it works. Tough nose. Tycho Brahe had silver nose. Lost it when he shook his head. Held breath too long and died.

Dragging feet through the thick, soft dust. It slides over the toes, lovely. Other things to think of. Shoes are in my hands. Thoughts on *Captain Grant's Children*.

"Tup, tup, tup," he's calling. Over in the deep shadows by the house. Much closer now. House hidden among trees. The old man calling his chickens. I know him. My friend, almost my teacher.

Have other things to think about. I saunter slower still so he won't see me. A couple of chickens come over the road just ahead of me. They're running, pouring it on. But they're old, so worn-out they can hardly keep their feathers on.

When he calls his chickens this way, he's in a good mood. Probably has something new going. But my mind is elsewhere: on *Captain Grant's Children*. And my day is ruined.

Last Sunday I was reading it. I came to the place where Lord Glenervan sends two men for help. That's what his name is, I don't know how to say it, because it's English; but the boys laughed when I said Lord Glenervan—they're not as smart as they think. It's in the Australian savannah. He sends them after help, and then what? Uh huh, what then?

We know the gentleman who owns *Captain Grant's Children*. We visited him last Sunday, and I got quite a lot read. Came to the place where the two men ride out into the savannah. But had to put it on the shelf again, for the family was leaving, saying goodbye, thanks, and all that. There are nine or ten other books by Jules Verne on the shelf. They're good books. A few times the old gentleman has asked if I'd like to borrow one. I never ask him myself; our family doesn't ask favors. He keeps a sharp eye on me for a while, and if he happens to feel like it, he loans me one. But not often. If for no other reason, then because he thinks I'm too crazy about reading. He can't stand that. If I want to borrow his books, I have to act for a long time like I can't stand books. It's not worth it. I get a lot more by reading his books on the sly. I've read most of them.

"Tup, tup, tup," calls the old one from just over there. Standing still behind an elder bush. Can't see me. The sun burning down, the sunshine is heavy. Seems strange that the leaves can take it. The elder leaves are shiny from the juice of aphids. Further down they're gray with dust from the road.

I stand thinking about Lord Glenervan and the two men he sent off. They were on horseback. Where did they ride to? It's too bad I didn't know. I told a couple of my schoolmates part of the book. Today at lunch. I just couldn't stop there where the men rode off. That's not how a book ends. I had to keep going. There was a bigger boy standing there listening. He started to laugh, he'd read the whole book. But I wouldn't change my explanation. You just can't do that. I wouldn't admit anything. So I had to fight with him. He got me down, but I wouldn't give up. He got me a good one on the nose too so that it swelled up. But I didn't change a word of what I'd told them about Lord Glenervan's men.

I'll tell more tomorrow.

"Tup, tup, tup."

He's standing in the shade under the walnut tree throwing out crumbs to his hens. Just a few crumbs at a time so that the little old ladies don't fight over them. (Those hens were so antiquated, so ready to drop, they could have been widows of the cock Socrates asked Criton to give to Aesclepius.)

A big old man who is very proud and strict. Steelrimmed glasses that sit way down on the hooked nose. The long beard full of down. There's down all over his clothes, too, which are saturated with oil. The down comes from the leaky feather tick in his sleeping alcove. He sleeps with his clothes on.

But I have *Captain Grant's Children* to think about, so I stand quietly behind the elder bush. A lot of kids hide from him this way. He's a strange man and a hermit, and many are a little afraid of him, even grownups.

They don't know him. He's loaned me more books than anyone else. He's not like that other one last Sunday. This old man loans me gobs of them. Most of them are serious, informative books. He doesn't like novels, so I won't be able to borrow *Captain Grant's Children* from him.

"Have you learned anything today?" he says. He knew all along I was here. That's the way he is. Stands there in the shadow looking at me. Over the top of his glasses. Powerful eyes. If you don't have a good conscience you can't stand to look at them very long. Eyes are red around the edges, that's from the smoke that comes from the little stove he cooks his mush on.

"Like usual," I say, and I feel my big nose. That way maybe he'll ask about it. It's tender and feels like it belongs to someone else. Seems like it ought to be bigger than it is.

"Have you started to calculate with square roots yet?"

"Not just yet," I say, "but it probably won't be too long now."
"For you it'll be some time yet," he says.

He's tough, all right. Won't do to brag to him. But I'm pretty good at arithmetic, and I know what he's thinking. He'd like to have an assistant. In time he thinks I'll be able to help him calculate stars, where they stand in the sky by the day and the hour. He's calculated and written down things about the stars, about Egypt's pyramids, the Bible, and the history of the world. He's a thinker, but he could use a helper for the rough calculations. I'm not quite ready for that yet. He demands a lot, but that doesn't bother me. I have faith in myself. Have a long and a great life ahead of me. I'll be a thousand years before I'm as old as he is.

"I'm going to start up the lathe today," he says, and he goes in, pulling the crooked door shut after him. He has to fuss for a while with the door, always does, in order to get the crooked thing shut. He's an inventor and a thinker and a genius, but he always has to fuss a long time with that door. I've never known it otherwise.

This means that he wants me to help him today. So I hurry to get home. But I'm careful to walk with my toes pointed inward, that's the way the Australian aborigines do. I look back over my footprints in the dust. They're exactly right. And the dust is perfectly Australian. The sunshine too. But the trees are not shadowless, the leaves don't hang straight up and down as they do in Australia.

He's sure to have *Captain Grant's Children* some place. He has chests and boxes and sacks full of books. He buys them at auctions, along with everything else under the sun. The rooms in his old ramshackle house are completely filled with such stuff—machines, machine parts, instruments, everything you can think of. He can't find anything in it because there's so much of it. He built himself a motorcycle out of these odds and ends. The old man and I took a little spin on it. It ran, but not too well. We drove it home and took it apart. But in all that junk we lost a crankshaft, and so we never got the motorcycle put back together. Everytime we go through the junk in the room, we keep an eye out for the crankshaft. It was two years ago we lost it, but it's still there somewhere.

He'll have the book all right. But how can I manage to borrow it? He doesn't like to loan novels because he doesn't think they're worth anything. Sometimes he sorts out a bucketful of novels from the chests and boxes and uses them for kindling. I've sat and watched him do it. (I remember how it hurt inside as I sat and watched it, silently—or what was even more traitorous—with precocious words giving him another reason or two for burning the novels, yes, digging through my little anthill of a brain to find the most telling reason to burn the novels.)

The prospects are small, but I have hope. Hope that crows like a young rooster.

I'm back at the walnut tree again, on the way in.

In to his hideaway. Under those dense treetops his house is hidden. He hasn't touched the garden for many years, and now only very slender creatures can live in it, the grass snake and the ermine. Trees and bushes have grown up tightly against the house. The dilapidated walls couldn't fall if they wanted to, there's no place to fall.

I grope my way into the dark hall. Could knock over a Barnholm clock here worth ten thousand crowns. But you also have to be careful inside his sitting room. Out in the open the sunshine is completely Australian, but here inside it is always evening-dark. From the window one sees only the wild underworld of the garden. Leaves touch the panes, lay hands on the glass. If one sits and moves his head a little, branches and leaves undulate and flow, for the old panes are flawed. Small birds swim by. A gray sparrow is sitting out there. It stretches it's neck and wants to look in. But its eye rolls out like a drop of water. The other eye is as large as a cannonball.

He's sitting in the armchair by the stove. Acts as if he doesn't notice me. Sits there looking at a drawing. Once in a while he takes a spoonful of barley mush out of the kettle—it's sitting on the stove within easy reach. Around the rim of the kettle is a thick crust of mush. It's rock hard and very old.

You could think you were standing in the hold of a ship that had sailed around the world for over a hundred years. That's the way it smells here, of foreign places and ancient days. If you gave a learned man a piece of the air and he looked at it under a good microscope, he'd find a lot in it to interest him, a little Nile mud, dust from the world's history.

Tick-tocking everywhere. From many clocks. Mighty, giant clocks and little shrimps. They're his own clocks. The clocks which are there for him to repair don't make any noise. (Some of them would certainly never tick again. They'd remain there, for their owners—he'd forgotten who they were—never came to claim them—they were undoubtedly dead.)

The large worktable under the windows and the oak counter in the middle of the room are covered with glass, junk, and books, so he can't work on either of them. He uses two chairs for tables. On the one his Bible is always lying, along with his loaf of rye bread, his knife, and his milk pitcher. On the other chair is his paper, for when he works mathematical problems or writes down thoughts in his heavy hand.

There is no chair for guests. But the lowest drawer in the chest is always pulled out, and that's my place. I sit down quietly on the drawer. It's full of books, and I began carefully to turn them over. It just could be that *Captain Grant's Children* is in here. I've rummaged through the drawer before without noticing it, but I'll try again.

He shows me the drawing. "Yes, I see," I say, while I continue to turn over the books carefully. He explains the drawing, and I say "I see" and keep looking. It's the drawing for a machine part. I know already what the machine is going to be, so I can go on rummaging in the drawer, very quietly of course, while he's explaining. He had to make a lot of precise and difficult calculations before the plan could be finished. But now he can make a new kind of machine for producing fine clocks. First he has to turn models of the machine's parts in wood on the lathe. Then they'll have to be cast in metal. "Yes," I say. I've heard it all before.

We're going to start up the lathe today. Get the big motor going. I always like that, that is, the times we can get it going. But

today it's hard to pull away from the chest of drawers to go with
the old man out to the motor. For I have Lord Glenervan on my
mind. I'm thinking about his two men.

The motor stands by the outer wall of a little courtyard where
there is a bit of green space under the trees. The motor turns
belts and pulleys, which drive the lathe inside a little shed. It's
an upright motor, mounted on an old millstone. The motor is
huge; it's like an elephant pulling a baby carriage.

The old man has already given the motor a trial run. Today is
one of the good days. We warm it up again with the little burner,
and he fusses with the flywheel, pushes his arm into the motor
here and there, caresses it. And yes—it's coming. Now it's running, though not smoothly. It drones.

He likes me to stay a little distance away until it's clear that the
motor isn't going to blow up. But you have to watch your step
here. The motor stands close to the well, and the green, rotten
planks cover only half of the well opening. You could easily
slip on the smooth stones, fall in, splash! And it's all over. Lovely
to think about that.

Our motor is frisky today. It rumbles and coughs, hammers and
thunders, rocks and bounces on the millstone. We look into the
shed, where the pulleys and belts spin crazily. The walls and
roof vibrate. Odds and ends fall here and there. They always do,
and we're used to it. We get spiders and earwigs in our hair—they
rain down from the dark loft. This whole shed is alive. Mice
scurry to their retreats, a couple of rats flee. But one of the ancient
hens strolls calmly at our feet—her nerves are gone and she can't
tell the difference.

The old one engages the lathe, and yes! it runs too. It sounds
like a bunch of women hurrying off with rustling skirts. Everything is right today, and the old man nods. I can see that he's singing, but I can't hear it. (It was the best lathe in Northern Europe,
and there were always collectors trying to get it. That much I
knew. But what I didn't understand as well then was that all this
was just a game for him, just a relaxation for the thinker. To in-
vent a new machine that would turn the clockmaking trade up-
side down was for him only a recreation, as grinding lenses was

for Spinoza, or sewing tents was for Paul. What his whole being desired was to demonstrate in a magnificent work the oneness of the universe and God's purpose in all history, all science, all wisdom. For that he needed at least two lives. Mine was to be the second.)

Usually I like to be in by the lathe, but today I'm glad to do as he prefers and stay out here by the motor. I have a lot of important things in my head right now, and out here I can stand and think in peace. I'm standing close to the huge, droning motor with my back against the quivering wall. You have to bite your teeth together, or else they chatter. The cobblestones under my feet tremble, and there's a quavering in the thick, green water of the well, which is only a meter below the lip. I often lie on my stomach here and look at all the creatures that live in the well. Watch funny, skinny fellows legging it over the water. Watch old snails come up from the depths, rising slowly and strangely, as in a dream. See them chewing with their little red, grandmother mouths. Look square into the eyes of toads. But now there are tremors traveling over the water. It's like the flank of a horse when he shakes off flies. The toads are nowhere in sight.

I stand here to keep an eye on the motor. The exhaust pipe sticks up through the straw along the eaves. Once in a while a spark flies out of the pipe and past the straw. That's not so good. But nothing has ever happened; it'll be all right.

I don't pay too much attention to any of it though, for I'm thinking. I'm full of longing, and I stand here singing a little song in my mind: Away I'll go, away so far, so far . . . To a place where something happens . . . To a place where there's something to see . . . To a land of adventure . . . To Australia, yes, to Australia.

I stand in deep shadows under a roof of leaves. These aren't Australian trees. Only a couple of slender light rays slide through them. On the other side of the well is a hollow willow tree. Up in the black crown of it under the leaves sits an owl. He's a big one, I know him well. A few times I've thought about catching him or shooting him. But really, I could never bring myself to hurt the old man's owl. There he sits, up in the crown of the willow, rocking and turning. He tries to turn his back to me, but there's not room for him to do it. Now he almost stumbles, almost topples overboard into the well, so clumsy he is. He's calmer now, he's settling down to rest. But the owl face is not calm. His large piercing eyes blink and blink.

Oh, oh! The motor cuts out. Grinds to a stop. Everything is still. The owl's large eyes glare without blinking; the stillness bothers him.

The old one comes out and pokes his arms into the motor. A piston! Well, we can't do any more today. Tomorrow, the next day, maybe the day after that too, we'll be making a new piston for the motor.

We go into the house and sit down, he in the armchair, I on the drawer of the chest. His glasses are pushed up on the dark, deeply furrowed brow. He looks toward the window, continues to stare at it. Some great thought must have come to him while he stood at the lathe. He has instructed me in the art of silence, and we can sit this way for hours. The large head, with the stern face, doesn't move. But my hands rustle like mice among the books in the drawer. I don't see anything of *Captain Grant's Children*, but I keep hoping.

The sun has gone down, it's getting dark, and he starts talking to me. Today he doesn't talk about history or astronomy; he talks about man's foolishness, about his great ignorance of spiritual things, about the great disasters that lie ahead. I've heard all this before too. Often he talks to me as if I personally were stagnant, apathetic mankind. I listen to him because he's my teacher. There's strength enough in me to listen and put up with it, for I have an inexhaustible life ahead of me.

Yes, darkness is coming now. Such a day. I keep hoping, but in the meantime I've had to give up and read another book. In the poor light I can feel my eyes straining. My ears follow his words just enough so that I can be ready if he asks me a question or starts to talk about something else. I hear his voice a long way away, and I hear the owl cry out there.

(The owl cries now over the naked field where we sat then, where the Jebusite's threshing place was. It has all been razed, it is long gone. Though I eventually found the book about Lord Glenervan, I can't tell you what became of the two men. But the piercing eyes of the owl and the old one are more perceptible to me now than they were then when red-cheeked innocence saw without concern the shadows of coming disasters darken the thinker's eyes.)

THE BOOK

BEFORE MATTIS had come to the end of his parents' wind-blown garden, he heard his mother calling again from the door-way. He limped further.

"Mattis! Mattis!"

He continued another three or four steps before he turned.

"Are you sure you can remember everything?"

"Of course," he shouted, irritated, "coffee, sugar, tonic."

"Take good care of the money."

"Of course."

"Take care of your leg."

"Uh-huh."

"And don't be too long!"

He didn't answer again but stalked on, looking grimly at the willow trees along the road as if they too were women full of admonitions. Why did she have to shout after him like that so that everybody heard it? Didn't he have any sense maybe? Was he merely going on a simple errand like any fool? I should think not. His purpose was that of a scholar—or nearly so.

A little further on he turned to look back, and he saw that his mother had gone in. At once his mood softened, and as he stumped on toward the church corner his thoughts filled with good intentions. This extra fifty øre, he thought, I really shouldn't spend it on myself. I'll think about her and the little ones. I ought to, hum, let's see . . . Should I go look at a pressing iron while I'm in town? She's always complaining that she has to run out and borrow. But maybe I couldn't get that for . . . no, of course not. Still it doesn't hurt to think about it.

When he reached the corner, the last spot from which he could still see the house, he stopped again. Yes, now his mother was standing by the front gable, as if his generous thoughts had called her out once again. She waved, and Mattis answered with his cap. And though he flapped it but once, he grew hoarse in the throat and depressed—for how could he build her a castle with fifty øre?

The houses there on the sandbank, where his mother's tiny form could be seen waving, could hardly be called picturesque. They stood there in the pungent spring air looking a bit dispirited, justifying the description once given of Slaraffenland as the place with gray, windblown huts.

Of all Slaraffenland's limitations, the scarcity of books was the worst for Mattis. It had been really bad during the long winter months while he lay in bed because of his knee. A cow had kicked him, severe infection had set in, and so he had become quite a fine person who stayed home, was taken care of, and had leisure to read. But the neighborhood couldn't satisfy his hunger for printed matter. If a newspaper came inside the door, the result was war between Mattis and his mother. She'd want to use it to pack lunches or cover kitchen shelves. To Mattis that was sacrilege, and he'd try to hide the paper in the straw of his mattress. What did he miss in a newspaper? Nothing! He devoured it all.

But now things had brightened for Mattis. There was something giddy and shimmering about the future, indeed about this heaven-high, shimmering day. He was about to enter upon his studies, he stood on the threshold of a golden time. His father had cut wood for the old lawyer, the town's queer snail and bookworm. And the lawyer had said: The boy can borrow books from me.

Mattis advanced slowly. The leg was not entirely well yet, and this was his first long walk. Yet he went more slowly than the leg absolutely required. How often during those winter months his thoughts had raced this way like a flock of frightened starlings. But now the time was come, he meant to enjoy every step. Besides, it wouldn't do to go hurrying along like a fool. Mattis might well have waited until the next day. Several times he began to wish that he had; maybe he wasn't quite ready yet. But then there was his business with the lawyer, who was a fine man as well as a queer snail. He had more books than anyone else in town, they said. And if Mattis measured the power and greatness of a man according to the number of his books, wasn't that quite as it should be?

Yes, he limped along, vaguely despondent. Soon he saw some boys playing and shouting in the meadow. Light as hares, they danced past peat cuttings, leaped over anthills. Mattis couldn't follow them in that, but it didn't bother him. On the contrary he felt the defect in his leg as a mark of distinction. The bad knee caused his light to shine. People paid attention to him, they noticed his intelligence, they came with flattering offers as the rich lawyer had done. What will those other boys ever amount to with minds like theirs? thought Mattis with some arrogance. In time I'll have books myself, a whole shelf of them, I'll have just as many or more than the lawyer. I'll be somebody, while those poor devils there . . .

Then as quickly as it came, his arrogance was gone, despondency returned, and he didn't understand why he was so insignificant. Maybe after all because he was from Slaraffenland, had a bad knee which was slow to heal, and was little for his age. Or maybe because the day was simply too momentous.

With downcast eyes he continued on his way, mildly uneasy, though the weather did much to cheer him. As the morning advanced, it became milder. One could not see so much as feel that spring was coming. The trees were still winter-bare, while the herbs seemed to be considering the matter. But now and then one could hear a fly, could smell the mould from the fields, and here and there the sun had hung a lark up in the sky.

A little past noon Mattis was limping along the road that led out of town and toward home. Naturally he had remembered everything. In his pockets along with the items his mother had requested were gifts he had purchased—some candy for the younger children and a package of hairpins for his mother. And under his arm he carried the book.

It was a heavy book, awkward to handle, a history of the world. On the way out of town, the urge to stop and open it was so strong he almost gave in to it. But it wouldn't look good to simply sit down on the curb and start reading right in the midst of the busy townspeople.

Half an hour later he had reached the forest along the shore. And still he had not opened the book. But he began to look about for a good place where he could sit down with it. In among the red trunks of the firs he could see one sunny spot after another. Yet he continued past them, further and further, for he must find the most golden spot in the whole forest. In the meantime, it was lovely to anticipate.

Finally he stopped, for the forest was less dense now. He chose a spot along the outskirts where the long, withered grass was dry and warm to the touch, and he made himself comfortable in the sunshine. But no, still it would not do to open the book. First he must take out the lunch which his mother had sent with him, and he removed the bread and butter from the piece of newspaper in which it was wrapped. While he munched, he read the columns from top to bottom and from bottom to top, even though he knew almost by heart what they contained before he started. From time to time he glanced down at the book lying beside him. Then he carefully folded the paper, tucked it inside his shirt, crept carefully down to the ditch to wash his hands in the cold water, and dried them on his pants.

Finally he took up the book and weighed it in his hands. Never before had he held one so large and heavy. And he began to turn the leaves, carefully—the lawyer had shown him how—yet with increasing eagerness. There were many pictures, but he wouldn't take time to look at them fully now. Besides, Mattis didn't care for pictures as much as for the printed words.

He turned back to the beginning again. The Egyptians. He read. The pyramids. Read further.

In spite of the sun it was cool there at the edge of the wood, for after all it was still early in the year; and Mattis soon began to shiver. He lay there trembling slightly as he read. A couple of times he shook himself, lifted his head, and looked about with a satisfied expression, as if he were thanking the trees and bushes for good company.

Mattis didn't read as other people do. For him reading was like a fever. His glance swept over the lines like wooden shoes on smooth ice, while the letters themselves were transformed into small living creatures who scurried into his brain, pricking and tingling there, causing the blood to pound through his body. And when the content was powerful and moving, as with this book, then the people and events rose up as if from his own inner self, as if he in fact had created them.

A long time passed, and Mattis was into the Persians. Suddenly he came back to the present with a jerk, rose up with difficulty, and started off with the book under his arm. Once up on the lonesome road between the ditchbanks, he tried to read as he walked along; but the book was terribly heavy, it made his arm ache and his chest too, there where the book rested against it. And then he became alarmed when he saw how much he had read already. Even assuming that he would read the book several times, he had to be careful, for he must make it last at least a month.

But when after an hour he passed an opening in the scrub brush and saw how enticingly the afternoon sun flamed in the field there, he could no longer resist. So he slipped into the sunny spot, sat down by an ample, dark hawthorn, and plunged again into the book.

He read about the Greeks.

And now it was clear to him that he wouldn't be able to stop before dark. Whether he lay on the commons under a dignified hawthorn or at the outer edge of the earth made no difference at all: he had to read. It did not matter that his mother at home had grown anxious wondering where he was, for he had become one who no longer has father or mother, family or anyone else who knows him, he had become a spirit called away to ancient times. How could it be that he at twelve years had not heard of the Greeks, of Thermopylae and Leonides, of Themistocles? Peoples came alive in his mind, working, wandering, warring, sailing the seas, discovering glass, dying their clothes in purple. Carthage, Rome! Alexander, Caesar, Augustus, the Cimbrians and the Vandals. The catacombs. The catacombs.

One hour followed another without Mattis being aware of it. There he sat, teeth chattering from the cold. The sun was long gone from the hawthorn, falling now behind the sandbanks. Out in the open field the partridges cried at long intervals. A solitary lark circled once in the evening air, trilled a couple of times, and sank heavily toward the spring-curled rye. With that the larks were still. Mattis had heard nothing, however, for he was in another world. He wandered up through ancient and medieval times, like a smith he toiled at Europe's hot forge. But around him it was cold.

He froze. And now hunger pinched him, so that—continuing to read—he began to fumble with a blue, numbed hand in the sack of candy. He drew out a piece and began to chew it. The little ones' candy! Mattis threw the sack out of reach, plucking out temptation. But the root remained fast and reminded him that he also had sugar, his mother's sugar. He chewed a couple of the small lumps. But then his teeth began to ache, those confounded decaying teeth! He lay there in the grass, whimpering occasionally, but in spite of cold and toothache he read on and on, transported, lost. His mind was a gigantic space in which the history of the world unfolded, where Granger-Rolf met Charles the Simple. "When Rolf approached the French king, who was called Charles the Simple, he should according to the custom have kneeled before him and kissed his foot.

" 'I have never bowed before anyone,' shouted Rolf, 'nor have I ever kissed anyone's foot.' Therefore one of his men was to do it for him. The viking came forward, grabbed the king's foot, and jerked it so roughly to his mouth that Charles fell over backward. At that all the vikings laughed." At that Mattis Mattiassen laughed. Neither have I ever bowed before anyone, said Mattis loudly to himself, nor have I ever kissed anyone's foot. But then, suddenly quiet and startled, he stopped reading. It was not true, he had bowed down, had knelt with his mother and the others when his father stayed at the tavern, or when there was bad sickness in the house. And as Mattis lay there in the grass with the huge book, he raised himself and folded his numb hands. "I thank Thee I can read," he whispered.

Once again the magnificent music played in him, again he was breathless, captivated. Columbus, Vasco da Gama, Columbus, Columbus!

Day waned, and the evening now was very cold. Mattis had been shivering for a long while. His throat was dry, it hurt, and his joints ached. And then there were those holey teeth. Slowly the darkness stole over him, but he could not stop. Like one of the damned, he hung over the book, so close that his eyelids almost touched the pages. The words danced before him, hid from him, with difficulty he must catch them one by one, guessing as he proceeded, giving birth to them in pain. In truth, it was as though in all his suffering he created the history of the world within himself.

Finally he could not go on. He stood up on trembling legs, near to tears with weariness and disappointment. With his inserted forefinger he marked the page where he had left off. Around him everything had changed incredibly since last he looked on it. All was dark and mysteriously still, oppressive as an empty church. Mattis was tired, his mind mortally exhausted from his prodigious travels, and yet sorrow welled up in him because he could not journey further.

Strange things occurred on the road home. As he stumped along—the good leg seemed little more obedient now than the bad one—it seemed to him that Granger-Rolf and Martin Luther came and walked with him. They talked with each other and they talked with him, and he became lighter at heart and laughed when they laughed. He heard many others too. Out in the fields he heard struggling legions, far off the muffled sounds of countless feet and hoofs. He saw peoples on the march, great ships sailing in the gloom through the fields, and cities with strange roofs and spires towering above the sandbanks.

His mother was sitting there in the dark when he came, his father was not home. "He is out looking for you," she said. She did not punish the boy, nor did she say more at first, but he had the feeling it would have been otherwise had he returned a couple of hours sooner. Now she had been afraid for a long time. She stroked him once on the cheek, and her hard fingers were moist. She has been sitting there squeezing her apron between her fingers and drying her eyes with it in between, he thought.

"Where have you been?"

"I was reading."

The mother asked nothing further but wrapped a shawl about her shoulders and said that she'd be gone for a little. She was probably afraid the father would stop someplace and have something to drink, for that happened readily when things were not going well. She slipped into her wooden shoes and left, and Mattis climbed with some difficulty up on a chair and laid the book on top of the wall clock where the smaller children could not reach it. But first he removed his forefinger, his bookmark. The finger was dead, completely without feeling. He took off his clothes and lay down in the foldaway bed beside his younger brother who was sleeping soundly.

He lay there listening to the slow ticking of the clock. At the same time there was a queer ringing in his ears. Cold shudders passed over him. It's probably fever, he said to himself, I'll probably be sick. Maybe I'll die. But oh! haven't I read! Faint and weak he snuggled against the warm sleeping brother, whose moist breath smelled of herring and potatoes.

Somewhere out in the night his mother is searching for his father, and she is afraid—afraid of the tavern, afraid of the dark, afraid of the father's wrath, afraid for the boy's health. Mattis could hear her in his imagination, wandering here, wandering there. It's my fault, he thought, and the tears rushed forth; he cried until the pain was eased, then dozed.

But then the visions came. He is Christopher Columbus, standing on the deck of the Santa Maria, staring with strained and smarting eyes out over the sea. The foldaway bed is the Santa Maria, and Mattis can feel distinctly the waves of the Atlantic, for everything pitches and rolls about him. Then he sees something far off in the distance. Is it perhaps the headboard of his parents' bed which he has sighted in the dark room? No, it is the first island rising up out of the sea. The new world! And Christopher Columbus drops to his knees on the deck planks of the Santa Maria, and with tears in his eyes gives thanks to the Creator for His great gifts.

THE MORNING HOUR

SOMEWHERE there is knocking, and consciousness—which belongs to the day—lifts its hare ears above the lovely grass. But the sound is gone, so awareness stretches out again in the grass, settling once more against the bosom of dreams.

The man is calling. I raise myself and stare at the darkness; now I am simply myself and alone.

The son is up. He strikes a match, and a dark giant—his shadow—rises up behind him. The giant strides with bent neck into the corner of the room, while the son moves over to the alarm clock. It's a little past one thirty. Suddenly the good and faithful clock clatters shrilly and glares back at me. But now I am as wide awake as the clock, twice as awake as ever before. To be routed out this way in the middle of the night suits me just fine.

The son blows the match out, and I throw the blanket from me. But the glow of the match lives a moment longer, and the dream turns on the threshold and looks at me briefly before the door closes on it completely. Again the bright grass and the white bodies of girls, as if under water. Hey, you! they whisper enticingly. But who is it that whispers? And where have I come from? Don't mention it to anyone, boy.

Rise and shine, the man has called. Pants and shirt are heavy and damp from yesterday's rain, but it feels good to put on wet clothes, suits me fine. The soft and forbidden disappear. Devil take them. Drenched clothes and chattering teeth, is there anything better?

The son and I come down from the creaking loft, where the smell of grain and mice is more than a hundred years old. In the kitchen the man stands measuring coffee into the can. He is in his shirt and undershorts, and he has raised his crooked toes from the cold stone floor. I manage to keep from smiling at him. I read a story about the Circassians who shoot each other in the name of the Father, and the Son, and the Holy Ghost. The farmer looks like an old Circassian, and even though the son is taller and broader, he resembles his father.

We don't say good morning, don't say anything in fact. That's how the man likes it. The son takes out the bread cutter, and I look quickly about me. There is the propane burner; I clean it and pump it up. Then I take cups from the cupboard, three pair. If you're worth anything, you'll find something to do yourself, those are the man's words. He doesn't like to give orders. Your mind must be as wide awake as an alarm clock. I go into the pantry and bring back the large thermos, just by instinct I guess, for I've no experience to tell me how things will go tonight. The man takes the thermos and pours steaming coffee into it. God bless my soul, what a wide-awake mind I have.

We pack bread, thermos and cups in a basket, and the man adds a flask of whiskey. Heathens, I think to myself, scandalized, for I'm used to abstinence. But then immediately I'm a little embarrassed with myself.

The womenfolk are not to be seen. On such a morning the housewife will probably not venture out in the kitchen, but she's lying in there listening, no doubt. When are they going to break something? she thinks. But Anne is sleeping, young Anne.

We walk through the field down toward the stream. The July night is fresh and humid. Things are so hazy you'd think there was mud in the air. The cloud cover is drifting a little to the northeast, but down here in the damp grain all is quiet. The fences are dark and strange to walk past, but the barley field is light as a fish belly. It's a muddy night, and that suits me just fine.

It's like someone breathing cold breath down your back, I like that about the night. I'm a night person. I like walking by my-self at night, and I go out a lot. Usually I meet the night cuckoo and help him set out his traps in the stream.

Oh, devil take it, that's just talk, I admit to myself shamefaced. You ventured away from the farm one night, and though it's true you met the night cuckoo, he wasn't at all sociable when you didn't have any cigarettes. You slunk home soon enough after that.

The night and everything else is like your own sorrowful mind. They're asleep. Somewhere out there your own people are sleeping. They've forgotten you. And the housewife is sleeping, and Anne her young daughter is sleeping. Gosh, it seems like she's always sleeping, always smiling like she was aleep. She looks at you across the table, but you could just as well be a figure in the carpet. And she never looks at you any other way. In a seemly and indescribable way she goes about smiling at distant, pretty things.

Sometimes it's not easy to keep yourself under control. Sup-posing you suddenly decided to kick one of them? I ask myself, full of resentment as I shuffle along behind these two big men who as yet have not uttered a word. I might just do it. Which of them? If I were to do it, I'd kick the man. Yes, it's going to happen, it's inevitable now. But my foot twists, and I manage only to step on the son's heel a little. He doesn't say anything, doesn't even turn around. But I've had enough of this stupid game, I'm tired of it. And now I wonder what in the world was I thinking of? For God's sake! I'm overwhelmed with shame, it burns the eyes, I'll never get over it.

Then I notice my lip trembling childishly, and I bite my teeth together, hard so they hurt. The molars are strong, and better than the man's, I'm sure of that. And so I follow along behind the backs of the two large men, grinding my teeth, rolling my eyes, throw-ing punches in the air. I try to be fierce, and I ask myself if I could make myself so fierce that I could go out of my head and be someone terrible to meet in the night.

But damn, there I go again. Really I'm a nobody, a nothing, only a minus walking along behind the man and the son. Just a

spot on the carpet to her who sits on the other side of the table.
For you Anne, I need to be a whole head taller. You, who come
from big people, and I, who am little for my age. So what would
it help, even if you could see me, Anne? Because I'm too proud,
I couldn't stand to be shorter than my sweetheart, I've got to
shoot up there. Well, it will come with age, won't it? Yes, of
course. But too late. For I'm afraid I won't be able to remember
you very long, Anne. I'm afraid I'll soon come to like someone
else better. That's the sad outlook for us two.

The meadow is pungent, and now I can smell the stream,
the sluggish, muddy water. Yes, now I feel at home.

There are no reeds along the edge in this stretch of the stream.
You could walk straight into the black water without even seeing
it. I have the feeling that sometime somebody must have walked
straight into the water here, and that it wasn't so terrible as you
might think. You walk out in it, you sink, and that's that. To hell
with everything, you think as you pull the blanket of stillness
over you. Goodbye world.

Yes, even a minus can know more than people would think.
Though he may be an outcast on the earth and a minus, he understands the stream. That black stream glides through his mind with
fish and dead men. And look, there are quiet enticing eddies, with
large, bright eyes. And you begin to feel the sweetness, and the
dream arises from the water like a lily. Hey, you! comes the enticing whisper.

Ah, to hell with it! Now we must get down to business. We
stow the lunch in a scaly, old box, and we fetch the tools from
the willow hedge, scythes and rakes with enormously long handles.
We begin at the lower end and work upstream with the scythes.
The son goes first, cutting farthest out, then comes the man, and
then me. The plant growth in the stream is dense, and one has
to get a good grip on the heavy scythe handle. In spite of callouses,
my right hand is soon torn up a little. Good, that pain is just
fine. Get a better hold and pull harder. You feel better if you have
some kind of sore, gives you an excuse to swear once in a while.
You can look at a sore like that and be proud of it; it's a badge of
courage, a medal for manliness.

Tonight I easily keep up with the man, who has fallen a little
behind the son. The farmer doesn't worry any more about measuring himself against others. I pull hard, and I keep right on his
heels, in fact I have to stop now and then to wait for him. Is
there anything better than getting up a good sweat from your work
and being able to feel your strength growing from one day to the
next? No, nothing in the world. You pull hard on the scythe,
cutting deep down there, you tromp through the soft grass tufts
along the shore and into the mud, wet half-way up the thighs.
It's good and refreshing. What was it now you were so preoccupied with a while ago? Superstition, dreams, and sorrows.
For hell's sake. No, I'm a hard working fool, and strong. Work all
day, work all night, work in all kinds of weather—that's just
what I like.

Tangled plants rise to the surface, milfoil and water thyme, I
know them, bladderwort and water lily, I know them all. Maybe
there are one or two I don't know.

After we've cut along the bottom, we let the current carry off
as much of the plant growth as possible. The rest we have to pull
out with the rakes. Lying on the banks, the water lily with its
thick, slimy stem looks like a snake. All of those wormy plants lie
there glistening faintly.

It would be good fishing tonight. Sometimes they even bump up
against us. They must not be very smart. Does anyone know anything better than fishing?

When we reach the reed patches, dawn is beginning. It makes
our faces look pale and flat. But both the man's and the son's eyes
are strangely dark, and no doubt mine are the same. Posts and
bushes creep together and shrink down in the gray beginnings of
the day.

Now we haul the tarred pram up to the reed patches, and the
hard part begins. The stream slings itself wide here, and here the
forests of reeds grow, their sharp blades all bristling in the same
direction. In front of the reeds there is open water, and the son
takes me on his shoulders and wades out into it. Very quickly he
is up to his armpits. At first it seems insulting to be carried, but

then I happen to think of Kristophoros,* and I feel—as if I were
the carrier myself—the strong man's joy in bearing something
through the water.

He sets me off among the reeds. Here I stand in water almost
up to the crotch. My naked feet feel their way over the tough
roots of the reeds and bulrushes which bear me over the depths
below. I wade further out until I am surrounded by the forest of
reeds. If it weren't so cold here, I'd think I was in a jungle. What
if a crocodile were to raise its great eyes there ahead of me? No,
that's childish nonsense.

The barge is out in the stream now, and the farmer extends the
rope to me at the end of a rake. I can't see anything, but I can
figure out that the son is standing on the opposite bank. From
there he's pulling the barge diagonally across the stream, while
the man is dragging a horserake through the water. I don't
need an explanation to figure it out. The severed plants tend to
jam up here, and since in the course of the morning great masses
of them will come floating down, cut by folks further upstream,
we have to keep the channel clear.

Now I can tell it's my turn. Slowly I heave at the rope end, in
the process sinking in clear to my stomach, for the swinging net-
work of roots gives gently under me. The son would surely break
through here, heavy as he is. Here I'm worth something.

As the rope plays out, I move a little to the south through the
reeds. It doesn't matter how cold the water is, I wouldn't trade
places with anyone. Working here like this, hovering above the
bottomless deep, it's the life for me. No need to say more.

The son is doing something else for the moment, and the farmer
drifts completely over to the reed forest. I bend the stalks a little
to the side and look out. It's a lot lighter now, and I have never
seen the meadow more green. But there is haze over it a little
way off. The barge comes drifting along slowly with the man. He
is filling his pipe, and he looks at me once with that severe, calm
look. Then he has drifted past and I can't see him any more, but

* literally "Christ bearer"

I hear him ask: "What's the square root of a hundred and forty four?" "Twelve!" I answer. Time passes, and I look out at the meadow, which is so green I can hardly believe it. Then I hear him say from somewhat further off: "What's the root of two thousand three hundred and four?"

Oh my gosh, now don't get all flustered. "It's got to be under fifty but over forty!" I shout. He grumbles from somewhere down there. "Closer to fifty!" I shout, my mind in an uproar. It's jumping around like a skittish horse, and I've got to get a firmer grip on the forelocks. "Forty eight," comes his voice from farther off. Damn it all! I just about had it.

Once again we pull the barge slowly back and forth.

The cloud cover is thinner now, with flecks of red beginning to show in it as we finish up. The haze is denser over the meadow, but the higher ground lies visible in all its amazing greenness. Way above us, gulls come sailing along. The light strikes them brilliantly, the sun is coming up.

I'm freezing now, so off over the meadow to get the circulation going. There's nothing else to do here besides watch to see that severed plants don't jam up in the channel. Later in the day the inspector will come floating down the stream.

Well, this has been a morning like no other. Before we go home and change clothes, we must eat and drink—that's the man's custom. Dripping wet we sit down by the old box, and he takes out the bread, the dark, firm rye bread and the fat slices of wheat bread. He butters them and hands them to us with thick slabs of cheese. Next he pours the coffee and brings out the whiskey flask. He pours himself a shot and downs it. And another. The son also drinks two. Then the man fills a third glass. I turn away, as if I didn't notice a thing, chew energetically and stare at a madly flapping lapwing. "It's to keep off the cold. Your father hasn't anything against that," says the man. I turn and empty the little glass as they watch. And I turn away again at once so they won't see the tears that come to my eyes. It burns all the way down, and I can feel the heat spreading out in me. Soon it seems we're sitting here so very light and elegant in the grass. Just a little nudge, and you could float off until you gently landed again. I

feel a strong inclination to talk coming over me, but I hold it
back. Fish are jumping, birds are on the move, a mouse pops up
a little way off in the shining grass.

Both father and son pour a shot into their coffee. They're feeling
pretty good now, but neither of them utters a word. The son just
lies there and smiles as he eats. It's the same sleeping smile as
Anne's. Mmmmm, Anne. But to heck with it, Anne. You'll find
someone in the east, I'll find someone in the west. That's the
way it goes, Anne.

The farmer really feels fine now. He takes his cap off and
lies there in the grass chewing with his hand under his cheek.
Maybe he's figuring quadratic equations. He's a gruff old Circassian or Cossack, his head is squarish, you could easily figure out
its volume—and it wouldn't be so little either. Gray whiskers,
heavy mustache, and a fierce brow above the eyes like a goat or
an eagle. But he thinks like I do. It could occur to him to count
the grass blades in a clump and then figure out how many blades
there were in the meadow, or even the whole country.

As we lie here enjoying ourselves, we hear shuffling footsteps
a little way off behind us. Some one is coming through the damp
hollow. The two grown men don't turn, and so I keep my head
fixed tight. Soon a man and a woman appear beside us. I've
never seen her before, but I know who she is, and I move back a
little.

The man I know. It's Mads, the one they call the night cuckoo.
He poaches fish, gathers lapwing eggs, and is generally considered a fool. The parish has to take care of his wife and children.
The night cuckoo is interesting at night; in the daylight he's just
trash.

Mads sits down casually on the box, and the farmer cuts a bit
of bread for him and gives him a shot. He offers bread and whiskey
to her too. She sits there and laughs, biting into the bread with
large, wide, white teeth, while the son watches her obliquely
through small blue eyes.

They must have met each other by accident in the meadow.
He's just a poor wretch, but she's a handsome, well-kept woman.
The rings on her soft hands, necklace about her white throat,

flowered dress, thin silk stockings, yes, she's altogether a different type. Is she pretty? The nose is maybe a little broad, the mouth is large, but she's terribly good-looking, though at the same time maybe she's the opposite, disgusting as the mud under the bulrushes.

"You must have things pretty good where you come from," says the farmer.

The woman laughs, she opens that big, red mouth and laughs. It disgusts me, and I turn away.

"What's this one you've got here?" she asks. "How old are you?" So I have to admit my age, not quite fifteen.

"Think of that!" she says.

They all grin. There is something in those grins that disgusts me. The night cuckoo, that riff-raff, has lewd wrinkles in place of eyes. His face looks like a rump. He's dirty, he smells like a fox. And her? I've heard about her, at least if she's who I think she is. She's the housekeeper on a large farm, but she's wild and doesn't care what people say about her. A real slut. And here we are eating together.

We sit for a while longer, and she laughs at everything they say. I don't even want to look at her, but now and then I do, fleetingly. Like a whiplash my glance flies past her. She's not wearing too much, and the dress doesn't even cover her round knees. You can't be yourself here now.

The haze has thinned out, and the sky is wasting a bit of sunshine on the meadow. The woman sits there so white and red and imposing; she blots out more than half of the sky.

The farmer and the night cuckoo get up and go over to the stream; the son still lies there, dripping wet to the armpits. Teasingly she pulls the straw out of his mouth. But the heavy man is quick, he catches her arm and twists it so that she gives a little cry. Then he too jumps up and goes over toward the stream.

There's no way I can get up now without it being obvious. What if she doesn't go away, can I leave anyway? Resentfully I lift my head and look into her eyes. What do I see? Her eyes are clear and soft, and they are so strangely familiar. I know you, and I know just how it is, her glance says. And then I have to turn away. From behind me the dream of the night puts its arms around me and whispers in my ear.

She has risen and is walking away, I see, walking toward the bridge. I hear her singing 'good morning' and the sulky replies from the men. And I cease to watch the strange woman. The countryside is green in the morning light, and now I have eyes to see it.

Part Two

Part Two

SACRIFICE

THE SUN smiles on all things. The weather is delightful, but the times are not. The moor is yellow with fair flowers, but in the torper's house there has been no butter for a long time. The barley is up, thanks be to God! But the field is small, for they have used the seed-barley for bread. It is possible that better folk still have a little flour, well hidden. The others must get along without. And how will they do it? Only He knows, who knows all.

It is the day after Ascension. All things flourish in the splendid weather. The field has put on her flowers before Whitsun, and she has a goodly selection from which to choose. The forest is a bride selecting ornaments for herself. Be a mirror for me, sea! Here is a small leaf, does it not become me?

But the smell of burning is in the air. Over the greening forest the smoke hangs suspended, dark as anxious thoughts.

Marie is the name of a little girl who was considered a big girl when she was almost twelve years old. She is walking out around the torper's * small field toward the moor where his cattle are grazing. The sun, which reflects yellow from the dandelions, wishes also to shine in the child-woman's hair. It is newly combed and braided, but the sun can do little, for the hair is dull and grayish.

"Oh, just look," says the girl to herself, "it's almost as if I have gloves on."

Her red hands are much darker than the thin, pale arms. She

---

* Archaic Danish for a small farmer in medieval times who left the farming village to establish himself on his own land, thus creating a *torp*. A variant of the occupational designation was also often used as a last name, as in Niels Torper.

walks without stockings in her wooden shoes, and her arms are bare. This is the first bare-armed day of the year, and the torper's wife has cut off the sleeves of Marie's dress. A pair of pants for the smallest child can be made from them.

Marie has a ball of yarn pinned on her breast, and as she walks, she is knitting a stocking and humming:

> If father has no trousers to put on . . .
> May is welcome;
> Let him put on mother's dress . . .
> May is welcome!

And then Marie drops a stitch: "The cows are in the rye," she screams, and Jacob's bristling hair pops up from behind a flower-covered knoll. He is ready to cry. Doubtless he has been lying asleep. But he must watch carefully, for the cattle would much rather enter the rye field than make do with moor grass. Every staff of rye counts, each one is precious. It will become black, sweet bread—just for special occasions, of course; for when the torper has given the sheriff his share and has set aside a half barrel for seed, there will remain only a good barrel for bread. And there are so many mouths.

"You've got to watch them close," she shouts as she begins to pick up her stitches.

"I am watching," he whimpers, "they're all three here."

"I saw one of them sneaking over toward the rye, and it made me drop stitches."

"You're just saying that."

"You weren't lying there asleep, were you?"

"No, I wasn't sleeping, Marie."

"Now what is that you're chewing on?" she says sternly; "spit it out!"

"Nothing," answers Jacob, even as he spits out a greenish pulp.

"You know very well that you're not supposed to just go and eat anything. You'll get sick and die."

"Ha, then I'll be up with Mother."

"Oh yes, you think so!" says Marie, "but Mother won't be glad to see a boy like you. She wants you to be a decent person. So don't always fall asleep, and don't always go biting into every-thing."

"Don't you believe me, Marie?" says Jacob, his lip trembling. He resembles a little drenched bush. Only touch him and the tears drop from him. He is just eight years old and has very thick, light-colored hair. It bristles over his ears so that the birds could build nests in it. But Jacob doesn't have a face big enough for his tufts of hair, it is so small and pinched and always wet under the nose.

Marie, the strict sister, takes a little green package out from the lining of her dress, a dock leaf folded about a little morsel of bread. Jacob munches, and naturally he gets tears in his eyes, those two never-failing fountains. The bread is bitter, made of acorns and elm bark.

"Did you steal it?" he asks.

"Oh, for shame, Jacob!" And Marie suddenly becomes very busy slinging the yarn over her needles. But then he picks a sorrel leaf for each of them, and they enjoy the good, bitter-sweet taste.

"The cows are in the rye!" she screams. Now it is serious, and Jacob runs after the lean cow. He runs with a stick; "hu, hu, hu," he howls. And the tears, the tears—Jacob can scarcely see the naughty cow. The strict sister scolds too; "hu, hu, hu!" And so the lean animal turns about and trots its creaking skeleton down into the moor.

"Marie, Marie!" he screams from above, "there's a wagon com-ing."

Marie does not put down her yarn and needles as she goes up to the edge of field to look.

"Isn't that a fine wagon!"

"It's somebody important," says Marie. "I recognize the other one, him in the green coat. It's the parish clerk."

"When I grow up, I'll be clerk and wear a green coat."

"For shame, Jacob, you shouldn't talk like that."

"Well, I will anyway."

It is the parish clerk, out driving with one of the district's notable landowners. The cart with the high wheels rises and falls over the stones, through the holes, so that the clerk must hold onto his high hat. The torper's lane isn't much good for wagons; seldom is one seen here.

"What have we there in those two?" asks Paal, the farmer, in a low voice, firm and calm.

"Those are the two orphans the torper has in his house."

"Ah, yes. The mother died in the last epidemic, and the father too, I guess."

"No, I think he died since. But there were more youngsters, some of them died."

"Probably for the best. I wonder if Nils Torper gets anything for them?"

"Oh, yes, certainly. At times he's managed to get something from the poor box."

"And so they have their usefulness. He knows well enough what he's up to, the torper does."

"He's a scoundrel. He never makes an offering."

"Well, yes, people do talk about Nils Torper."

"Never even the barest offering, neither to priest nor clerk," says the tall parish clerk with the bowed back and the large blue nose. "The smell of burning is strong here at the edge of the woods, eh?"

"It drifts over from the parishes to the west. They're all burning."

"A lot of good it'll do."

They drive into the forest, following the narrow tracks where the farmer must carefully avoid boulders, tree roots, and fallen branches. The clerk removes his tall hat. His furrowed forehead is covered with greasy drops of sweat.

"I don't like this ride," he puffs.

"How could anybody like it?" answers the farmer, "but they chose us to do it, and you can best speak for yourself."

"I wonder where they're going?"

"I don't know, Jacob; maybe they're going to see the wise one."

"What would they want with the wise one?"

"Probably they have somebody sick at home."

"Who is it that's sick?"

"Oh, for heaven's sake, it's probably a little child with consumption."

"But what's the child's name?"

"Oh heavens, her name is probably Magdalene. That's such a pretty name, don't you think?"

"Yes . . . but where do you know all this from, Marie?"

"For heaven's sake, Jacob, questions, questions; you'd drive a person crazy. Why don't you lie down and sleep a bit and I'll watch after the cows. Besides, I'm not going home to the little ones until I've knitted a thumb's length."

"But Marie, why does it smell so funny?"

"Because they've lit fires round about."

"Why have they done that?"

"You know why it is, boy. To work against the plague."

"That's what Mother died of, isn't it?"

"And Lisa too, but you can't remember her."

"Yes I can too. And big Hans."

"You can't really remember them, you just think you can."

"And Father, I can remember that."

"Father died afterwards. See, that proves you can't remember."

"And there was the little one too, that didn't have a name."

"Ah lordy yes, that was a shame. She wasn't baptized, so I guess she's not in heaven with the others. But lie down and sleep, Jacob. I have a half finger still to go."

The wagon had reached a clearing deep in the forest. Here there were several small fields, and further away one could see above the undergrowth a gable with chimneys crooked as horns.

"That's where she lives," said the farmer.

"God the Father protect and preserve us," said the clerk.

"Amen, but I guess we have to . . ."

"She's a condemned witch," said the clerk.

"Hey, what's this now?" exclaimed the farmer. The horses had come to an abrupt stop in the midst of the sun's bright light. He flicked the reins, and the horses shuffled their hooves but did not move forward. Again he tried, again without effect.

"There's nothing on the path ahead," said the clerk; "give them a little rap."

"Oh no, I'm not in the habit of hitting them," answered the farmer.

"Just a reasonable little rap," said the clerk, who was also a schoolmaster and understood these things.

The farmer touched the horses with his whip. They trembled but remained standing. So he stood up quickly and laid on a pair of whistling blows. They reared but did not move forward.

"God a mercy, look how I struck my beasts," muttered the farmer; "what in Satan's name came over me?"

"Don't take *his* name here," whispered the clerk. He made the sign of the cross and chanted: "Saint John baptized Jesus in water. When the Lord Jesus was baptized, he arose straightway out of the water. In such manner shall ye also be redeemed! . . . Now try it!"

"It's no use, they can't go," answered the farmer. He got down from the wagon.

"I can't go forward either," he said from where he stood.

"In nomine patris et filii et spiritus sancti," chanted the clerk; "take the headgear off the near horse and peek through it. That way you'll be able to see who's holding them back."

"I'm not too keen on that," answered the farmer.

A woman came walking toward them. She was small and fine featured, her eyes were brilliant and blue as forget-me-nots.

"What seems to be troubling you folks?" she asked.

"Well, sure enough it's Mother Else," said the farmer. "It might be you can turn us loose."

"Just what is it you believe about me, Paal?" she said, smiling at him.

"Dear Mother . . . good Madam Else . . ." stammered the clerk, "you must help us."

"Perhaps you're simply paralyzed by evil thoughts," she said, fixing him with her eyes.

The farmer tried again, and now both he and the horses were able to advance.

"You've got to help us," said Paal Farmer, "for now the sickness is spread among the people. Some are already buried. It's coming on from every side. In eight days we'll all be lying in the ground, every last one."

"Do you really believe I can stop the plague?" she said. "There's only one who can. Get you to the priest."

"The priests are praying in all the parishes. It changes nothing."

"Then get you to the dean."

"He's reading and praying night and day. But they die like flies."

"Well, I can't help you."

"If only you have some remedy for us," said the farmer, "we won't be stingy with our thanks—and with that that goes with it."

"I know your thanks," she answered and smiled as she pounded one wooden shoe against the other. Staring at her little foot in its red wool stocking she added: "Afterwards one of you would try to have me burned."

"Which of us would want to do that?" said the clerk.

"That one who is not plague blackened in the face," she answered without looking at them.

Each man glanced sidelong at the other. Neither of them was black in the face, quite the contrary.

"I do know an old remedy, one which has been helpful in the past," she continued, "but it is costly. Very costly."

Honeybees droned by. The young leaves of the oak unfolded themselves, and the sun stood great and warm, beaming over all.

Little Jacob slept yet amidst the buttercups, his pudgy nose in the air. Marie had hurried with her knitting so that now she could afford to play a little. The cows were lying down, chewing the cud, and it was easy to watch them. Between the sun and the play, she had almost forgotten what time it was. She had found an alder branch with a pair of twigs which she broke off in suitable lengths. "My sweet child," she said to the remnants of the branch, "you are just as naked as was our Savior in the manger. My poor little Magdalene. But now I shall put some fine clothes on you. Oh, my little princess will be so fine, so fine."

And so she plucked a coltsfoot leaf for a dress; to be sure it was not a very big dress, but there were flowers enough to stick here and there to decorate it, marsh marigolds and saxifrage. "Sweet, sweet little mite," she purred. And in this manner she played when she was alone. Jacob wanted so much to join her in such play, but in relation to him and the other children she must be grown up.

As the wagon came lumbering out of the forest, Marie arose with the doll in her arms and stared at it. A wagon was a rare sight here; even so she did not disturb Jacob from his sound sleep.

"Well, there she is again," says the clerk in order to say something.

"Oh, you mean the little hussy?" mutters the farmer.

The clerk feels suddenly hot, suddenly frozen. He has never hankered for a drink so much as he does now. And with the farmer things are not much better.

"She's rather little for her age," the clerk continues, for it is sometimes better to be talking about nothing than to enter the company of one's own thoughts.

"She seems a little bent too, doesn't she?" says the farmer.

"Probably from hauling the torper's children about."

"Poor sparrow," says the farmer, "for someone like her it's almost a misfortune to exist."

"True. And they're not much older before they begin to drop children of their own."

"Well, in any case, she must still be a virgin," says the farmer.

The clerk turns and glares at him, and they stare hard at each other for a moment. Then Paal turns his eyes away and spits over the wagon wheel. "God's body, clerk!" he says.

The clerk brings his fist down hard on the wagon frame. "This is serious, Paal, this is serious now," he says. "What if we were to cast lots, what about it? What would you say if . . ."

And as the farmer suddenly starts the horses into a trot, the clerk screams above the rumbling: "What would you say? This is serious now . . ."

Late in the day the bells began pealing over in the village. The torper climbed the hill beside the house and stared in that direction. He was bony, worn, and windbitten, resembling one who, having been hanged, is brought to life again. His heavy, bow-legged wife, whose wet lips were always open, followed after him with three of the larger children hanging at her skirts. Marie wanted to come up too with the two small ones. She carried the youngest, but the second would also be carried. When he bawled, the littlest one also began to cry. The torper yelled angrily that she should keep them still, so Marie had to stay at the foot of the hill and find sorrel leaves for them.

"What is it?" said the wife.

"It's not a fire," answered the Torper, "it's probably the bigwigs making war or some other madness."

The bells fell silent. They heard the distant sound of a horn. Shortly after, the pealing began again.

"They're summoning everyone," said the woman, with some effort holding her mouth shut for a time.

"Why should I care," he said.

"You'll be fined, Nils," she said, and she shushed the children. The air was altogether still. The sun stood low in the sky, and all the bees and flies flitting about appeared to shine like pieces of gold.

"What do I care," said the torper, "they only have use for me if they need to fleece somebody, and here there's nothing left to fleece."

He walked down from the height, his wife following. Marie sat and played with the little ones. A five-year-old, following on the heels of his mother, was chewing as he walked. "Oh, for shame," said Marie, "spit it out!" And the child spat the finely-chewed grass out.

It is evening but not yet completely dark. The torper's wife and children have gone to rest. Jacob lies naked and sniffling on a folddown bench.

"You're pinching my stomach," he whimpers to Marie. She is lying in the same makeshift bed with her head in the opposite direction. "You're sick in the head, Jacob," she whispers, "I didn't touch you in the least."

"Yes, you did, you're kicking me."

"Hush up," says the torper's wife from the alcove.

"Hush up, Jacob," whispers Marie sternly. She pushes her arm out and gives the hanging cradle a shove so that it swings back and forth, and the wooden hook creaks pleasantly up by the roof rafter.

The torper passes through the room. He is reaching for something high up on the stone fireplace. There is the sound of iron scraping against the chimney.

"What is it, Nils?"

"They're coming. On horseback and on foot."

"What do you mean to do, Nils?"

"You just lie down."

He has taken down the rifle. Over the alcove hangs the powder-horn, and many dark and large eyes watch him reach after it.

"Jesus Christ protect us," breathes the wife.

The torper rams the charge into the gun. Then he takes the straw chair with him out into the entry and seats himself there behind the bolted door with the weapon over his knees.

Yes, now they can be heard outside. And now there is someone at the door.

"Nils Torper!" sounds a voice—it is the sheriff's. But the torper doesn't answer.

"Nils Torper, come out here!" says that authoritative voice.

The torper is as quiet as a dead man. And everyone within is quiet as the dead.

"I'm telling you to come out here!" shouts the sheriff.

But as no one answers, they talk out there in subdued tones among themselves. Then another voice is heard at the door. It is the parish clerk.

"I know that you're standing there and that you can hear me, Nils Torper. I want you to know that we haven't come here with any evil intention, Nils. But we've got to talk with you. Now be a reasonable man and come out. You haven't made an offering in the past several years, and our pastor hasn't seen you at the communion table in a long time. And there might be other things that we could call to your attention. It's still not too late for you to make amends, Nils Torper. But if you're going to be stubborn, then I'm afraid our patience—"

"Be off, jackal," says the torper, banging his rifle barrel against the door boards, and outside there is the sound of hurried movement.

"Nils," comes the wife's whisper from the alcove, ". . . Nils . . . Nils . . ."

"We won't stand out here and beg!" shouts the sheriff.

But then a man steps up on the door step and speaks through the planks: "This is Paal. I'm not happy about all this, Nils Torper. But I give my word, nothing'll happen to you and yours."

The torper has gone out to the men. Within the room, they can hear indistinctly now and then the stamping of a horse, otherwise nothing. But the stillness is peaceful, and after the terrible fear, they feel exhausted. They lie staring up at the ceiling. The open hatch in the roof is blue as a wave on the ocean, but the room is dark. The small children breathe unevenly in their sleep, and Jacob, who had been nervously crying, has fallen fast asleep. Marie too is drowsy. She gives the cradle a little shove. So pleasant to sleep, to snuggle down under the hide. If only she can now dream about good food—barley bread, roast, sizzling fat, or best of all, chicken wings and honey.

"What can they be after?" whispers the wife from the alcove, but Marie doesn't hear. Dozing, she suddenly pulls herself up and folds her hands, then relaxes again and slumbers off in the middle of her evening prayer.

"You've children, too, Nils," says a voice, "you've many lives to protect, and so has each of us here. Every one of us has more than his own life to consider."

The torper glares at the speaker's face but says nothing.

"But this can save our children, our women, and us too," the voice continues, "it's a necessary penance."

"The judgment of God requires it," mutters the parish clerk, who stands in the circle of dark forms.

"Nils Torper," says the subdued voice, "you're a poor, ignorant man. Will you pretend to be wiser than everyone and oppose His judgment, whose ways are unfathomable to us all? We need your help, but you must give it willingly. Surely a poor man like you isn't going to bring misfortune and death on all of us here and on your own innocent children by refusing us your help?"

Morning had come. Marie awoke and looked about. Suddenly she was frightened. The sun had been up for a long time. She could hear the younger children quarreling outside, and she began to cry for shame of her negligence. She shook Jacob, who gradually opened his brown, puzzled eyes.

"Jacob, we've slept too long. Just imagine . . ."

"I've been dreaming . . ."

"That doesn't matter, hurry up now."

"I dreamed I got a lovely piece of bread. But then I dropped it on the ground, Marie . . ."

"Come on, hurry up, boy!"

The door creaked open, and the torper's wife entered carrying a dish in which there was a little thin, warm milk.

"Oh, have you milked already?" said Marie. "I'm sorry I . . ."

The housewife walked past without looking at them and set the dish up over the oven. Standing there with her back toward them, she cleared her throat several times before she said: "It's all right. You can rest a little longer."

"Yes, Mistress, but . . ."

"Today you don't have to do anything."

The wife went out, and Jacob lay down again.

"What do you think, is it a birthday?"

"There isn't anybody who has a birthday now, Jacob. Think again."

Again the door creaked open. This time it was the torper. He sat down in the straw chair, something which he ordinarily never did during the day. There he sat, peeling thick pieces of skin off his palms. Every hair in the torper's beard could be seen, and it looked as though the skin underneath had been scoured white.

When the housewife reappeared, he said: "Don't you have something or other?"

She nodded, cleared her throat and said: "A little honey."

She brought a small dish in which there remained a spoonful of honey. Then she took Jacob's and Marie's wooden spoons and divided it between them. She handed the one to Marie.

"But Mistress—should I really?"

The woman stared at her, not answering, not nodding.

"Take it," said the torper.

"And Jacob too?"

"Wake him!" said the torper. And Jacob was roused so quickly that he had to fight back tears, but that passed.

"You can lick the bowl," the man said.

"You can do it, Jacob," said the girl.

Sunbeams slanted down from the roof hatch, revealing every movement in the restless, sooty cobwebs under the rafters. It was going to be another beautiful day.

And this morning the torper's wife helped them get washed. She looked in their ears, combed Jacob's wild hair, and braided Marie's.

"But why is this, Mistress?"

"You are going away today."

"Yes, but what kind of a celebration is it going to be?"

"Well . . . you'll just have to wait and see . . . you can borrow my bodice . . . you'll look really fine, Marie."

She kissed them, which ordinarily she never did, and stood outside the house, watching them go. The small children cried, for they wanted to go with Marie. As for the torper, he had gone earlier into the forest.

"It isn't much fun to be going when it makes them cry," said Marie.

"Oh, it's only because they're too small," said Jacob.

"Well, just remember that you're a big boy, and you must behave like it."

After the torper's house was out of sight, Marie's spirits lifted. But she had continually to remind Jacob to hurry, for he was forever stopping to put this or that in his mouth.

"Well, I'm hungry."

"You can wait well enough, boy. There'll be food to eat, she said so."

"Will there be real bread?"

"Bread and sausages and everything you can think, she said so."

The young leaves glittered in the sun, and the grass was fragrant. At a spot where there was heather and juniper bushes, the children heard the church bell begin to peal, and they paused to listen. As they were about to continue, they became aware of a woman, dark and poorly dressed, coming toward them.

"Mother . . . Mother!" cried Marie and ran to meet her. The woman took her in her arms and kissed her. But Jacob remained standing.

"Look, Mother! That's Jacob standing there. Hasn't he gotten big? Come on, Jacob! Can't you see it's Mother?"

Hesitatingly, Jacob came. The woman kneeled down before them and they inclined their heads toward her. "Mother!" sighed Marie softly. Then, "Mother's gone."

"I could tell it was her."

"I really don't think you could, Jacob. But that's all right, because you were so little then."

Dreamily they went onward. Jacob began to be tired. Then they emerged from a grove and stood looking down over the clear sea. The sheriff's field stretched all the way down to the water. And that was their destination.

"Look, Jacob, there are so many people there."

"Yes, but I can't see any other children."

"It doesn't matter."

"Why aren't there children, Marie?"

"I don't know the answer for everything, boy."

At the edge of the field were many wagons. People wearing their best clothes stood about in groups near the fence, but there was no talking among them. All watched the two children as they came, hand in hand, down toward them.

A group of the women began hesitatingly to go out to meet them, but most of them stopped short, and several retraced their steps. Only one large, splendidly dressed woman continued forward to Marie and Jacob. She wore silver ornaments, and her bodice was much prettier than the one belonging to the torper's wife.

"God's peace be with you," she said, "we've been waiting." Her red mouth set firmly, she turned abruptly and walked before the children toward the spot where most of the people were gathered. As they approached, those nearest stepped back to give plenty of room. There were gathered here both young and old adults, especially old women who had brought stools with them, and they sat waiting like dark birds. Here and there some dried their eyes. Two women joined hands momentarily, then suddenly both ran with rustling skirts away from the others, over the field, away. But the men were either very red or very pale in their faces. Some of them drank now and then from flasks they carried with them.

In the midst of the cluster of people near the fence, many spades had been pushed into the ground. Past them the woman led Marie and Jacob, past heaps of straw and earth to a deep oblong hole, in one end of which a step had been cut. It appeared to be a drying hole for flax. Here she stopped, and put her arms gently around the children, at the same time sending a searching glance back at those who stood about. The men cringed before that look; some flinched as though they would turn and run. But she shook her head.

"Children," she said, and as she bent over them, smelling of lavender and roses, Marie could hear close to her ear how the silver on the woman's breast tinkled, oh so nicely, "I'm going to tell you a story . . ."

Marie lifted her head, gazed over the pit at those who stood there, then turned her eyes slowly toward the woman, whose cheeks were flushed like two red flowers, though her skin otherwise was very white. There was such a strange movement about her mouth, but her eyes, large and sparkling, did not turn from Marie's.

"You mustn't do Jacob any harm," said Marie. Everyone could hear her, for it was very still.

Then someone in the midst of the cluster said: "Yes, why him?"

"They belong together," came the whispered reply.

The woman had released the children. "Where is the clerk?" she asked fiercely.

Some murmuring could be heard, and then the parish clerk lurched forward. He had been drinking.

"You tell the story," she said.

"Why should it be me?" he snarled, "why are you trying to push it all on me . . . I had to go to the damned wit—"

"Shut up!"

"So, now you can't . . . well, all I know is, it's got to be a virgin."

"Will you read a prayer then?"

But he could utter only incoherent drivel. "Take him away," said the woman.

She bent over the children. "Aren't you little ones hungry? Here, look at this." And she opened a green chest on which rose vines were ingeniously entwined. It was filled with food—black bread with butter, wheat bread, cheese . . .

"See, it's for you to eat."

And Jacob cried.

The woman stood up with the chest and descended the steps into the pit. There she spread a white cloth on the clay, laid food out on it, and then knelt down beside it. "Come down," she said softly.

"Don't do it, Jacob," said Marie, looking about her without raising her head. But Jacob cried and pulled at her hand, and so she relented, following her tearful brother and supporting him as they descended.

"Sit down here and eat," said the woman. They kneeled down beside the cloth, and Marie looked up at the large, handsome woman, whose eyes shone brighter and brighter. Jacob took a piece of bread, the smallest, not out of tact so much as habit. There was meat on it, and he had difficulty biting through it because he had lost most of his front teeth. Marie sat quietly with a piece of bread in her hand, but she did not eat.

"You're a good girl," said the woman, "you've taken care of the torper's small children, haven't you. Do you like them?"

Marie nodded weakly.

"What would you think if they were to die?"

The girl looked up shyly, then bowed her head.

"You can help them so that they don't get the plague and die," said the woman whose eyes shone so brightly. "You can help all the children, my children too. You can help all the people. You can come before Almighty God and pray for all of us sinners, you two unfortunate little ones."

"Anna, that's enough now!" came a voice from above them. It was the sheriff. The woman, becoming more pale, stood looking up at the others. "Cowards," she said.

Then turning slowly to the children she said: "Wouldn't you like to drink a little more?"

"Ah, won't you take this to our mistress?" said Marie. She had removed her bodice and held it out to the woman. But the latter shook her head, tied the bodice again about Marie, and kissed her on her hair. Then, tarrying slightly, she climbed the steps. At the same time, Jacob was reaching for another piece of bread.

"Now it must be finished," said the woman, and tall and erect she walked away from the grave.

A wall of men appeared about the hole, and waves of dead earth pounded down.

"The straw, first the straw! Are you mad?" screamed someone. They hesitated slightly. Whimpering, Jacob dug into the loose earth; "Oh, please not on my food." Marie, with dirt in her hair, embraced her brother.

Hurriedly they threw in straw. Then earth. Men and women, old women—with spades and shovels, with hands and feet they pitched the earth in.

"You are mad, I can't do it." screamed one.

"Who was that? Make her come here!"

"One and all must be with us!"

"For our children . . . For us all . . ."

"Some must die in order that all . . ."

"You didn't prepare them! You didn't read a prayer!"

"Where is the clerk? He's got to read."

"Where is the clerk?"

He was dead drunk.

The sun shines mildly over field and grove. The people begin to disperse. Some drive home at a sharp trot. But many are as if lamed and cannot bring themselves to leave. Old men set wattles on the grave, and a very old woman with bent back plucks flowers—dandelions and daisies—and, muttering to herself, casts them on the grave.

The sheriff approaches a cluster of women. "Did you see if Anna went home?" he asks. They have not seen her.

"Where is Anna Sheriff?" The question goes around, and the sheriff refuses a drink which the men offer him. "Yes, now I remember," says one, "Anna Sheriff went down toward the sea . . . while we were . . ."

"To the sea?" cries the sheriff. The powerful man runs, and none dares follow him immediately. "Anna, Anna!" The echo of his voice rolls back from hills and woods. "Anna, Anna!"

Here is the open shore, where once he saw his wife bathing, naked and beautiful. She had stood there smiling in the June night, water dripping from her long hair: "If things should ever go badly, look for me here," she had said.

The man calls, and the echo answers like the bellowing of a stag, but the sea says nothing. She has not gone out here by the open shore. There are no footprints here. But among the alder bushes he finds the place, and creeping out on an overhanging trunk, he can see her beneath him. Her white bodice and her silver shine up through the water.

Stillness over the field and in the sea. The sun is smiling, smiling on all things.

THE SOLDIER
AND THE GIRL

IN THE compartment sat a soldier, an old woman, and two
fat men who were playing cards. With the more bloated of these
two was a pretty little boy. His hair was curly and black, and his
eyes were just as dark. The little boy sat looking at the soldier,
and the soldier looked at him.

The soldier's brown uniform was old and worn. It was already
missing a button, and he sat there twisting the next one as he
looked at the little fellow. On his chest he wore a medal.

The old woman was sleeping. Whenever the train slowed down
or stopped, it sounded as if she were the engine in it.

The little train stopped often. If it wasn't for someone to bring
aboard a lunch pack for the engineer, then it was because a crow
was sitting on the track in front of them. The train reminded
one of an old dog who trots a hundred steps along a ditch bank,
stopping here and there to remember how it smelled in his youth.

"Never in my life have I seen such a pretty boy," thought the
soldier. "Odd that he should have got such a father, or more precisely, that his father got such a son."

Clearly the man was even more of a sponge than his companion.
He had been drinking, one could see and smell that, and he
hadn't just begun either.

"I wish he were my son," said the soldier to himself. "He looks

like a musician, or someone who could write music. Yes, I remember seeing a picture of a composer when he was a boy, and
this one is just like him. I'll bet the little fellow is musical. He
probably plays the flute. I'll give him a button."

The soldier pulled the button off his coat and handed it to the
boy. "It's been through the war," he said, "but you needn't worry
about that, the button is just fine."

The child was delighted. He didn't doubt for a minute that it
was a gold button and that it would show to better advantage if
he rubbed it a little on his sweater. He touched his father to say
something, and the father put his arm around him and stroked
his black locks. It was then the soldier saw that the child had
deformed ears.

"Well," thought the soldier, "obviously he can't play the flute.
I was wrong about that, just as I always am."

Yet the man was not a bad father after all, even if his heart was
pickled in liquor and his beard stubble so heavy that one could
transfix a fly on every whisker. He lay his cards down and began
to play with the boy and his button. They had fun together.

The men and the child got off at the next station.

"Hey," shouted the soldier after them, "I wanted to give you my
medal." But they didn't hear him, and this time the locomotive
was eager and wanted to get out of there at once.

That left the soldier and the old woman alone. She was awake
now, and taking two apples out of her basket, she tossed one of
them over to him.

"Thanks," he said. "It's too bad I didn't think to give him my
medal; he should have had it."

"You ought to keep it," said the old woman, "because you probably received it for bravery."

"For running and hopping," answered the soldier. He bit into
his apple, which was the larger and sweeter of the two.

And so he sat there, looking out at the passing scene. There
were fields wherever one looked. Red fields, brown fields and,
where they had been plowed, black fields. At a distance there were
houses which looked toward the soldier with gable faces and win-

dow eyes. And beside the distant houses a forest began to run toward the railroad tracks in order to swallow the train. It did. A little afterwards, they came out again into the open. The clouds on this side were the same as they had been on the other. You can take the sky with you across a new land.

"This is it, it must be!" shouted the soldier suddenly. Picking up his medal, he arose and opened the compartment door.

"Wouldn't it be better if you got them to stop?" said the old woman.

"Probably so," he said, "but in any case I must get off here."

The compartment they were in was isolated because it was old fashioned, and so they couldn't get hold of the conductor.

"It's right up there," said the old woman; she understood how urgent it was.

"You're a peach," he answered as he jumped up on the seat and pulled the emergency brake.

The train stopped—but some time passed before anyone came. First of all they had to find out if any grass was bound up around the axles.

"I want to thank you for the apple and for your help," said the soldier.

"Don't mention it," she said; "are you going to visit somebody hereabouts?"

"No," he answered, "I've never been here before. Except maybe in dreams. I saw a pond back there, and the hills behind it. And so I have to get off."

"I know just what you mean," she said.

"Yes, you do, don't you," he said. "When I was in Hell, I thought a lot about just such a pond with hills behind it and nothing else around. Exactly like here."

"But why are you still wearing your uniform?" she asked.

"I just can't get it off," answered the soldier; "I'll never be able to."

"Well," said the old woman, "if I were thirty years younger, dearie, I'd get it off of you all right."

"You're a delightful girl just as you are," he said, and he lifted her up and kissed her. Since he was a tall soldier, the old woman became quite dizzy before he set her down again.

"For the time being I'm not going to forgive you for that," she puffed.

"That was actually only a sample," he said.

At just that moment the engineer arrived, and since the old—but happy—woman stood nearest the door, he said to her: "Was it you who pulled?"

"Oh good gracious! At my age?" shouted the old dame. "But it is certainly sweet of you to think so!" Her cheeks were now as red as her apples.

"It was me," said the soldier, "this is my destination."

"Well, this is a damned expensive business," said the engineer. "We can't just stop anywhere. We've got regulations to follow. Have you got any money?"

"Oh, yes, scads of it in prospect," answered the soldier. "I had a position in a big place where they buy skeletons. There wasn't any use for mine just at the time, as you can well understand. But they gave me a commitment, and if I can just come up with some kind of interesting injury, which has grown together again, preferably crooked, they'll give me top priority. And of course that can easily be taken care of."

"Yes, of course," said the engineer.

"Here, take a couple of my sweet apples," said the old woman.

"They're just as sweet as the girl herself," said the soldier.

"We're talking about regulations here," said the engineer, "but there's that medal you have there. If you wouldn't mind letting me have that, I think we could settle this amicably."

"Alas," said the soldier, "had it been a button I could have considered your offer. But there is also a set of regulations for medals, and it says that medals may only be given away to little, black-haired boys who are deaf and dumb."

"You ought to be ashamed," said the old woman to the engineer. "If I had the money, I'd be glad to pay for someone who has fought for the fatherland."

"Now my darling knows how to run and hop," said the soldier. The engineer sat down on the step to think things over, and since the conductor now arrived and likewise sat down on the step, the engineer didn't say anything more about the medal.

"The thing is," he said, "we have to proceed according to schedule, and now we have to write this up and make a report. If you can't pay for this stop, I'm afraid we'll have to take you along to the end station."

"Then I'm afraid I'll have to start a civil war," said the soldier, "and that's too bad, since I'm inclined to be law-abiding. But now there's no need for me to delay you any longer." He pressed the old woman's hand and said: "Promise me you'll be faithful and wait for me."

"Yes," she said, beginning to cry.

Then the soldier shook hands with the engineer and said: "You've taken this splendidly. Now don't worry about it any more. I'll come and pay you just as soon as the business with the skeleton is taken care of, and that can't be so very long. As you know, a soldier always keeps his word."

After likewise shaking hands with the conductor, he saluted, turned, and started back along the tracks. The old woman stood with her head out of the compartment window, looking after him as the train pulled away. And then she got a cinder in her eye and had to search hard for her handkerchief.

The soldier walked on, looking about and chatting to himself. "This does resemble it. Amazing how like it is. It must be here. What luck that I came this way. I might have looked for a long time, even until I didn't care any longer. Awfully nice of them to let me off that way. It's remarkable how nice people can be sometimes. Yes, this does look like it. Some woods that close up just there, the hills behind, without houses about. And the clouds there. It really occurred to me first when I saw the clouds. They came along with us from over there. Yes, they're certainly right, but don't they look cold. They're not going to last forever, but no doubt they'll last long enough."

In this way he went along chattering to himself until he was opposite the pond he had seen; then he left the tracks and struck out over the plowed fields. He was tall and tough, but still it made him breathless to walk through the heavy earth. "There it is," he thought; "I've come further than most of the others, but before long I won't care any longer. Ah, how good the earth smells."

As he came closer, he saw that the pond was a large marl pit. There was water in it and rushes, and also some water lilies which had seen better days. Up along the marl pit ran an old fence and an embankment with a couple of trees.

"Yes, indeed, this has to be it, and isn't it fine to be in such good company," he said, referring to the rubbish which floated at the edge of the pit and even further out in the water. The remnant of a mildewed feather mattress, rotten sacks, buckets with holes in them, a broken shovel, fragments of plates and glasses— these were what one noticed first. From the branches of a little alder tree, which reached out over the water, hung a tattered dress.

"Good day, madam," said the soldier to it. "Thank you for the invitation. I know I'm going to feel at home here. I'll certainly 'fall in' with it."

He sat down in the grass under one of the willow trees and unlaced his boots. Without using his hands, he worked the muddy things off and then gave them a push with his foot—one of them rolled all the way down to the feather mattress. "Wasn't that fun," he said, at the same time removing the medal from his chest. "Honorable marl pit," said he, "this is a perfectly good medal, and it wasn't so cheap either. It may not have been as useful as the other things in your collection, but what does that matter?"

With that, he flung the medal out into the water. It sank, and the water rings spread over the calm surface, bobbing the individual straws which floated like a flock at the edge, the only participants who were moved by the spectacle.

Lighting a cigaret, the soldier lay down on the slope with his hands under his neck. Evening was coming on and it began to be chilly, but he didn't notice. Lying there, he could look up at the hillsides. There were no houses, no trees, no planted fields, nothing but the bare, quiet earth.

The clouds had moved and there was a little red in them now. They had changed, would never again be what they had been, but still he could recognize them.

And then he fell asleep, his homemade cigaret going out by itself. He didn't sleep peacefully, but soon twilight came and united him with the marl pit and the other things, and now he too resembled the bare, quiet earth.

When he awoke, it was almost completely dark. Groping about, he caught hold of an old kale stock lying there and pulled himself up very cautiously. With both hands on the stock, he looked around on all sides. His cap had fallen off, and the delicate fingers of the evening wind played a little in his hair. The moon was some distance above the hills; having followed the sun for much of the day, it was now descending.

The soldier felt himself to be sure it was he. Then he lit a cigaret and lay back again. Often he had awakened believing he was lying in a place like this, only to find he was somewhere else. But this time it was really so. "I didn't think it could happen," he said. And so he lay there listening while a mouse, or some other small creature, rustled about down by one of his boots.

"Who are you?" said a gentle voice from the ditch by the embankment behind him.

The soldier lay there staring. Again he took hold of the kale stock, but he was puzzled. "I'm a soldier," he answered after a pause.

"Should I be afraid of you?" asked the voice.

"No," he said.

"But you've hurt people, haven't you?" It was a girl's voice— not very loud but clear. And the soldier still could not see anything.

"Can you see how the moon is shining," he said, "it must have just come up."

"I lie here and can't see anything," she answered.

The soldier quietly turned up his collar and pulled his coat more tightly about him. There were two buttons missing now, and it was cold.

"You needn't be afraid to say it," said the girl's voice, "but you were a soldier, and no doubt you couldn't help it."

"Tell me something, my girl," answered the soldier.

"Oh," she said, "there's so little to tell."

And then it was quiet for so long that the mouse dared once again to begin his work with the boot.

"Say it again!" she said.

"You can have whatever you want, my girl," said the soldier, "but what do you want?"

"Ah, now you've said it again."

"Oh, you women," said the soldier. "But this is a quiet and good home you have."

"Except that I'm so lonely," she answered. "Of course you're here with me now."

"Yes," he said.

"You've probably traveled so many places, seen so much, and tried everything that's bad," she said, "while I've just lain here and yearned for so long, so long."

"Well, this is where I get discharged," said the soldier.

"Ah, there's so little to tell," said the girl-voice; "I wasn't very old. And I wanted so much to live and be happy."

"Glass shards and sacks, at ease!" muttered the soldier.

"And to think that you've come!" whispered the girl. "No one has come to me at all since they put me here."

"Tattered dress, dismissed!" muttered the soldier.

"I wanted so much to live," said the girl-voice, "but then I became afraid and ran down here to the water."

"I'm not questioning you about anything, my girl," said the soldier.

"My dear, I'm lying peacefully now, and it seems to me now that I can see the moon."

"I was wrong about that before," he said. "The moon hasn't just come up; it's going down. I don't like the red color it's taking on. But it will soon be down."

"Then I'll just lie and think about your being here," she said.

The moon was almost down, but it still reflected in the marl pit in front of the soldier. It looked as if his medal had come up out of the water and was lying there being melted down.

THE JUST

IT'S STRANGE to think that you found the bust, still more strange that you found out where it came from. I can scarcely believe it even now.

Do you mind if I look at the picture again? Yes, that's it all right. It's his work, no doubt about it. I hope you'll excuse me, this is so unexpected. Yes, it's my father's work. He did it so long ago, very long ago. That's my sister's head, you understand. She wasn't alive then, so he chiseled her in stone. My, my, that was long ago.

It seems so incredible that you could discover who made it. He wasn't known in that sense, not at all. Back there in my hometown I'm sure everyone has forgotten him. Or in any case they don't remember him on account of his work. You can see that from the churchyard, most of the gravestones he chiseled are already gone.

No, I didn't think that I would ever see that bust again. I remember it so clearly, how could I not. That is, by the way, an excellent photograph you've taken of it. I'm grateful to see it again, I can't thank you enough.

Yes, I searched for it for many years, traced it through several of the first owners, who apparently didn't value it much. I don't think they realized what they had in their hands. But then I lost the track. And so it's most strange suddenly to see it again, if you know what I mean.

The large gravestone which he chiseled there at home, I found that myself some years ago. He got rid of that large memorial and the little bust on one and the same day. I remember it very clearly. Frankly, I've sometimes wished that I could not remember it. I guess I was eleven-twelve years old then. Maybe nearer thirteen. He gave up other pieces that day too, some of his best things, but I don't remember them so clearly, even though there weren't all that many. It hit him pretty hard. I don't think he ever made anything really good after that day.

Actually it unbalanced him. The whole thing was completely crazy. But then I'm not the one to judge. For that matter I could tell you a great many peculiar things, but—no, I'll not bore you. Incidentally, he didn't live to be very old.

Yes, thank you, I'd be glad to visit you and see the head, as soon as I get an opportunity. I searched for it a long time. Look! Even here in the photograph you can see how warm the stone is. It's sandstone. I can picture it before me, as if I had been acquainted with the head during this whole time. It must be thirty years now. Yes, I'd have been between twelve and thirteen.

I'm glad you think it a good piece of work. In my opinion it was his best. One could of course consider the large gravestone. But the little bust is nobler. It's simpler. Can a thing be nobler by being simpler? But of course it wasn't just for that reason it hit us so hard when he acted as he did. We probably had no idea then how much it was worth. Well, maybe she did. I finally stopped searching for it when she too was dead.

As I said, I found the gravestone. It was standing in the garden of a pub—it actually was. The place was a long way from our hometown. And of course, not everyone could see that the monument was intended as a vault cover. I do wish it had been me personally who found it, but I don't get out and around so very much. It was an acquaintance of ours who came across it, a salesman, who travels a lot and cares about fine things. "Say, didn't your father sculpt that large stone that stands at such and such?"

he said to me one day, and it was the one. I had never said a word to him about my father. And that is queer, for now you too have ferreted out my father, who otherwise is quite forgotten. Maybe there's a little justice in the world after all.

For that monument he had chosen a coarse-grained block of granite, of that kind to which lichen attaches easily. I believe he planned on that. On it he sculpted a person, heavy, bent, a man reaching down to something before and beneath him. But it's chiseled in such a way that one only senses the form, or perhaps something more than senses, I don't know quite how to say it. But if you should happen to be going that way sometime, you ought really to stop at the churchyard and see it. It's standing on their graves now. Or to be more precise, it's standing on her grave. When he made it, they were both living, actually they weren't too old, younger than I am now. That's strange to think about. But I understood already then that he had made it for her grave. Children can understand so much. Unfortunately.

Lichen had grown on it while it stood in the pub garden. I saw to it that it was protected as much as possible during the moving. A couple of years ago when I went there I discovered that the church gardener had cleaned the moss and lichen off the stone; such an excellent and dedicated man, naturally he couldn't conceive of it belonging there. I had to explain to him the intention of it, and the man felt just terrible about it. But now it will be years before it looks as he imagined it. We have arranged that the stone will stand over them for a very long time; the extra cost to us is a financial sacrifice scarcely worth talking about.

I don't think I have the ability to explain how that monument affects one, but I believe you'd be glad to see it. He had had that stone at home for years before he touched it. It was not one of those he sculpted for the sake of profession or income. By that time he no longer had his own workshop; there was just a little shack at home standing out in the nettles. The stone had stood in that shack for as long as I can remember.

She has told me that he could sit for whole nights simply looking at the stone; as it was; before he had even touched it. Many times he called her out at night so she could sit there for a while and look at the stone. He said that he didn't dare to wake it yet, not before it called, he said. "Does it call to you?" he would ask. "I don't know," she would answer. But when he asked her once, and she answered that she thought there was something now, he began chiseling immediately. That same night, at that very moment.

You'll see for yourself how little he has actually chiseled away, and how wonderfully it is done. Perhaps that seems to you a strong word, but I use it advisedly. He "looked" that figure out of the stone. It is wonderfully done.

But the little head, I was never able to find it. Let me just see that photograph once more. Yes, that's my sister. She was a little older than I, she was the eldest. Actually I remember her most clearly from the stone. I had only just started school when he sculpted it. It too came straight out of the stone, mother said. He had often said while my sister was alive that she should sit for him. But it never came to anything, and that in its way was typical of him. And then she was gone, and he had to create it out of his memory. He shut himself up in the shack night and day. The master stonecutter, in whose shop he worked, sent for him, but he didn't hear a thing. Mother found him the third night sleeping on the dirt floor. He had finished it, as you know it now. Perhaps it was that that unbalanced him.

I notice you've been looking around. But there are only a couple of his small things here. The rest that you can see I've done myself. If you look carefully, you can't mistake the difference. I putter some, but I don't put a lot into it. I know better than others that there isn't much to what I do. Oh, yes, there's a certain facility there. I'm not afraid to show these things to people who visit. But I don't take them seriously. It amuses me if people get any pleasure from these little pieces I carve in my free time; I'm glad when people like them. But if they turn away fastidiously, I'm not hurt. I don't see anything in them myself.

Yes, my wife likes them. You can see she uses them to decorate here and there. I don't think she does it just because she and I get along well; I believe she really finds them pretty. My husband is actually an artist! she sometimes used to say. She doesn't do it now, because I asked her not to. It's a hobby, it's enjoyment, but nothing more! I said. But then sometimes she might say: My husband inherited it from his father. No! I'd reply, no! My father really could. He was one of the fools of this earth. My mother was one of the unfortunate of this earth.

As I said, I don't take it seriously. I just sit and carve in my spare time, mostly in the evening, and mostly during the winter. My children often sit around and watch. Sometimes they borrow a knife and a piece of wood. It makes the time go. My wife comes with the evening tea, she looks over my shoulder, and she can always see that the work has progressed a little. Then we drink our tea. My wife says that we live peacefully, happily. We retire early, for I have my job to look after in the morning, and I'd hate not to do it well. No, there's nothing I could wish otherwise, absolutely nothing.

Sometimes in the evening as we sit around the lamp in the living room, I take a thoughtful look at the children. There they are, each with a piece of wood, a lump of clay, or paper and crayons. My father never gave me anything like that, it never occurred to him. But the children are serious, they take pains with their creations, and they have no anxieties. I think they're happy. I think they're as well off as I can make them. I say to myself: that's the way it should be, that's the right way for it to be. But they'll never have as much to remember as I do.

My father never showed anyone a piece of work that was unfinished. Sometimes he'd hammer one to pieces before anyone saw it. Except maybe Mother. He'd come in late at night to get her. One would wake suddenly, aware of a small lantern shining from the doorway. He'd be standing there tall and still, you could just see his face. He'd be self-conscious, as if he'd just been in some kind of trouble. Marie! he'd say, so softly it could scarcely be heard, are you asleep? And of course she wasn't, for the slightest sound woke her—she never really slept properly, not until after he was gone and she was old did she learn to sleep. No, she'd whisper. And then he'd mumble: Marie, you've got to come out and see if it says anything to you.

She always got up, and she always followed him when he

came in this way. She was stronger-willed than he, but she always indulged him in this. Does it say anything to you? he'd ask after they'd gone out to the shack. That's what he always said, time and time again. She was the only one he asked. Does it say anything to you? Well, what does one say to a question like that? It's not so easy as that, is it? One can of course come up with some reply or other, or just repeat the same thing over and over. But do you see what I mean? It's a very difficult question to have thrown at you continually, and especially when it's asked by a person like him.

I don't have any judgment in these things, she'd say. Oh yes you do! he'd reply. In a way they were both right. There was probably only one artist in the world that she could judge, but I believe she was not in any instance wrong about his work.

When he had taken her out to the shed, where sometimes he would chisel or carve the whole night through, she'd stand a long time looking at what he'd done. There was nothing I could do but simply wait to see if any impression came to me, she explained to me once afterward. She stood often and looked at the work with closed eyes. Yes, I mean that, she looked at it with her eyes closed. And he would stand there saying never a word, simply watching her, for he knew how delicate her perceptions were. Often they both stood there freezing, shivering with cold. There was no stove in that shed, and so it could be terribly cold. But it was there that he sculpted his last pieces. Earlier he had been a master himself and had owned a stonecutting business; there in his workshop he had plenty of room, and everything he needed to use was at hand. But I was not very old when he had to sell it and work as a journeyman under the new owner. And so it was at home in that leaky old shed that he worked on the things he really cared about. It was extremely damp out there, partly because of the dirt floor. The stones he kept standing there always sweated. But actually he didn't do that much out there. Sometimes months would pass between his fits of activity in the shed, and even then he broke up much of what he started. I never do that. What I do is just to occupy my time, nothing more. And so it's impossible to compare us. From a purely technical standpoint I'm perhaps not much inferior to him, and I've had the good fortune to see a lot more than he did. But these facts are not decisive. My father lived in about the same place all his life, and he didn't see very much. He was in some of his things old-fashionedly romantic, don't you know. I wouldn't want to say that he was a great artist, and now of course he's completely forgotten. But I will say that he was genuine—in his best things. You can't compare us at all. He was "right"—in his best things. And always in stone.

The shed leaned, hanging on its bearing posts. The boards on it were rotten, the panes were broken, and there was a strong draft. Mother would stand there in her nightgown shivering. And he always shivered whenever he was showing her something. She would stand there for a while, and then maybe she'd say: Yes, I think it says something to me. —Well, he'd say, well, it does say something then? —Yes, it says something to me, she'd repeat. —I see, he'd breathe, almost in a whisper. And then she'd go in to bed. She could lie there shivering with cold for a long time after. But if she had answered him in this way, we could be almost certain that before long we would hear him working out in the shed, the blows of the hammer, the bite of the chisel. He'd be finishing up, or he'd have begun something new. We could read him according to the blows. When they came calmly and at long intervals, as if they were ripe, you understand, then we could lie quietly and give ourselves up to sleep, for then we knew it was well with him. But if the sounds came rapidly, then we were always afraid.

And sometimes it could happen that after Mother had stood there for a long time freezing, she would say at last: I don't know! She wouldn't say it soft and low, but vehemently, for she knew what was at stake. —I don't know, Vilhelm, I don't know! —No, of course not, he'd say. —No, I just can't, Vilhelm! she would almost shout, standing there terribly pale and erect. —I see, he'd say very gently. —Why do you always come and ask me? she'd say in a loud voice, and Father would retreat a little.

You mustn't feel bad about it Marie, don't take it in that way, he'd say quietly, what does it matter if it's not particularly good?

It doesn't matter. But we'd better think about getting some rest, Marie. You just go in and lie down, and I'll be along. —No, she'd answer, I'll get some clothes on, I'll just wrap a blanket around me. I'll sit here with you while you work. —No, he'd answer, that won't do at all. —Listen to me, Vilhelm, Mother would say in that loud voice, I'll get dressed, I'll sit here with you, and you can go on working, do you understand! —No dear, that's no good, Father would say, smiling, no, I'm tired, very tired.

She'd stay with him until he went in. All the same, as a rule he'd break up any piece of work that didn't say something to Mother. As the years passed she learned of course how costly that could be. It got worse and worse, and so one can understand why from time to time she began to embellish her responses somewhat. It was not easy for her, for she was an honest person, but sometimes she just let on as though his work said something to her. Yet though she was brighter than Father, he wasn't easily fooled, he could tell. And so in spite of her he would give up on the piece, or knock it to bits. Then for a long time he'd be strangely self-conscious with Mother; I think it was very harmful to their relationship.

That's how it went during the first years. When he broke up a piece, he'd stay away from the shed for a long time, and he'd be gentle and kind to us for a while. It was as if he'd wronged us in some way and had to make it up to us, as if he'd discovered his family. For there could be long periods when we didn't exist for him at all. He wouldn't even see us. —May I use that knife? I might ask him out in the shed, and though I hadn't said a word before, he'd reply: Will you stop plaguing me with all these questions! And if I reached over to pick up the knife, he'd shout: Will you stop it! I can't have you out here!

But after he'd had bad luck with a piece he seemed to wake up, he'd be lively, he'd work hard for the master at the workshop during the day, and in the evening he might play with us, joke and sing maybe, or tell us stories. And Mother would sit in the living room like a flower that has needed water for a long time and now has been watered. In just one day she could seem years younger. They'd look at each other, and suddenly they could begin to romp and play, the two of them. I've never known anyone to play so joyously as Mother and Father when the impulse came over them. They'd laugh and dance about, tipping over chairs, rattling the hanging lamp. We'd all get wild and crazy.

The good time could be short or long, but in the last years it was always very short and it always ended with him drinking heavily.

Many times I sat on the steps and waited for him, on the steps of the pub. Mother sent me there when he stayed away. As I think about it, I believe it was just one of the first times that she sent me. After that, it seems to me that I went by myself. The whole town knew him, so we were sure to hear when he went on one of his binges. There was no lack of women who were more than glad to come and tell Mother about him. They held something against her, many of them. It was because she was more of a woman, she outshone them, she was warmer and stronger than the others, that was it I think. I'm afraid I'm not giving you quite the right impression of her. Yes, that's her, the picture on the wall there. No, one doesn't really get the right . . . you know what I mean, don't you, there are people who have something about them that just never comes through in photographs. But you could see it in her. She moved gracefully, was proud. Precisely when things were worst, she held her head highest.

There was probably just one person who sometimes saw her break down. He's sitting here. I wasn't very old when it happened the first time. You must remember that when Lily, my sister, died, I was the oldest. I became actually a hard little nail. I can feel it in me still, how hard and bitter I became inside whenever it happened. At those times she needed me. And I hated him; worse yet, I think I despised him, because he was weak and drank and cried and broke down miserably. And all the same . . . Yes, I was there between them, and each time I felt I was being torn in bits and pieces. I sat there like a little lump of cement between them, and I had to make myself hard and unfeeling like a stone.

My mother there? Yes, she was a lady. Men continued to stare after her, and when Father was in a decent frame of mind he was terribly proud of her. But when things fell apart for him, he'd start looking for trifles he could be jealous about. Once in a while he'd get violent, threaten her, and then cry. I've often thought that perhaps he relied on mistrust and jealousy to justify himself; he had to hide his weakness behind something. But Mother never gave him any cause, of that I'm sure. She was just one of those people who can't pass through this world without having an impact. There were those old busybodies who gossiped about her, who said it was her fault things went as they did with him. But I'll say this, and I believe it's true: she was the only person who could really make him happy.

Yes, how well I remember it, sitting there on the steps, and then him coming out of the pub. Finally. And we'd be alone.

"Manuel, what's this, are you sitting out here?"

"You know I was."

"Manuel," he'd say, standing there on the steps and staring up in the air, as if he only understood what was far away, "was there someone sent you, Manuel?"

"No, there wasn't."

"Manuel," he'd say.

Then he'd take me by the hand and we'd walk toward home. After I got a little older, I remember, I'd only take his hand if it was dark and no one could see us. We'd never go straight home. As we neared the house, he'd begin to talk of this or that and we'd turn off on a side street, walking back and forth hand in hand. Finally we'd go home. The house would be still, they would have gone to bed.

"Manuel," he'd say, as we came near the house, "if only it weren't so quiet."

Yes, that's how one remembers it. And especially the last time, but I suppose one shouldn't even get into that story. Of all the times I waited on the stone steps of the pub, that was the worst and hardest to forget. Afterwards he never went to that pub again. When the mood came on him and he had to drink, he'd go farther away. And he'd stay away for a long time. But that, incidentally, didn't last for much more than a year, and then he left for good. We never learned the reason why, but I suspect it was because of shame. He couldn't stand to see us, and it was tearing him apart. Besides, he knew very well we could get along better without him. Yes. When he died, he was a long way from home.

But on that day I'm speaking of, it was along in the afternoon, I think. I'd been sitting there a long time—at that age one never knows exactly how long. It was spring, but cold; the sun was shining but with a cold, thin kind of light, you know. I was shivering because I was bare-legged, but I was proud to be bare-legged so early in the season. There I sat huddled on the steps, gritting my teeth and feeling proud of the goose pimples on my bare legs.

Then someone came out on the steps, a dark little man in filthy clothes all too large for him. His sleeves hung down over his hands so that you could see only his blue knuckles. Everything hung on him, and he staggered and bounced; it looked as though he would topple down the steps. But he didn't fall; that was just his way of walking. Like a hen he hopped down to the next step. His nickname was Wienerbassen; I don't know why he was called that. He was from another town, but we knew him. He often worked for The Just, driving around buying berries and eggs and chickens.

I had been able to see from the steps that Father was drinking with Wienerbassen and several others. You could see them every time they went into the latrine. One got to despise those men because they swilled so much and had to be continually running in there, flushed in the face. Yes, I despised my father. He never looked out on the steps when he knew I was there, even though many another man came out to chase me away. Personally I never would have stood to have a son of mine sitting out there. I hated him because he'd begun to keep company with persons like Wienerbassen. And there stood Bassen on the steps above me, bouncing and spitting, so close that I could smell his alcohol breath.

"Well, are you here, you little informer!" he said.

"You're one yourself," I responded. I was sitting so close he could easily have grabbed me. I glared up straight at his little black hen's head, into the yellow eyes. He spat out a black glob which glistened in the sunlight like a swallow's back and flew far out in the street.

Then I could hear several of them coming out through the

corridor, and I knew I probably wouldn't be able to get Father away. Not when he was in company. If only he'd been alone, for I was the stronger at those times. He'd stand on the steps with that faraway look in his eye.

"Manuel," he'd say.

"Let's go now," I'd say. And I'd take him by the hand, that is, if it were dark.

"Manuel," he'd say now and then as we walked along. And as we neared the house he'd stop: "Listen, boy, there's something we should talk about." And we'd turn off on a side street, walking back and forth. "Look here, son," he'd begin, but it never came to anything; he'd just manage to say, "Look here, Manuel." And we'd keep walking.

Then he'd stop. We'd stand there a long time listening. Maybe we'd hear something moving a long way off. It was usually late, and the lights would be out in most of the houses. Maybe there'd be a rushing overhead, birds flying over us. You couldn't see them, but you could hear the wings.

"Manuel," he'd say, "do you ever wish you had wings and could fly?"

"Yes, I wish it a lot," I'd say.

"Manuel, things will turn out fine for you. The world is very large."

And we'd walk back and forth. Suddenly he'd stop again and say: "A stone, you see, a large block. That piece of granite with the large crystals. I ought to call it the boulder. That boulder is lying there waiting for something, can you feel that, Manuel? It's waiting to become a person. Your little sister, Manuel, she was there in the stone. Jesus Christ, we found her there in the stone, Manuel."

And then we'd walk further. Sometimes I could tell he was crying. He'd try to keep it quiet so that I wouldn't hear it in his voice. But when he'd squeeze my hand, so firmly I would have cried out if I hadn't been a hard little nail, I knew he was crying. That was the worst thing I knew. I hated it. He was a big strong man, he oughtn't to have done that. He was a handsome man, yes, you see him there by the side of Mother. It's strange, he appears firmer and stronger in pictures than he actually was, just opposite from her. But at least I never saw him break down and blubber.

I think I understood at the time why he cried sometimes as we walked together in the dark. It was because he wasn't my father. I don't mean in the literal sense, for of course he was my physical progenitor. But he was not a model for me, at bottom I didn't respect him. Many a time as we ambled along in the dark I wished it were me, the boy, who had wandered astray and that my Father, now strong and stern, would lead me back. Don't get the idea I was a model child; on the contrary. But I knew that my father could not honestly regard himself as fit to lead and guide me. He had authority over me, but he didn't have any moral power over me—and I wished that he had. He should have been to me like a lighthouse in the world until I was old enough myself to give off light. But as we trudged back and forth on the streets late in the evenings, it was me who had the power, it was me who was most reasonable. It was as if I was my father's father, and that's a hard thing to be.

He'd stop and say, no, he'd shout: "Manuel," he'd shout, "remember this now, always remember it, until the day you die, Manuel! Remember now that everything you hear me say to your mother and about your mother, it's all lies, Manuel. Remember, it's always fantasies and lies, Manuel!"

Then he'd crush my hand and say: "Will you remember that, Manuel?"

"Yes," I'd say.

"And you understand me, don't you!" he'd say, holding me under the chin with his big stonecutter's hand. But I could never answer that, for I'd be all queer in the throat and not able to say anything.

It's probably hard for anyone else to understand, but those walks are still somehow among the best memories I have. I won't attempt to explain it.

I seem to remember many, many such walks. No doubt that's an exaggeration. Maybe there weren't actually so many times we came home together. And yet it seems that much of my childhood was

spent sitting there on those stone steps and waiting. The memory exaggerates that way.

It looks as though I can't avoid telling you what happened that
last time, though I probably shouldn't. Well, Wienerbassen was
standing there on the pub steps.

"So the little tattletale answers back, eh?" said the filthy little
man with the hen's head. I sat there on the lowest step looking
him straight in the eyes—they were yellow. He wasn't a human
being. Maybe he had been once, but he wasn't any longer.

He grinned and spat, and the black glob fell on the step beside me in the shape of a disgusting black star. I had scratched
a picture in the stone step in just that spot, a flower taken from
my imagination.

Whenever I think about my childhood, I always see the steps
of that pub before me. It's almost as if they were a stage on which
it all took place, a stage which (as is typical in dreams) is much
larger than in reality. Yet in this vision I see those steps just as
they were. At the sides there was an iron railing which had once
been painted red. The round iron above had been worn clean and
bright as the sky, but that was just on the top surface; underneath
it was black with rust. At the end, where the iron turned up into
two spheres, it was likewise black, but in this case from grease
and dirt. Between the bars of the railing, the old paint sat in thick
clusters which had been red earlier but which with time had turned
black. They ripened like cherries, and if you wiped the dirt from
them, they were really smooth and pretty like berries. But where
the bars were cemented into the stone, they had thick roots, or
knobs; that was rust. There on the steps the stench of beer and
urine always hit one through the open door, but what the pub
looked like inside I can't say, for I never went in there. I just saw
people going in and out, and I could see how they wore down the
step surfaces. The steps were made of a soft stone, apparently
some kind of limestone, a strange choice for a spot so frequented.
The stone seemed almost horny, there were many small round
pits and long valleys in it. In rainy weather, water stood in them
like little lakes and streams, though the stone absorbed this
moisture quickly. Generally it was gray with dirt, while along the

sides it was cheese-green from a kind of moss. But if you scraped it
with a piece of glass, the light color of the stone became visible.
It was easy to scratch pictures in it, and when you blew away the
white dust, they looked clear and handsome. But already the next
day dirt from people's feet, together with spit and tobacco juice,
would have ruined the pictures.

"Well, I suppose that slut at home sent you down here after
Dad, huh?" said the subhuman. He stood there bouncing and
spitting. Tobacco juice ran out of the corner of his mouth, collecting in a black pool below.

"I'm not afraid of somebody like you," I said, looking straight
up at him.

The next one to come out on the steps was a superfluous man,
you could see that immediatcly. He was like leftovers, no one even
bothered to notice him. I didn't know him, but he wore decent
gray clothes, had a round head, was red-cheeked, and smiled continuously. He was a superfluous man who was just glad to be
allowed along, glad if he didn't get a kick in the backside, but if
he couldn't get anything else, he might even have been glad for
that.

Father came next, followed by The Just. Wienerbassen hopped
like a hen all the way down to the street. The other three stood
there on the steps blinking and screwing up their eyes. Their
eyes were red and watery, you'd think they'd been crying, but it
was just from the drink. They couldn't get used to the sunlight,
so they didn't see me at first.

"What weather! What weather!" they all said, one after the
other, with Father and the superfluous man echoing The Just. He
dominated them, I could see that well enough. I knew too that
now I'd have a hard time getting Father to go with me. But I
stayed all the same, I wasn't afraid; the stone step was my fortress.
Because of my father, I often had to fight with bigger boys here
by the steps. They'd come over and say something about him
while I was sitting there waiting, and I wouldn't take that. They
could get me down, but I'd never give up.

"Manuel!" exclaimed my father suddenly.

"Well, is that yours?" said The Just.

"They say he's mine," said Father.

"But you're apparently not wholly sure?"

"Well now, is that really yours?" asked the superfluous man.

"But you're not really certain, is that it, little Vilhelm?"

"That's my Manuel, by God!" said my father. "Isn't that right, Manuel?"

"Please come and go home with me," I said.

"What's that you're saying, little Manuel?"

"You should come and go home with me now!"

"What kind of way is that for a little fellow to be talking to you, Vilhelm?" asked The Just.

"That's the kind of person I am," answered Father and laughed.

"Hasn't he been taught respect for you?"

"See what I am!" said Father, slapping himself on the chest.

"You should come home to us now!" I shouted.

"He's my guardian, as I understand it," said Father. "My conscience, because I'm a slack and despicable person. But I like you, little Manuel. We've been through a lot together, haven't we?"

"Let's go now, Father!" I shouted.

"Hold on a minute, I want an explanation here!" said The Just.

"It's because the slut sent him down here," said Wienerbassen. "Vilhelm can't keep her in her place."

"What was that?" cried my father, striding stiffly down the steps. "What was that? What did he say?" and he went for Wienerbassen, whose rat eyes began to blink rapidly. At that moment he was really my father.

"Yes, hit him!" I screamed.

"Listen here, you two clowns," said The Just in his very deep voice, "you know very well I won't tolerate a brawl. I'm a peaceable person, and I intend to have order. But that rascal there is going to have a lesson from me!"

He came down toward me. The Just was a huge man, with layers of fat on his neck, with cheeks and eyes like a boar pig. You could see there was plenty of blood in him. He always wore a leather jacket. He made a living from every possible kind of trade.

He slapped me hard on the cheek. I probably could have

stayed on my feet, but I let myself fall and as I lay there I screamed: "That was wrong, you haven't any right to hit me!"

"Oh don't I, don't I!" said The Just, lifting me a little and hitting me in the face with the other hand. I could smell his terrible breath. "Yes, I have a perfect right, my little friend. They've neglected to teach you properly, so now I have to for society's sake. Do you know why you got the first one? Because you don't respect your father. But why did you get the second? Because you don't respect me. I'll see that you learn order."

And I could hear my father behind us, in a craven voice: "He doesn't mean any harm by it, little Manuel. Don't worry about it, just forget it."

The Just drew himself up and said: "Mark me, Vilhelm, for apparently I must remind you of one thing! You know as well as I that I *always* mean what I say. And you know that I always intend it for all parties concerned. You must know by now that I'm a serious man!"

I got up, there was a whirring in my head, and I had to blink my eyes to get the tears out of them. I said: "You've no right to do that, you're a man who worms money out of him and cheats him!"

"There you see—Manuel can give it back as well as take it," said Father.

"It's not for you to talk about anybody after you've drunk up my money."

"What money was that, little Manuel?"

"You took my two crowns to put in the bank. That was a week ago, but you haven't done it."

"Well, I'm only human, little Manuel."

"Have you used his money, Vilhelm?" asked The Just.

"Not sure about that," said Father. "It's not written on each coin what it's to be used for. But if Manuel says so, it must be right. It's like me anyway."

"There has to be order in things!" said The Just. "You give him a two crown piece right now while I'm a witness to it."

"I'm afraid I can't do it just now," answered Father smiling, "but tomorrow, little Manuel, or day after tomorrow at the latest."

"You can give him this one right now!" said The Just, holding out a coin. "Consider that you've borrowed it from me, and we'll just add it to our little account."

Smiling, Father handed me the two crown piece, his eyes clouded and red, sleepy. But I said: "You can wait and give it to me when Mother can see!"

"All right, Manuel," he said and started to stick the coin in his pocket, but The Just prevented him and took the money back.

"It's probably better for me to put it away," said The Just, "but this all seems a little mysterious to me. Answer me truthfully about one thing. Was it your mother who sent you down here to order your Dad about, even though he's the head of the family?"

"That's none of your business!" I said, jumping back so he couldn't reach me.

"Of course the slut sent him!" said Wienerbassen. "She's so high-assed she won't have anything to do with the likes of us."

"What did he say?" shouted Father, his hackle suddenly rising. But after all he was too craven, there was no real force in him now.

"I wonder if we hadn't ought to go look over the situation?" said The Just. "I could accompany you home, Vilhelm, if you'd care to have me. You did once in an amiable mood invite me. And as for Marie, I remember seeing her once upon a time, way back then."

"I don't recall if I ever did remember to invite you," said Father. "I ought to have done it a long time ago, that's sure! But this is a devil's unlucky day, I don't have a thing in the house!"

"Vilhelm, you know that it's not for the sake of a well-laid table I look in on friends and acquaintances," said The Just. "And for that matter we can simply stop off at a shop on the way home and take a few small things with us."

"A devil's unlucky day!" said Father, "for when one invites guests he ought himself to have something in the house. It's too bad, but I'll have to invite you another day. And I hope you'll come, you'll be truly welcome."

"In other words, you don't want to have us in your home, Vilhelm! Well, well, well! I haven't anything to say to that, not at all, that's a private matter. But then you ought to consider your-

self too good to play this comedy and invite us! Of course, you're
an artist, as they say, and maybe one has to overlook some things."

"What in the hell did you call me?" said Father, "I'm not an
artist, I'm a dog! But I'll invite you, by the devil. Come along!"

"Remember now, you invited us yourself," said The Just. "I'll
be delighted to see how you live at home, and then we can always
sit there comfortably and talk about our little account."

At that Father laughed to high heaven, and they went over to
The Just's car. Wienerbassen took out a crank, spit on it, and
winked at me with one eye. He was chauffeur for The Just. It
was an old car, tall and green. But if the others had forgotten me,
not so the superfluous man. He smiled at me without meaning
anything by it, as if he'd only just noticed me.

I lit out for home. They had to drive a roundabout way to
reach our house, and they also meant to buy liquor somewhere.
I ran along the path past the pond, going as hard as I could. Tears
were coursing down my cheeks till I almost couldn't see, and I
cursed loudly as I ran.

By the willow bush next to the pond stood a large, fat boy—it
was Poul. He was nice, and really smart in school. In fact, he often helped me with arithmetic problems. But now I just swore and
ran past him.

"Why are you crying, Manuel?" he called after me.

I stopped and shouted: "By damn, I'm not crying!"

"You are too! You've got red stripes down your face!"

I flew at him and hit him as hard as I could.

"Ow-ww!" he bawled, "you hit me in the face!"

"Yes," I cried, and then I hit him again on the mouth. He
wailed and looked all gray in the face, and when he put his hand
to his mouth and discovered blood on it, he howled with fright. But
I was gone. Now there'd be trouble I knew, but I didn't have time
to think any more about him. I raced on, and there was the house,
our house! It stood on a corner, and in the sharp spring air you
could see clearly all the places where the plaster had fallen from
the walls and where the paint was peeling over the windows. By
the side of Father's leaning shed lay old stones and piles of rock
chips, and out of the stone heaps bristled dried nettles. But the

front steps of the house were scoured, the front hall was orderly and clean, and the old coats hung neatly on pegs. From the kitchen came the smell of clean clothes, fresh and warm and a bit scorched. Mother was standing at the ironing board. She was all in white, and there wasn't a spot on her. Her black hair glistened, and her face was a little flushed. When she was warm from her work like this, you almost couldn't see that she'd grown thinner. She'd look young and pretty. She washed and ironed for other people, it was mainly she who provided for us now. But she didn't go out to do the work, and she didn't have to tolerate any woman giving her orders, for she was so skillful she could wash and iron those things scarcely anyone else could master.

"I'm to say hello from Grandma!" I shouted immediately. "I stopped by her house. She and the children are fine."

"Manuel, what have you been up to?"

"Nothing, I haven't done anything! Grandma also wants me to ask if you won't come over there right away . . ."

"Manuel, what are those red streaks on your face?"

Then I cried in hard, short bursts, almost like barking.

"He's drunk again!"

"Who's he been with?"

"Wienerbassen and The Just."

"That louse," she said.

Mother swung the iron so that it jumped from the handle and slid along the range until it rested directly over the fire. I admired her for that art. Then she removed her white cap and untied her apron.

"Manuel," she said, "put on your brown shoes and your blue shirt, it's clean and lying in the bedroom. Then take your night clothes and roll them up and put them in the old baby carriage. You can put the girls' night clothes there too."

"But I don't think we need to move," I said, "I don't think he's so bad today. He really didn't want them to come home with him."

Then Mother came over and stood directly in front of me. She put her hands on her hips and looked down at me as if she was scoffing at me.

"So, you still believe in him, do you?" she said.

"I don't know."

"And you can't imagine having a better father?" she asked.

"I don't know," I said, "another might not be any better."

"So, and you think then that things can go on like this?"

"He's awfully nice when he's not drinking," I answered.

"He's his true self when he's drinking," she said; "what he is when he drinks is what he really is!"

I stood there and stared at Mother's one arm. It was shaking, she was terribly tense. Then she knelt down in front of me so she was lower and put her brow against my chest: "Manuel, whatever shall we do?" she whispered.

Right then they arrived. I heard the car stop outside the gate, and I went over to the door. Father and The Just were the first ones to step out of the car.

"Well, and here we have Manuel," shouted The Just. "Hello there, my boy!"

I didn't answer.

"What is it with you, boy?" shouted Father. "Can't you speak when you're spoken to?"

He came striding rapidly up toward me. He was much agitated, I could see that. But The Just shouted: "Don't be too strict now, Vilhelm! One should never lose one's temper with children. Incidentally, the roof on your house isn't too good, is it. Naturally you owe a lot on the old box, eh?"

"It's mortgaged up to the chimney," answered Father swaggering. "In fact, up to the sky."

"I think you ought to sell the old box while you can still make a good deal on it," said The Just.

"And if you were to buy it, that would certainly be a good deal," said Father. He was speaking in a loud, blustering voice, and now he shouted: "Why the devil don't they bring the oasis?"

Wienerbassen and the superfluous man came shuffling, carrying a box filled with bottles.

Father stopped outside the door and shouted: "I hope my dear wife will be good enough to come and receive these guests. They're my friends, friends for life. Moreover, I've brought an important man whom you know already, but he says he hasn't seen you for many years. He says that you danced with him once. You'll never forget that, will you?" he said to The Just.

The Just shook his head. "No, indeed," he answered, "there are some things a man doesn't forget."

Then my father shouted in a terribly loud voice :"Marie, come out here!"

I became aware of Mother standing beside me in the doorway. I took her by the hand, and she said: "Vilhelm, take your friends, as you call them, and go away. Don't make us miserable."

"Miserable?" said Father, "what's that supposed to mean? By the Lord, we've truly come to make you happy! Truly we have. And these are truly my friends for life, and that woman there is truly my sweetheart. Maybe we can get up a little dance here, eh? I'll play the harmonica."

"Well, I may not be so light on my feet any more," said The Just, "but I still know how. I do remember well that I've danced with you before, Marie."

"And it was unforgettable!" said Father.

"I don't know that person," said Mother.

"That's embarrassing for me, isn't it," said The Just. "Usually people manage to remember me very well."

"Don't let it bother you," said Father. "My wife has met so many, and so it's not easy just on the spur of the moment to re-member someone in particular."

"She's a catfish," said Wienerbassen behind him.

Father turned around, laid his hand lightly on that man's shoulder, and said: "For the moment you're my guest and my friend for life, and so it's impossible for me to beat you. I'm as hospitable as the bedouins, you might say. But bedouins don't forget. I'll come back to this matter when you're no longer my guest."

"Just leave Bassen to me, I'll take care of him," said The Just. "But now, Vilhelm, will you kindly explain to your wife that we didn't come to cause inconvenience. Maybe you can get her to understand that we're not intrusive and impudent people, but that you yourself invited us. And if you regret it now, we'll cer-tainly be glad to leave. But then perhaps you ought to think it over a little better another time."

"What kind of nonsense is that?" said Father. "Of course I invited you. Step inside!"

"Vilhelm," said Mother in that calm voice I was most afraid of, "you'll not bring these people in as long as I'm here. It's never come to that before, and I will not tolerate it in my house."

"Your house?" said Father.

"Aah, it's your wife's house then, Vilhelm?" said The Just. "In that case you've acted very wrongly, for you had no right to invite us."

Father said nothing. He stood there, looking with clouded eyes over the garden toward the shed. His glance moved slowly from one stone to the next. Everyone stood there silent, for his behavior was so strange. He turned his head and looked at his guests one after the other, as if amazed. Then he stared at Mother. They stood there looking at each other for a long time, and he smiled. It was so strange one could scarcely breathe.

"Vilhelm," she said softly.

"Yes," he answered.

"It's not too late, Vilhelm."

"Maybe it is." And he smiled.

Mother turned from the door, and I followed her out into the kitchen. She sat down on a chair and stared.

"Welcome to the house!" we heard him shout. "Come on in where it's warm, for you are truly our friends! Let's see now what the house has to offer."

Father came out into the kitchen. He poured water in the kettle, sat it over the fire, and said: "I won't ask you to do anything. I'm not going to trouble you to make coffee. By all means just stay sitting!"

When the kettle whistled, I took the whistle off and sat down again by Mother. It was getting along toward evening now, the light was fading. The whole time we could hear them in there. Finally Father came out to the boiling water. "So, you don't like my friends, eh?" he said as he filtered the coffee. "That's understandable, they're swine. But they're my friends. I invited them."

Later on he opened the door to the kitchen and shouted at us: "I'd better forewarn you, the parlor may look a little different after this blessed day is over. We're having a pleasant card game, and we may be playing for a few of these things. I've had a little account with him which I wish to dispose of in an honorable way—unfortunately for the moment it's gotten somewhat larger. But I want you to know I'm only putting up the things which came from my home!"

Behind him the boar head of The Just came into view, and it said thickly: "It is true, dear lady, that in order to make the hours pass more entertainingly your husband has in several exceptional instances put up furniture and such things. But I do assure you, that if something or other belonging to the lady should happen to get mixed in, naturally it will be returned with apologies, as is only right."

They drank a lot, and they made a lot of noise. Mother sat straight and stiff in the chair, and I sat on the woodbox beside her. It was almost completely dark, so Grandmother would soon be coming with the younger children. I knew I should probably go over there to stop her.

Father came out in the kitchen again. He had drunk a great deal, but he was very calm. "Manuel, I want to speak with your mother," he said. "Take the basket and go get some wood!"

I went with the basket, but I stopped by the door. Father sat down on the box where I'd been sitting, and I heard him mumble: "Marie, can you see what it's all coming to?"

She didn't answer.

"Marie, does it say anything to you?"

Mother drew a breath heavily, but she didn't answer.

"Marie," he said again, very softly and calmly, "you're going to have to help now. You're going to have to finish it. You're going to have to help now."

"I don't see how I can help."

"Yes, you can. Yes, Marie! I don't know how you'll go about it, but I know you can. Yes, you can, and no one else."

"No," she said, "maybe I'd like to, but I can't, Vilhelm. Everything's dead now."

"I see," he said, getting up. And I hid myself behind the door. "Well, then," he said, stepping out into the hall and lighting a lantern. Then he knocked on the parlor door, threw it open and shouted: "Come out here, you misers, and I'll show you an artist. Come on out and look at the junk."

They went in a staggering, noisy procession out to the shed. An hour later they returned, each of them carrying something or other of Father's work. All of the best pieces.

He stood in the doorway and lifted the lantern.

"We can't bring the large gravestone in to take a closer look at it," he said, "but it's not bad at all, though I say it myself. I had thought it would mark the grave of someone in particular. Ha ha, sometimes one thinks too much. But I don't doubt it will stand over some good person sometime."

He lifted the lantern higher and came in to us. In his other hand was the little stone head, my sister, she who had Mother's large, smooth forehead, she who was dead. "Look at it!" he said. "Look now!" he repeated, turning the head in the light. "You must say goodbye to her now!"

Then he disappeared with the bunch of them into the parlor, and the kitchen was dark around us. We sat there silently for a long time.

"Manuel," she said, "who do you think is unhappy now?"

"I know very well."

We remained sitting there in the dark. Mother had scarcely moved, and she had not cried.

"Have you ever wished you were a bird and could fly?"

"Yes," my mother said.

I had come back from telling Grandmother that the children could stay with her for the night. Again I was in the dark kitchen with Mother. We sat there as still as the dead.

"Manuel, I wonder if you too will find people in stone?"

"No," I said.

THE BIRDS

ONE DAY young Espen came home and announced that he had resigned his position and taken another.

"Wagtails must wag," said his father. "It's not so very long since the last time, and the time before that. Who's to have the honor now?"

"The priest at Kyndelby," answered Espen.

"The one they call the fool priest, eh?" said the father. "It's nice to have a sensible son who feels compelled to look out for lost sheep. How much will you get in wages?"

The boy was to have half as much as in his last position.

"This gets better and better," said his father. "I suppose you've also committed yourself to pay his debts?"

"You can cancel the arrangement if you want to," said the boy.

"I wouldn't dream of it, especially when I'm so lucky in having a shrewd son," answered the father. "Besides, you're seventeen now, and that's an advanced age."

"My father is forgetting that I'll be eighteen," said Espen.

"Not at all, if you don't mind my correcting you," answered his father, "for if you're going to be eighteen, it is quite obvious that you *are* seventeen. But will you look around now and find a cloth to wipe up the floor with, for I'm quite sure your mother is going to shed tears over this."

"Have you forgotten all the good sermons you've heard here?" said his mother, who had overheard them and was in fact crying.

"I always fell asleep," answered the boy.

"What's this you're saying to your mother?" she lamented.

"I'll just say it straight out," said he, "I like the priest at Kyndelby better."

"His sermons are frightful," said the mother.

"Yes, they *are* pretty bad," said Espen.

"Have you actually heard him, child?" she screamed.

"Three and a half times," he replied, "the half is because I fell asleep in the middle of the first time. I was in the habit."

"My poor child, this is almost more appalling that if you had become a pimp or a Catholic!" said she. "But if you're going to do it anyway, couldn't you get us some good preserving apples from the rectory garden? They ought to be exceptionally fine."

The boy promised he would, and when November came, he went over to Kyndelby.

"How is it that you clear your throat every time I look at you?" asked the priest after Espen had been there fourteen days.

"Well, that pile out behind should have been hauled and spread long ago," answered the boy. He was referring to the stable dung.

"Is that so?" said the priest. "That is annoying, isn't it. Why haven't you spoken to Mads about it?"

"You've got to collect it, you've got to collect it!" shouted Mads. He was an old fellow who puttered about the farm. The priest himself cultivated the ground, and he did a poor job of it.

"It's a shame we haven't done it," said the priest; "is it too late now?"

"No, I can take care of it, provided that Mads doesn't get in my way," said the boy.

"I'll hand in my resignation!" shouted the old idler.

"Oh, that would be too bad," said the priest. "Mads has nothing else to live on. I've thought many times, Mads, that you're an impossible loafer. But I could never bring myself to fire you."

"Give praise and thanks for the crumbs," shouted Mads, "and

be sure to wag your tail; give thanks and praise and remember Lazarus."

"What did you say, you old swindler?" shouted the priest. "Are you insulting the man who's sacrificed everything for you, you scoundrel. You talk about Lazarus: do you dare to think that Lazarus stole eggs and cheese and sold them in town? I wonder if Lazarus emptied the tobacco can, you thieving wretch."

"I don't give a damn what you say about me," shouted Mads. "I haven't seen a shilling in nine months, God knows."

"One gets nothing but trouble and ingratitude for one's pains," shouted the priest, "trouble and ingratitude. But the truth is," he said to the boy, "I've done old Mads a bitter injustice. He's faithful, and he is excellent. He's as nice and as patient as a person could be, and I really owe him a lot in back wages. Did I accuse you of stealing, dear Mads? I'm sorry about that, Mads, really sorry. I'm going to increase your wages. Say, couldn't we give Mads wages without his having to do anything for it?"

"Yes, that would be a good arrangement," answered the boy.

And so Espen hauled out the dung and spread it. He was a hard worker in the field.

The priest came out with the horses to plow. "I love to plow," said he. But his furrows were so crooked that the birds who swarmed down after worms got dizzy walking in them. As the priest passed Espen, who was spreading dung, he heard him say:

"This is simply unspeakable. Amen! This is terribly bad farming. Amen!"

"What is that you're saying?" asked the priest.

"I'm preaching a sermon," answered the boy.

"Well, it's a strange sermon."

"A priest ought to know," said the boy, "and if I may say so, that's strange plowing."

"That makes me feel bad," said the priest, "but perhaps you can teach me something about it."

The boy plowed several times around the field, straightening the furrows; and though it was foggy, as if they were standing in a deserted island, he made the furrows so true that one could have shot a rifle ball through the length of them.

"That really looks good," said the tall priest, "obviously one has to know what one is doing. Won't you explain to me now how you do it?"

"It isn't something you can explain," said Espen, "you just have to have it in you. But the horses must learn to step out and to hold the swingletrees even. That way they hold their necks high, and they become proud. Otherwise they become sullen and obstinate like Mads."

"I really wonder if there's anything I could teach you that you don't already know," said the priest.

"When you swing the plow, the traces should be tight," said the boy. "That way you can set the plow in the furrow with two fingers. Like this. It rises easily out of the ground and lands again like a gull."

"That must be delightful," said the priest, "but frankly, when you're as clever as you are, I can't understand why you're willing to work here for me."

"Once in a lifetime you should do something crazy," answered the boy.

"Of course," said the priest, "but it doesn't have to be *that* crazy. Don't you have other reasons?"

"Well, since more than a few had quit on you," said Espen, "it gave me courage to try."

"You're making my conscience bother me," said the priest, "for it's just possible I won't even be able to pay you your wages. Is there something else I can do for you? Do you want to learn Latin?"

"Yes, thanks," answered the boy.

"But I still wonder if there aren't other reasons?"

"Well, ye-ess," said Espen, drawing it out, "to be honest I don't think your sermons are particularly good."

"You have some judgment in that too, and you think that my sermons are bad," said the priest sorrowfully. "Well, you're completely right about that, it's true, God help me."

"I've fallen asleep in many a good sermon," said the boy, "and I'll trade them all gladly for a bad one."

"I'm no Demosthenes or Abelard, alas," said the priest. "I'm well aware that my superiors are very dissatisfied with me. You're right. I feel completely inadequate when I stand before the altar or in the pulpit. But what was that just then?"

"It was a toad," said Espen. They saw the fat little fellow twitch his arms and legs in the furrow just before the plow plunged earth on top of him. Quickly the priest began to dig with his hands in the dirt.

"We must save you, little brother," said the priest, and when he could not find the toad, he went home to get shovels. Finally, as it was darkening over the plowed field, he stood with the toad in his hand—and it was still alive, its heart beating so that its breast steadily rose and fell.

"Tell me now," said the priest that evening in his study as they began to read Latin, "is it because of my daughter that you've come?"

"If that were the reason, I'd have been smart to stay home," answered the boy.

"Good," said the priest. "Nevertheless, we'll begin by conjugating the verb 'love.' As a matter of fact, it's the most important of all words."

The progress with Latin was very slow, for the priest had a thousand other things to think about. But the boy did not lack aptitude, and since he had a good head for figures, he began to keep books on the farming operation. It looked pretty bleak, but Espen worked like a Trojan in order to brighten the picture.

One evening as they were sitting about, the priest wanted to read to them from the works of Homer. "I love Homer," said the priest. "Since the coming of the Gospel, there haven't been any real creators in the literary arts. No doubt they're superfluous now. But Homer was a creator. Wouldn't you just love to be a Homer?"

"Well, ye—ess," said the boy. But sometimes he fell asleep in the middle of the books, just as Homer does.

"I'll see to it that you get your eyes opened," said the priest.

One night during the winter he woke Espen and insisted that he get up and dress himself warmly. Outside it was storming fiercely. The priest also woke the three tramps who were sleeping in the parlor (there was always someone coming there for a meal and a place to stay overnight). "Now you're going to see God create a poem," the priest shouted in to them. "Get some extra clothes from the hallway." The priest's wife and daughter came out in thick cloaks. He bowed to his wife, who was a good woman, and he offered her his arm. "You can take Helena," he shouted to the boy. After the priestly couple came the three sleepy tramps, and then came Espen and the daughter. She held tightly to him, which made him a little nervous.

Along they went toward the coast, directly against the wind. They had to lean forward in order not to be blown over. Helena squeezed the boy's arm—she was a year older then he and lively—and it was not long before she stuck her hand in his pocket.

"Oh, how delightfully warm," said she, "but what is this you have here?"

"It's just some snail shells, they're not worth anything."

"But there's also something larger, what is it?"

"Oh, that's nothing but a lobster claw."

"You're going to be my knight, aren't you?" said she.

"If only I'm up to it," answered the boy.

"You're quick and strong and handsome, you have clean nails," she said, "you'll make a wonderful knight. But you ought to play for me on the harp or the flute. And you must wear my color on your armor."

"What color is that?"

"Red," she said excitedly.

"Red like rust?" he asked.

"No, like blood," said the girl, "and you must come riding with beautiful, priceless gifts for me."

"I have nothing but snail shells and a lobster claw," said Espen.

"Ah, if only we were engaged," said she directly into his ear so that it tickled. It was blowing so hard they had to scream that which ordinarily one whispers.

"Yes indeed," said the boy.

"You're welcome to come and sing beneath my window at night," said she.

"Thanks a lot."

"It's all right if you knock on the window."

"Thanks," he said.

"Ah, it's hard walking against the wind," said she. "Lover, put your strong arm around my waist. Yes, like that. No, hold tighter, my own sweet boy."

The boy held her more tightly, and he couldn't help noticing that she was shaped to the purpose, for she was slender there but plumper both above and below.

As they approached the sea, great damp clouds came flying against them. The priest led his little flock forward to the cliff edge where they came to a stop. Below, the heavy surf pounded against the rocks. A piece of the cliff before them suddenly slid away, and one of the tramps just managed to save the priest's wife. A great tree leaned far over, too far, and plunged into the sea without their even hearing the splash. And every time the ocean took a breath, a mile of stones ran up the shore. It was very dark, as if both sea and clouds had just come flowing out of the Kingdom of Death.

The priest stood there at the edge like a tall beacon in which the light has been extinguished. He reached forth a long arm as if he meant to tear down the ragged edges of Heaven. His hat blew off and flew like a great bird away into the dark. But no one could hear what it was he was shouting and explaining.

The oldest of the three tramps likewise felt impelled to communicate. The blanket, in which he was wrapped, billowed about him and made him appear enormously fat. He and the priest shouted many times to each other without the priest understanding him.

"I'm just saying that it's sure windy," bellowed the tramp at the top of his lungs.

But then they saw a light moving far out at sea, and the priest wanted to get home and telephone the coast patrol. Helena and the boy brought up the rear of the procession, and once again she slipped inside his arm. As long as he held her tightly, she said not a word.

"Oh, but that was a wonderful walk," she whispered in his ear as they came into the shelter of the trees, and then the boy realized that he was kissing her. "Longer, my knight!" she said.

The boy obliged, though he couldn't understand how she kept it up so long. Neither could his snail shells, as he discovered later.

"Lover," said Helena, "I am an ocean with lovely, large waves. But watch out that Mother doesn't see us."

The priest wanted them all to come in to the church; they were to pray for the sailors at sea. He lit the candles and said: "Have any of you been to sea?"

"Yes, I have," said one of the tramps.

"I too," said the second.

"Then it is fitting for you to speak to God," said the priest.

"I'll pray God to keep them abeam of the seas," said the first.

"And keep them cheerful," said the second.

"Amen," said the priest.

But the priest's good wife fell into ill health after that nocturnal excursion, she wasted away, and along toward spring she died.

"I'm guilty of my wife's death," said the priest to everyone he met.

"Oh, don't look at it that way," folks replied, in order to say something.

"Yes, my boy," said the priest to Espen just before she died, "I knew she wasn't strong, and in spite of that I took her out to see Homer's Superior compose hexameters. She's the finest soul that ever walked the earth, yet I've always been irascible and inconsiderate toward her, don't you think so?"

"Yes," said the boy.

"It's right for you to say so," said the priest, wiping his nose. "But go in to my wife now; she asked me to call you."

"Take care of him," said the wife to Espen (who scarcely dared to breathe in the sickroom; he was afraid it would blow out her flame of life, so weak she looked), "take care of him. He has a bird in his breast; take good care of it."

The boy went home to see his parents.

"Well," said his father, "your clothes are still shrinking. You ought to buy a new suit that is large enough. After all, you're getting good wages."

"I haven't been paid anything yet," answered Espen.

"What does that matter, as long as you know the money is

there," said the father. "I've been thinking that the next time you wag your tail, you might come home and dig us a new well. But apparently you're not leaving your place yet?"

"No," said the boy, "and I've come to ask if you'll loan me several hundred crowns."

"Why, of course," answered the father. "I don't have them, for things aren't too fat around here just now, but I'll go out and borrow the money for you immediately. Your father is well thought of, that's a good thing for a son to know, just as it's a good thing when a father can say about his children: Look here, even though the oaf has some rough edges, I know that there's good wood in him."

"I've a stone here with a peculiar hole in it," said the boy, "I'll lay it here on the chest. It'll be security for the money, and when you see it, you'll know that I'm going to come home and dig the well as soon as I can. But you haven't asked me what I need the money for."

The father did not reply. He combed his few remaining hairs, put on a dark coat, and went out to borrow the money.

"I'd like to know, Espen," said his mother.

"I just want to see that the priest's wife shall be properly buried," said the boy.

"Poor woman," said the mother, "she was the daughter of a bishop. That's the way it goes. But anyway, you have my blessing."

The boy paid for the casket, and he helped to bear it at the funeral. He could scarcely tell that there was anything in it, so wasted away she was, so strong had he become.

"From dust you came, to dust you shall return, from dust you shall again come forth," said the priest. Around him stood many poor folks and vagrants. They were a people unto themselves.

The home came unglued after the wife was gone. The priest was deeply in debt, he gave away much, was cheated out of much, and didn't take care of the rest. Furthermore, he became queer. He didn't want to see anyone at the rectory, he locked himself into his study, and there he sat trying to draw his wife's face. If there had been pictures of her earlier, they could not be found in the present disorder. The priest couldn't draw her, but he kept trying. He tore up the papers and threw them out the window, then he began again, After a long time had passed this way, the boy knocked on the door.

"Don't dare to disturb me!" shouted the priest.

The boy went around to the window.

"What do you want?" shouted the priest.

"There's much to be done," answered Espen.

"How dare you camp outside my study, you lout," shouted the priest. "You're intrusive and ill-mannered in your nature. I doubt you can even say the Articles of Faith. And how did it go with Latin, not even to mention Homer, whom you fell asleep over. Go on back to your work, you're getting good wages, you know."

"Is that so?" said the boy. "That is good to know."

"In addition to everything else, you're impudent," shouted the priest.

"I'm just glad to know that I'm going to get my wages," said Espen. "I'd like to be paid now."

"For God's sake," shouted the priest, "then take one of the cows in the stable! How many are left, aren't there still two? Then take one of them and disappear."

The boy went and packed his belongings together. As he was leaving the rectory with his bundle, he met Helena. She had a garland of dandelions about her throat.

"What have you there in the bundle, my worshiper?" she cried.

"It's only my armor," answered the boy.

"Are you off on a crusade?" she asked. "Oh, you must return very soon and set me free. For the days of my tribulation are almost past, and I had thought that day after tomorrow we ought to marry. But for now I must have a love pledge from you."

"Here is my lobster claw," answered Espen.

After a little, the priest caught up with him. He was carrying a hoe. "Would you be willing to show me how I should do the weeding?" asked the priest. And so Espen carried his belongings back, and he showed the priest what to weed.

"Now I can see my wife's face in the flowers," said the priest when he had worked a while. After that he no longer locked himself in his study.

But it was the boy who did most for the place. He did the work of three men in the field, and sang while he did it. "Ready, set, fire!" and he attacked the thistles and couch grass in the neglected fields. When the weather became fine, Helena came out with the boy. Not that she helped him very much. "Actually I'm a poppy," she said. "I must be careful so as not to lose my petals, but of course you'll be twice as strong when you have a poppy to look at."

She didn't wear a great many clothes, and she became brown in the sun. When the boy was cutting hay down in the moor where no one could see them, she was like a wild enchanted thing.

"I know now that my days of sorrow are past," said she. "Aah, let me be an ocean again. Kiss me, my Prince Paris." And then: "Ooh, how playful we are! You're like a thousand handsome knights, and now I am going to cut you up the middle, for I am a scissors."

The boy left the hay standing a little too long, and they played Adam and Eve all the while.

"We really should tell your father about this," said Espen.

"Do whatever you wish, my sweet Lord," said she.

Espen hesitated for several days, but then he went to speak with the priest. "I'm sorry to say it, but I've broken one of the commandments."

"Have you, my friend?" said the priest, "just one of the commandments? Which one was it?"

"I'm quite sure it was the fifth," said the boy.

"Espen, Espen, Espen, oh my," said the priest, laying his hand on his shoulder, "then you must have been very confused and unhappy. And you did it in a fit of temper, isn't that right? Temper, temper, it's the most terrible thing in itself, Espen. Lord God almighty. Not often is one as fortunate as Peter, who merely cut the ear off Malthus. My boy, my boy, even though you've done this terrible thing, which I've only thought of doing, I can't say that I'm any better than you. But tell me about it."

"Well, I'm afraid I made a mistake," said Espen, backing up a little to escape the priest's fatherly grip on his shoulder—but without succeeding, for the priest moved with him, "I think I should have said the seventh commandment."

"You mean it wasn't murder, but stealing?" exclaimed the priest. "What are you saying, boy. Do you mean you came here to confess a shabby theft? And what's going on in your head, boy, that you mix up the commandments? Rooting around with your snout in our Lord's commandments like a lazy pig. And right to my face. You blockhead. If only I'd known that, I'd have seen to it that the commandments and their words were banged into your thick skull."

"I'm not at all sure that would have helped," said the boy.

"Oh, oh," said the priest, "this must be more serious than I thought. What did you steal?"

"Somehow I just can't bring myself to say it," answered Espen.

"Can't say it!" cried the priest, pacing with quick long strides back and forth in the room. "Then why in the name of heaven did you come here?"

"I didn't want someone else to come and tell you before I did," said the boy.

The priest stood at the window collecting his thoughts.

"Stealing? I never would have thought that of you," he said, "and I still don't believe you would. You've bungled again. Obviously you mean the commandment in between, the sixth."

"Yes," said the boy.

"I must be getting old," said the priest, sitting down in his chair, "I should have realized from the first that's what we were talking about. But tell me, Espen, do you think you can give up this sin if you tell me about it?"

"No, I'm afraid not," answered the boy.

"I'm afraid not also," said the priest, "I'm afraid not."

"But it's not quite that simple," said Espen.

"I know that, my boy, it's not so simple," said the priest, "but I hadn't realized you had reached that point. Still I must thank you for the polite and proper way you've treated my daughter Helena."

"Yes, some of the time," answered the boy.

"Oh, my God!" said the priest. "You're both so young. But we've got to get you married. That's what you mean to do, isn't it?"

"Yes," said the boy.

"Well, I'm glad of that," said the priest, "in fact, very happy! That lifts a heavy burden from me. Very heavy. I've been so concerned about Helena since her mother's been gone. But I thank God for the son-in-law I'm getting, indeed I do. So let's have a glass of wine!"

The priest called the kitchen girl and asked her to fetch Helena to him. Then he took out several dusty glasses, and from the bottom of a cupboard he took out a wine flask. "It's empty," he said. The next one was likewise empty. "They're all empty," said he, "but we must have a drink one way or another."

The girl came back and said that she couldn't find Helena, but that someone had seen her walking in the woods with the grocer's son, who was home for vacation.

"Yes, that's excellent, Anna," said the priest, "but will you help me now by looking everywhere to find some good wine."

The boy left. He too went for a walk in the woods. It was not a large forest, just a leafy grove filled with old trees, with thickets, and with hiding places which he well knew. But he didn't look into the hiding places, though he went entirely around the grove. He had become a solid lad, not small at all, and now he went around treading firmly on all the dry branches so that they crackled and snapped under him. Then he went home again.

Not until evening did Helena return, looking splendid. The priest called both of them in to him. He hadn't found any wine; instead he poured raspberry juice into the glasses. Lifting his glass, he looked at the radiant Helena and the glum lad.

"Children," said he, "I am very happy."

"I'm very happy too," said Helena, "but why are we drinking wine now?"

"I can already see in my mind's eye," said the priest, "how I'll be sitting here with my little grandchildren on my knee."

"You'll surely have them, delightful children," said Helena, "and they'll have a wonderfully beautiful father."

"Well, of course Espen is not so bad looking," said the priest, "—but wonderfully beautiful?"

"Oh, it's not Espen, my dear, how could you think that," said Helena. "Espen is quite nice looking, you really are, Espen! But you are, and you'll always be, a peasant. There's no denying that you have a handsome nose, and manly eyes, and a good mouth, but they're still a peasant nose and a peasant mouth, you'll admit that yourself. There are men who are much finer and much handsomer, that I know."

The priest emptied his glass. "Good night, children," he said, and he left.

"It's quite all right for you to kiss me," said Helena. "But you certainly can't expect me to marry you. You understand that, don't you?"

"Skaal," said Espen, and he drank his raspberry juice.

"I was terribly embarrassed for your sake," said Helena. "We heard you sneaking around in the woods. But you were so peasant-clumsy, continually stepping on dried twigs. The student got completely pale in the face, so angry he was. You must remember that for another time."

The boy watched over every seed and straw, slaving from sunrise till sundown. And the priest gave away everything the creditors didn't take. Furthermore, he began to increase his debt with wineflasks which arrived full but very quickly became empty. Perhaps he thought he could find in the wine some good advice for his romantic daughter. He counseled, he threatened, he pleaded with her. But Helena was mad about beautiful knights, and she made them happy. Finally she flew away, flew with one of her worshipers over land and sea to the big city. She sent little, brightly colored postcards, she was having wonderful adventures. And her father preached a great many very bad sermons in which he said that he was a bad, unhappy father and priest, a caricature of God. Be not as I am, good people, he cried. Many agreed heartily with these sentiments, and since there were shocking rumors about his daughter's life in the city, since he was not clever on the one hand, nor strict in administering the rituals on the other, and since he even seemed offended by extreme piety, they managed eventually to pry him from his ministry. By then he was frightfully in debt (Espen could not hold him above water, even though he worked his heart out), so that a forced auction of his possessions was held.

Now suddenly Helena came flying home to her father, whose nose had taken on a dignified bluish hue. She had heard that he was to be put out-of-doors, but she was here now and would help him of course. Several years had passed, and Helena, radiant and beautiful, came driving up in an automobile which was itself as beautiful as a ladybird—and her very own. It had been given her by a marvelous man who continually gave her the most expensive gifts, in fact, anything she pointed at. Her husband? Good heavens no! You can't think that Helena would be so egotistic and petty as to marry. To be sure, she had met a very poor but noble flute player whom she had wanted to make happy for the rest of their lives. What of it, she had left him; it had been impossible and trivial. But she would find means for her father. How much did he need?

"My poor girl," said the priest, "I can't have you do that."

"Why do you say poor?" said Helena. "I know now, of course, that there are not so many fine, true knights as I had believed earlier. But I assure you, there are delightful people who want to make me happy, and whom I want to make happy. And now you're going to be happy to."

"My poor little girl," said the priest. "I won't hide my poverty under your luxuriant shame. Would to God that you had come in impoverished humility to hide yourself under my rags."

"Did you say shame, my little Father?" she replied. "My dear, I am so jubilantly happy that I can give happiness. It's so wonderful to be a beautiful woman that sometimes, I must admit it, I'm even envious of myself. Oh, yes, to be a swelling ocean, to be a brightly colored postcard and travel by post to gladden someone who is grieved. I'm a flying bird, Father. Is that a shame?"

"My dear, my little girl," said the priest, "you've doubtless inherited your mania for flying from me, and you see before you how the feathers fall off and one is left sitting lead-bellied at the last. This vessel is so shattered that God's authority can never be poured into it again, and thus I can't say to you what I ought to say. But are you really happy?"

"I could fly up and kiss the sun," said she.

"Well, come back when you aren't happy," said the priest, "or when you've burned yourself."

"Dear little Father," said Helena, "you do look frightful in those clothes. I really must help you."

"Well," said the priest, "perhaps you could buy a flask of wine for me. Wine would be very good for my health."

Out of sheer happiness she kissed him, and then she asked: "Who is that singing?"

"It must be Espen," said the priest. "He's been paid his wages, that's probably why."

"Good heavens," she exclaimed. "Didn't he go to America years ago?"

"He's leaving soon," said the priest. "And he's been paid. I'm proud to say that I gave him his back pay. Not all of it, of course; well, in fact, very little of it. But you did see that all my books are gone. Yes, I sold them before they came and made up the list of all my things; Espen didn't know about it either. And I hung onto the money well enough that I could give him over half of it. But I didn't part with my Homer. On the sly I'm taking him with me, *The Iliad* in the right pocket and *The Odyssey* in the left, nearest to my heart. And naturally my Testament in the inside pocket."

Helena drove off to the grocer in her red ladybird and returned with a dozen flasks for the priest. Then she went over to Espen's room. He was sitting there tying a lump of lead to the end of a string.

"God in heaven, what a man you've become!" said Helena. "But what have you there?"

"A plumb line," answered the boy, "it's to be used for digging a well. How's the lobster claw?"

"What lobster claw are you talking about?" said she. "My but haven't you become a man. What a pleasing profile, and such arms. And your beard too, even though you're very nicely shaved. You *are* something to look at."

"How many knights have played the harp for you by now?" said the boy.

"Oh, many," said she, "but I've loved a thousand, maybe ten thousand beautiful men."

"This is a fine shovel for well-digging," said the boy. "I forged it myself and carved the handle. It's a very good one, even if it looks a little peasant-crude."

"You can leave whenever you want," said Helena. "You needn't worry, I'll take care of father. He'll be well-off with me, I'll spoil him."

"I don't think you should do that," said Espen. "He's at the end of his rope now, but he's still worth more than that. Let me help you to remember that for another time." With that he grabbed her and laid her over his knee.

"Espen," she cried, trying to slip free, "I'm a poppy, you know I am. I can stand anything if I'm happy, but you'll shake off my petals if you hurt me."

"I've worn your color on my armor," said the boy, and he struck her.

She crept up on his bed and sat there.

"Helena," said the boy, "don't sit there looking at me that way."

"You remember, don't you," said she.

"Helena," he said, "you're not to sit there looking pretty."

But she did, and the boy did not finish his plumb line.

Now Helena wanted nothing but him, and she decided to stay. But the boy left.

"You are no fatter than you were," said his father as Espen stood in the parlor, "your clothes seem to fit, and that's always an advantage."

"Here is the money I borrowed," said the boy, "and thank you very much."

"Don't mention it," said the father. "Just let me put on my shirt front, and I'll go pay it back at once. But there's too much here."

"That's the interest and the interest on the interest up to and including today," said the boy.

"Is the wagtail ready to wag again?" said the father.

"We can go and measure for the well," said Espen, "though I still have an errand to do. But the stone with the hole is lying there on the chest, isn't it. Where is Mother?"

"Lying down," said the father. "Until lately she's been lively as a roe deer, but now she's dragging her hooves a little. Go in and see her while I run over with this money before they add on more interest."

The priest was alone when he took his leave of the empty house. In the garden he plucked a rose from a bush his wife had planted, stuck it in his buttonhole, patted himself on *The Odyssey*, and left.

"Well, are you here?" said he.

It was the boy, sitting there on the stone fence beside the gate. The priest sat down with a sigh on the other side. He was already tired in the legs with just walking through the garden.

"I thought that you were through with being crazy," said the priest.

"One should be thorough," said the boy.

"You have underscored that point," answered the priest, sniffing his rose.

"There's just one thing I'd like to ask," said Espen. "Would it be all right if I say 'du' to you now." *

"My boy," said the priest, "that would make me very happy. I'd feel as if I'd just been named to the Royal Order."

"Where are you planning to go now?" asked the boy.

"I haven't the faintest," answered the priest, "but no doubt there's a spot somewhere for Lazaruses."

"I should tell you that my parents send greetings; you're welcome with them, and you can live there."

"Thank you," said the priest.

They sat there for some time, resting on either side of the fence.

"There was something else I wanted to ask," said Espen. "Just

* I.e, employ the familiar form of second person pronouns.

before she died, the good mistress said something to me. There was a person, she said, who had a bird in his breast, and that I should watch over it. I wonder what that meant?"

"My Adele," said the priest, "she believed in me too much. I don't know what she meant by it, though she said it often. But it was she who held things together here. Since then it's gone downhill badly, hasn't it?"

"Yes," said the boy.

"And what about you, where will you go?" asked the priest.

"Trees often bear their sweetest fruit just before they fall," said Espen.

"Ah ha!" exclaimed the priest, "I should preach some more miserable sermons, that's what you think, is it? Apparently you're not all there, you fool. Don't I deserve a little peace now that my knees will scarcely bear my dry-rotted body? Ha! I was welcome at your place, you said, and I was so touched I was about to faint and fall off this fence. But I don't believe you any more, sir. I won't accept your offer. No, I'm going to the Land of Nod, which no one knows."

"I can work," said the boy, "I can plow, forge, dig wells, figure interest, run errands, I can find food for the bird who can't find it for himself. But I can say nothing to people that they'd do well to hear that they don't know already."

"How should I be able to do it, failure that I am?" exclaimed the priest. "Before I could believe that, you'd have to explain to me how a poor sermon can be good."

"Right," said Espen, "well, you get pulled out on a stormy night, and a man stands there shouting, trying to explain something which you can neither hear nor understand. And yet somehow you come to know what you'd never known before."

"My boy," said the priest, getting up, "I'm nothing but a skunk in priestly clothes. I'll just plod along streets and roads until I drop over. I don't know precisely what I'll do. He'll just have to whisper to me along the way. Perhaps I'll screech like a crow about human corruption, perhaps I'll twitter like a lark about the light of the resurrection. And maybe He'll say, with this person don't say anything at all. I don't know precisely where I'll preach those miserable sermons—or even if I'll preach them. But I'm going now."

"I think I'd better go with you," said the boy.

"Such delightful old trees," said the priest as they walked down a road lined with lindens. "One would like to press every leaf in one's hand and then have a really good talk with those old sisters. One should read them carefully, for their trunks contain hiero-glyphics and legends from top to bottom. And look at the clouds, for they are—in truth—clouds, one sees them framed up there between the trees. And the grass out there, there is only one thing in the world that that can be, genuine green grass. And the oats there in the field, one has seen them so often that he knows them inside out, and yet they renew the heart, like seeing again a face one can never grow tired of. And look, there is Adele's picture!" said he, pointing to a little, white-starred flower on the ditch bank.

"And there's another picture," said the boy: he was looking at a poppy.

The flat stone with the peculiar hole still lay on the chest, on the white cloth which was always changed on feast days. But once or twice a week, depending on how busy things were in garden and field, it was dusted and wiped with a wet cloth. Then for a short time it was bright-colored, with red, blue, and yellow here and there and silver spots in between. As it dried it became gray again, its short Sunday over.

The stone had hundreds of Sundays. Finally it was allowed to remain gray; no longer did the woman's hand with the wet cloth come to interrupt. Now and then when the dust got very thick, a bearded face came and blew the worst of it away.

In the large city, in a hospital room with many patients, the fool priest lay. With half-open mouth and a nose that jutted upward, he lay sleeping. Aside from the nose, there was not much left of him. His account was nearly settled, and the other patients knew that he would not last the night—they could tell that by watching the nurses. In a hospital one becomes sharp-eyed.

There were two who came in and sat quietly with the sleeping priest, the woman on one side of the bed, the man on the other. They sat there for a long time; finally she touched him. His self could not really come up out of sleep; it crept up the slopes of consciousness, reached the edge, the tired eyes opened, but then it slid down again. At last he was awake.

"My little girl," he said, "I knew you were here, I could hear you singing out in the garden. It went like this." And the old priest tried to hum the melody, but it didn't come out right.

It was Helena. She kissed him.

"My little girl," he said, "so he has finally found you."

Just then he pinched his lips together in pain. Helena scarcely knew him, so sunken was his mouth. He no longer had a tooth in his head, a deficiency which cannot have made his sermons any better.

"You're just as young and fresh to look at as you ever were," he went on. "And are you still happy?"

"Yes, I'm happy," she said, kissing him. And so she seemed to the dying man. But Helena was not young any longer. She was dark under the eyes, and a little sallow. Frankly, Helena looked somewhat used.

"And I am very happy too," said the priest, "for now you are sitting here together. At last. God bless you."

"You must rest now," said the boy.

"Now just a minute," said the priest, "you surely don't think you can give me orders now, do you? Yes, Espen and I—we two have come a long way together, my girl. Good and long. Many roads, many streets. Did anything grow from it? Not fields certainly. Birds came flying with berries and seeds, and maybe they took root here and there in a crack between the stones. Yes—and my calling, he made me follow it. Really it was more as if I was his errand boy than he mine. I preached a long, long, and very bad sermon, and he took care of everything and helped everywhere."

"You must rest now," said Espen.

"No, wait," said the priest, "I want to read to both of you. I can still do that. First I'll give you a little of Homer."

But it came to nothing, for just then his eyes closed, and that was all. On his table lay Homer and the New Testament. They were worn and black along the edges. The covers had been lost, but the boy had put on new covers, solid they were, made of shoe leather. And on them he had hammered out a bird which looked a little like a bird of paradise.

Now it spread its wings and rose toward its lofty nest.

The boy followed Helena to the narrow street where she lived, up a great many worn steps, and into a powder-sultry, sweet-smelling room that he did not care for.

"May I sit down?" asked the boy.

"Do whatever you want," she replied. She stood at a mirror painting her gray lips.

"I've searched for you," said he.

"That was sweet of you, knight-errant," said Helena.

"Everywhere that we came," said the boy.

"You're sitting on my newly ironed bodice," said she.

"Sorry," said the boy. And he remained standing, for he didn't care to sit on the soft divan so covered with powder.

"You should come with me," he said.

"To your snailhouse?" said Helena, powdering herself. "There was a time I would have done it. But you shook the petals off me, and since then things haven't gone so well for the poppy. Now little lobsterclaw, I don't care any more."

"Helena," said the boy, "will you turn and look at me?"

Instead Helena looked at herself in the mirror. She gave her nose a couple of pats; now she was a work of art that looked very good in the lamplight.

"Don't you think some other knight will come along and like me now?" she said.

Espen's father was awakened early one morning by a sound he couldn't account for. As he came outside, he saw a large pile of dirt in the yard. On top of it lay heavy red clay, dug up in massive clods which glistened on the side. Behind the clay he saw the head and shoulders of a fellow he knew. And he went over to him.

"Hello, wagtail," said he. "Your spade has gotten a bit rusty."

"It's shining now," said the boy.

More snow had drifted in the father's hair, but he hadn't much of it left, and his crown was bright and cheerful.

In the clay at the bottom of the hole lay a large stone that Espen had dug free. He lifted it out and laid it on the edge.

"Not badly done for a shrimp," said the father. "We'll have to take that one inside and put it on the chest."

The sun was coming up, and the boy was four shovels deep with the well.

THE HARVEST FEAST

On a Michaelmas Eve many years ago a death occurred on a Zealand farm which abruptly and unpleasantly disturbed the harvest feast and stopped the busy din in the great house. As a result of this incident, a gloomy shadow hung for some years over the farm's low straw roofs and dark orchard. Clearsighted people could see it. Now it is forgotten. Farmfolk, guests, and servants have gone the same way as the blameless victim, who had had as little to expect of the world as the world of him. Had he lived a long life, he might perhaps have made an even fainter impression than he did with his tragic death, which subsequently, after the fresh unpleasantness had passed, became a crust for gossip and a peppercorn of memory, which all misfortune and suffering become before they are forgotten.

That evening, light gleamed out all the small windows in the long farm house; but the glow could scarcely penetrate to the outer edges of the damp garden, for the September evening was so foggy and dense that its darkness merged with the black of the newly plowed fields. Within the steaming kitchen, women filled bowls and plates noisily, almost beside themselves with hurry and anxiety. The housewife in her black, rustling silk dress hurried back and forth through the long house, her sleeves rolled up over her stout arms. Her place at the women's table was often empty, and with browned fat or red jam on her fingers she ran unceasingly to fetch this or that, driven by that hostess's unrest which can be worse than the fear of childbirth. Each time she passed through the little servants' hall, but dimly lit with two tallow candles, she would call out that everyone must be sure to refill his plate and take another dram.

The farm hands, those who belonged to the farm as well as the several visitors, ate and drank with enthusiasm. Already the liquor was working in them, so that they began to take liberties with the serving girls. They were teasing young Jens Otto, urging him to take yet another drink. Johan, the herdsman, was the leader in this jesting. He was master at the table in the way that a cock can reign in the henhouse without ever having to test his strength against rivals. Crudity accounted for his domination. The herdsman was not a handsome fellow; though in his mid-twenties, his long, bony face was angry and old, furrowed by that half-wild sluggishness which sets deeper lines than intellectual exertion. His nose was disfigured and crooked, so that he snuffled a little. This fellow, made boastful and malicious by liquor, had since boyhood born scars stemming from the crude amusements of adult farmhands and from ill treatment suffered at the hands of the notorious hag who had brought him up. Living up in the sandbanks in a dilapidated, stinking house, into which better folk came only to have their fortunes told, this old witch had supported herself for many years by caring for homeless children farmed out by the parish. Some did not slip from her fosterage alive; Johan had clung to life tenaciously, but he emerged from his ordeal with a rounded back and knobs on his skull.

The herdsman had much to revenge on life but little opportunity for it. And so he turned on the underaged; as so often happens, he forced the stigmata of the grownup servant on the defenseless young. Besides, he didn't like the twelve-year-old servant boy Jens Otto because he was handsome and came from the best house in the sandbanks. True enough, the father drank, and there were many children and poverty in the house; but the children were neat and well brought up. Jens Otto was handsome, with dark hair and dark eyes, though hardship had engraved a little dullness on the fine face.

The herdsman pushed his full glass over to Jens and shouted: "One more, and you can try on my high boots." The boy's cheeks burned, he was willing enough, but he didn't dare and he laughed with embarrassment. "Why not? Because of your father? He drinks enough himself," said the herdsman. "He's let you taste it, hasn't he, when there wasn't enough wood for the stove, eh?" "Yes, once," laughed the boy. "Be sure to help yourselves," shouted the housewife, compulsively pulling down her silk sleeves as she ran with fixed eyes through the room. "You'd better hurry," said the herdsman to the flushed boy, "because the priest is about ready to start preaching."

Up in the large main dining room, on the whitewashed walls of which there hung here and there tasteless old oleographs, everyone waited for the priest's address. There were at least forty guests in their dark best clothes, the men sitting at one long table, the women at another. The white, shining tablecloths almost disappeared under the great spread of beef, goose, duck, fish, cabbage and drink. All had eaten and drunk for almost two hours without saying much. But now one could stretch a bit, conversation and laughter followed steadily, the housewife was seated in her place with silk sleeves buttoned and anticipation in her face, and the priest's hour was overdue. Many glanced sidewise at his hand which already had picked up a spoon and might tap on the glass at any moment.

But the priest remained still. His light, shy eyes glanced over the men at the table. He reflected with satisfaction that he could no longer remember what he had intended to say. That seemed to him a good sign; it meant that inexhaustible resources of words would open up for him as soon as he arose and pushed in his chair. But at this moment, as he sat released from the necessity of riveting and filing on his sentences, he felt suddenly, as he had often done before, the inclination to speak in a very unconventional way. He knew what was expected of him. Perhaps his listeners had not consciously formulated their expectations, but it was true nonetheless. They would appreciate his speech most if it were easy to forget, one course among the other courses, out of the men's minds before the dinner was over, remembered by the women in the same way they would remember the hostess's pastry. The sweets of light Christian poesy were appropriate at such a large and fine harvest feast as this, and that is precisely what the priest could give them. But now as his fingers played with the spoon, the feeling came over him once again. His lips tightened a little, and he determined to speak in a way that would shake them. Again his eye swept over these rows of self-confident and self-satisfied men, and into his mind came the parable about the man who built his granaries larger, that parable which hides a fearsome kernel beneath its simple surface. He would reveal the horror in that situation and shock these satisfied farmers.

The young priest, who frequently was preoccupied and almost shy, knew little about men and much about himself. His eyes grew hard as he contemplated the judgment which already in his mind was forming itself in caustic sentences, yet not for a moment did he really believe that he would speak in that way. If nothing else prevented it, his tactfulness was sufficient restraint. He had sat and eaten with these people, he was a guest. If he now stood up and spoke the truth, it would ring false because he had begun by indulging himself at the feast table. Perhaps an evangelist of original and naive mentality might still do it, but such the young priest was not.

He knew that he did not stand on solid ground, and that deep inside he was afraid of these people. As he now contemplated them, he felt weighted down by his calling. There they sat, at first glance remarkably like one another, cast in the mold of their class, stolid, easygoing and inscrutable farmers, flexible as rushes, stiff as posts, an unimpressionable lot who could easily enough intimidate one like the young priest. And immediately thereafter they provoked a new, uneasy feeling in him. Their sameness dissolved suddenly before his eyes, and he beheld a confused multiplicity. The group was split into distinctly separate individualities, tall and sinewed men, short and coarse men, gigantic men with small heads, small men with large pointed heads. There were round and red faces, long, brown, hard faces, old faces without a wrinkle, young faces with deep furrows. Across from him sat a black-haired and black-bearded farmer, pale yellow and hard as a Castilian, by his side an old man whose close-cropped gray head had the round shape of the Slavs. And the host Anders Andersen would not be conspicuous among Mongolian Kalmucks. If one wished really to speak to this disquieting multitude, which seemed not to have gathered in a Danish parish but rather from distant lands and many foreign races, he must first realize a great Pentecostal miracle, so that he could proclaim in many tongues, in many dialects of mind. But the priest looked about again, and once more he was aware of the mysterious fellowship which bound the group together and transformed Spaniards, Slavs, Mongols, and Scandinavians into Danish farmers, that secret society and that old covenant into which one cannot be adopted but only born, to which one can never return, having once broken out, the chains of which nevertheless one cannot escape as long as he lives. The young priest knew that this conspiracy, which evaluates individuals not according to written or unwritten laws clearly apparent to consciousness, but rather by monstrously subtle sensibilities which one scarcely is aware of possessing—that this conspiracy was the most fearsome restraint on his preaching. He stood without and was not taken seriously by them. Even had he been one of their own, he would have alienated himself had he tried to preach with words from that dialect with which they were comfortable. The young priest was an outsider; that he always felt this and understood it clearly, in spite of all their friendliness, in spite of the good favor he enjoyed, was the clearest proof that he had once been a part of their fellowship. He must necessarily be an outsider because he was a priest. He bore still the chains, and they restrained him, for he had not that fire of conviction in the heat of which all is consumed.

The priest was a fair and well-formed man with a noble head; a stranger would guess that he was descended from old aristocracy, perhaps from a family of ecclesiastes. But in fact he was one of those farmer's sons who are born to books and spiritual agitation. He had been in the parish only a few years but had been liked immediately. The services at which he presided were well-attended, and his preaching was a happy blending of genuine worldly knowledge, livestock, and farming conditions with that gentle Christian lyric to which his listeners were partial but which they would consider fanaticism if it were applied on Monday equally as much as on Sunday.

He struck his glass for all to hear and began to speak. The busy farm folk engaged in the harvest, together with the poor who came to glean, had seemed to him an impressive sight, he said. But what significance did a full barn and rich house have if the owner's heart were empty and not filled with thanksgiving to Him who had set those heavy ears of corn on the stalks.

After a moment's silence the dinner continued more freely and noisily. The priest's words passed out of mind, but in a salutary way they had loosened tongues, released good spirits and, as it were, dedicated the draughts which were still to be drunk.

The priest had thought several times about leaving and was only waiting for an opportunity to arise when his attention fell on the hostess. She was walking up through the hall; her earlier bustling manner had given way to a quietness which caused the priest to wonder. Silently she went up to the host and whispered something to him. He sat for a moment, then threw down his knife with a crash and went out. Among the guests, only the priest noticed this. His glance met the housewife's, and she came over to him. The large, heavy woman smiled, but the smile seemed forced and small muscles quivered at the corners of her mouth. Her cheeks were flushed and her throat was full; a little time passed before she could speak. Then in a rather high voice she asked the priest to go out and say something to the young people.

After the upright, smiling woman had led him out of the main hall, she shut the door behind them and remained standing with her hand on the door latch. The talk and laughter resumed once more within. But the red disappeared from her cheeks, she appeared not white but gray.

"What can be the matter," asked the priest. "Come and see," she whispered. He followed after her through the many half-dark rooms until they stood in the servants' hall.

The table had been cleared, and on it they had laid the servant boy Jens Otto. He lay stretched out, still and lifeless. The glazed brown eyes stared up at the black ceiling.

Here and there about the room stood small clusters of girls, women, and farm hands. Some tried to stifle weeping in their aprons, others stood pale and still, as if they comprehended nothing. On the bench behind the table, the two visiting drivers and the herdsman Johan were still sitting. The two supported themselves against the edge of the table, staring at their large, rough workman's hands. Apparently they didn't know what they should do with themselves. But the herdsman thrust his broad, round-shouldered back against the wall and glared from one to another like a wild beast in a trap. The host went over to him and struck him hard in the face: "Damn, you, you . . . you . . . ," he muttered. Johan ducked with the blow, and his long arms flew up to cover his head. Then his eyes flicked even more abruptly from one face to another.

The priest saw it all as though in a dream. Going over to the wall, he took down a chipped mirror and held it over the boy's mouth.

"There's nothing to be done for it," said one of the cooking women. "How did it happen?" asked the priest. "They made him drink himself to death," answered the old cooking woman calmly.

Meeting the herdsman's wild, flickering stare, the priest turned away. He shut the dead eyes, then drawing out his handkerchief he wiped away a little thin froth from the corners of the boy's mouth. Absently he stood and looked at the handkerchief, but then he turned and put it in the cold stove. He knew that his actions appeared deliberate, consciously professional, and yet his mind was distracted. He had seen many people die, and many who were dead, but he could not remember ever having closed the eyes of anyone. No, I never have, he thought. To shut the eyes of one who has died is an intimate service of friendship, and I have often wanted to do it. But I have always avoided it when the moment was there. And why? I don't know. It always seemed so demanding and so incomprehensible. But now I have closed the boy's eyes, and it was like stopping a clock in the sitting room at home. What did I feel? Nothing, absolutely nothing.

Jens Otto appeared larger as he lay there in the patched but clean clothes which had been others' before they were his and which even now had become too short in the sleeves for him. The dark, curly hair stuck here and there to his forehead. He was handsome. But a sallow hue already covered his face.

They all stood quite still, and at length the priest realized that they were waiting for him. He could hear the gaiety up in the main hall, and it disturbed his thoughts and perpetuated his feeling of unreality. But finally he knew that beyond all the others, he had responsibilities here. He turned to the landowner and his wife who were standing side by side behind him. To the wife he said: "His parents?"

She opened her mouth but could not answer, and in her place the old, calm cooking woman spoke: "The little girl has run up with word to the sandbank. The little tyke was the only one who dared." "And the doctor?" asked the priest. "They've gone out to harness the horse," answered the old woman.

"They're surely not going to drive through the courtyard so people will hear?" exclaimed the landowner, and he started toward the door. "You can say that it's the Pastor leaving," said his wife. "Good Lord, that he should worry about that now—" she gasped as she pulled her apron up before her contorted face.

But the landowner turned, went back to the herdsman and struck him. "Why are you doing that?" asked the priest. "It was you, you did it!" shouted the landowner, but with a strange indistinctness as he attempted to stifle the sound from his furious outburst. "Why was it me, why . . . ?" stammered the herdsman as he covered himself. "I know you!" groaned the landowner. "Why was it me, why . . . you devil?" returned the herdsman. He sat straight up, did not move his arms nor shut his eyes as the owner once again struck him in the face. He stared at them all with the large, wild glance which they could not bear.

The priest took the owner by the arm and said with a heavy authority which seemed foreign even to himself: "I will not look upon this. There were others here also. And you are not doing this for the boy's sake, you are doing it because you are afraid of your guests. You should rather be thinking that a landowner has a responsibility."

The owner yielded, and his shoulders dropped. "What am I to do?" he said in a low voice. "What should I do with these strangers? What should I do with Jens Otto?"

The priest looked remotely at him, and suddenly he understood what all this time they had been waiting for. He went closer to the boy and folded his hands. The guests up in the main hall could still be heard, but the words of the prayer and the priest's subdued, hesitating voice established a barrier as between two worlds, so that stillness came. They bowed their heads, and only the herdsman sat there and stared.

In the stillness they heard clearly the heavy tread of wooden shoes out in the courtyard. They heard the steps out in the entry. Beside the kitchen door, someone removed his wooden shoes and in stocking feet came in through the kitchen. And then the boy's father was standing at the door. He was a tall, lean day-laborer in his mid-forties, wearing the dusty clothes in which he had returned that evening from work at the estate's harvest floor. His face was long and gray and hard. He looked toward the table but remained standing, his arms hanging at his sides. The housewife started toward him. "Poor . . ." she began, but she was unable to say more. The father looked at them, as though apologizing for having come, and the priest wondered, was he drunk or had he simply not yet grasped what had happened.

But the father passed calmly through them to the side of the boy. Carefully lifting the limp body in his strong arms, he bore it past them out through the door. They heard the kitchen floor creak under him, and they heard him groping after his wooden shoes at the outer door. Then the housewife gave a sob and followed after him. But they heard his heavy tread pass through the entry, through the courtyard, and into the night.

The housewife returned. With her was the girl who had taken the message, her eyes tearstained. Nearly everyone was crying.

The priest found his overcoat. "Can't you stay here a little longer?" asked the wife. "What are we to do?" said the farmer. "There is someone I must help," answered the priest, and he left them.

He knew that there was a path leading over the sandbanks up to the boy's home, but he could not find it in the dark. And so he had to follow the road round about. Without his really being aware of it, the road seemed to vanish, and he walked as if he had drunk much wine. Gradually, as his eyes became accustomed to the night, he saw clearly the curious shapes of the great willow trees; but even as he stared at the strange, somber form of a tree, it was suddenly gone, fallen far behind.

At the top of the hill he paused. "What was that I just said?" he muttered, for in his ears he yet heard the sound of his words, there is someone I must help. "God Almighty. How in the world shall I ever be able to help anyone?"

He became weak in the knees. And suddenly he felt on the verge of laughing at his inadequacy. He set out again, more briskly than before. It was just a sign of weakness, he thought, and again he almost laughed. It was as if one became stronger by taking vigorous steps.

As he now followed the narrow road toward the small houses on the sandbanks, he saw, notwithstanding the darkness, something which drained all the power out of his limbs, and he came once again to a standstill. He stood at a place where the path, which he had not been able to find, issued into the road. Beside the path there were two trees, and between them a pump and a watering trough. Sitting on the trough was a dark form. It was the father. He sat on the trough with the boy in his arms.

"I will help you," said the priest.

The man did not move.

"Let me help you," the priest repeated.

"Can you bring him back to life?" said the father.

He arose and went on with his burden, up toward the houses. The priest watched him go until he disappeared in the darkness. Then he sat down on the trough. "I knew it would be so," he muttered. He listened, but now all was still on the road and in the fields round about. He heard only a drop of water fall from a twig. It fell in the water. He sat for a long while, waiting for the next drop.

The priest did not know what he should do. Neither did he know how long he had been sitting there. When he arose, he did not know where he ought to go. But abruptly he started out with long strides toward the houses. His steps slackened as he passed the two foremost, which lay with dark panes in small, wind-blasted gardens. When he came to the third, he could see that light was shining out from the far side, and he stole about to it as though he were a thief. The grass absorbed the sound of his steps so that he could quietly approach the window.

He looked into a little, whitewashed kitchen. The father sat over in the dark corner by the hearth, under the dark open chimney. Over under the window was a table, and on it lay the boy. The priest could see his head. The mother sat on a chair beside the table. A tallow candle was burning by the dead boy's head, and it lighted up the woman's calm, wan face. She was dark-haired, and one could see that she had been pretty once. She sat dry-eyed, holding the boy's hand. By the weak light falling through the half-opened door into the sitting room, the priest glimpsed the heads of several children above the table edge, staring into the kitchen.

He crept back carefully and hurried away past the other houses. He heard a cart rumbling along the road. The doctor! He turned into the field, away from the road, and began to run. He plunged into heavy, plowed earth, but still he ran. He ran out around the village and toward the rectory. As he stopped for a moment to catch his breath, wild, agonizing thoughts overcame him, rising with gasping and groaning in his throat. But when he passed through the large, bare courtyard of the rectory, he clenched his fists and gained control of himself. What he had experienced at the harvest feast seemed now like a distant and unreal dream. But the heads of the children, which he had scarcely been able to see in the semi-darkness, that was reality.

Upon entering he lit a candle and slipped quietly into the bedroom where his wife and two small daughters slept. He went over to the youngest, who lay slightly feverish. She was sleeping peacefully, but he could hardly bring himself to believe it. He bent more closely over her delicate head, heard clearly her regular breathing. And still it was difficult for him to believe. He had entered the room with the mental certainty that she too was dead, taken from him because he was incompetent and guilty.

He heard his wife whisper, and when she saw him, she arose, wrapped a blanket about herself, and followed him into the study, where he lit his old paraffin lamp. She looked at his muddy boots, then seated herself quietly in a chair. They sat for a long time before he asked: "Little Tina, how is she now?"

"Much better. This evening she had only three degrees of fever."

"It is strange that Tina is alive," he said as if to himself.

He heard that the woman was about to say something, but he did not let her speak; loudly, as though he were near to laughter, he said: "Marie, I can't do it, I'm no good at it."

He had sat down with his back toward her and toward the light, but now he turned and looked at her. It seemed to her that he had become much older, furrowed, worn out. His smile, which usually made him appear young, remarkably so she had thought the first time she'd seen him, now made his face seem old. A feeling of anxiety for him came over her, but she remained sitting quietly with her hands under her shawl.

He told her what he had experienced. When she heard that the boy was dead, she arose, went to the window, and pulled the blind. Then she seated herself again quietly.

He began again with accusations against himself, but she said: "Christian, I have heard this from you before. That you are inadequate. That you are not worthy of your call. It isn't true. Why do people look up to you, why do they have confidence in you, Christian, why do they like you?"

"No, no," he said, and now he laughed, "I won't listen to that. Don't you become as false as I am. Marie—I'm sorry, forgive me."

"You needn't say that," she answered.

"Oh, yes," he said, "I ought to be excusing myself continuously. No, I'm talking drivel. But the crazy thing is just that, that I'm constantly offering excuses. I'm one of those charming preachers

who ask their contemporaries to excuse God for existing. A fine
type, don't you agree? What *do* you think about the type, Marie?
Give me your honest opinion."

He looked at her, but she stared at the soft, flickering flame in
the lamp and did not turn her gaze toward him. There is strength
in her eyes, he thought, she isn't weak.

"Marie, look at me now and answer!"

His wife stared at the light, steadily and silently.

She isn't pretty, he thought, not in the banal sense. But in
another way. Like a cool breeze.

"My dear, you're beautiful," he said.

She really is, he thought, and he turned again to his desk.

"The mark of a minister, Marie, is not that people like him, so
don't say that. You mustn't let yourself catch my mendacity, it's a
bad disease. You like me too. Maybe that's blinded you. When you
see faults and carelessness in me, you don't hesitate to give your
candid opinion of them. But in this other most important matter,
my calling, you've never evaluated me strictly. You ought to. Why
don't you?"

Falling silent, he dipped his pen in the inkwell and began to
draw on the desk pad, waiting.

"I admire you," he said quietly after a little time had passed.

"But you have a responsibility to speak out too," he continued
in the same tone as before. "That doesn't make my responsibility
easier or less, not in the slightest. But you have a responsibility to
the truth, completely, in all things. I can't believe that you're blind
in this matter. But you want to spare me. You like me too much.
You watch a sacred calling become simply an occupation, but
you don't say anything. You can't bring yourself to cut me to
the marrow, Marie, even though there's disease in the marrow.
And so you're guilty too."

"Yes," she answered.

He rose halfway out of his chair but then settled slowly down
again.

"The faces of those children behind the table," he continued,
"I couldn't endure them, I had to leave. Leave? I ran like a sur-

prised thief. Keep in mind that in a few years those children will come to me to be instructed in the way of truth and life. To me?"

"It was probably for the best that you didn't go in to them," she said.

"To me?" He repeated the question. ". . . But you said something?"

"It was best that you didn't go in."

"Best? Yes, perhaps. Yes, when one is so futile. One might have given offense to the young, and woe unto him from whom the offense cometh."

He sat still for a little, listening to the simmering of the lamp and the soft sounds in the house. "Is she sleeping now?" he asked.

She arose and went into the bedroom. He didn't look at her when she returned. She sat down quietly without saying anything.

"Thank you," he said.

"But I simply can't remain a priest any longer, Marie," he continued, "I can't be a priest even for the rest of this night. Do you understand what this means. That we can't go on pretending any longer, that we have to give up playing this delicate comedy of the heart. You can't prop me up any longer with talk about people looking up to me, having confidence in me. What kind of a minister is one whom everyone likes, but no one listens to? Just a church confectioner. And why should they? How can they believe me when I don't believe?"

From behind him came her reply: "Christian, do you believe that I'm the only one who hears you now?"

"No . . . no," he answered hesitating, "no, I can't avoid knowing that yet another ear perceives my pitifulness. But that's even worse, isn't it, to know that one's faith is just sentimentality, deadly habit, rubbish and nonsense. Because if I really believed, I'd have helped him. I'd have been able to help. I wouldn't have looked like I'd seen a ghost when he asked me if I could restore his son. Perhaps I'd have answered, yes, I can. But of course I'll never know, because I don't have that kind of faith."

He scribbled rapidly on the blotter.

"I can see it clearly now. The devil likes me too, he likes my preaching. He sits there in the organ loft saying bravo. I understand it perfectly now." A pause, and then in a strong voice: "Marie, do you know what night this is? Michaelmas Eve, Saint Michael's Eve, the night of the judge. The boy died on this night, but I wonder if it is he who'll be judged? Who will be judged? The herdsman perhaps, him only? Or those visiting farmhands, or the landowner, the guests? Or I? I sat there in the house where it happened. But did I have any thought for them, did I protect him? We are all guilty, but my guilt is so great that I cannot face it squarely for long at a time. And therefore, I shall be judged. I didn't help before it happened; I didn't help after it happened. But Marie, do you understand the terrible, meaningless loss? Can you understand it? And we are guilty in it. One thing I do understand: I understand now the words, 'Thy brother's blood cries out unto me from the ground.' "

"Yes," she said.

"It's strange," he went on, "that the plain and simple is always hardest to understand. Thy brother's blood cries out. That cry has always sounded, but I have certainly never heard it before. That's the result of not having lived. One hasn't suffered, and one hasn't lived."

"You, who have children," she said, "you, who have a sick little girl, you, who waken repeatedly in the night to check on her?"

He laughed: "Yes, I suppose you're right. And yet—so much of my life seems to me now to have been like a dream. I wonder if now for the first time I really know you, am aware that the three of you really belong to me. Really, I mean. First now. Of course, with little Tina—no, I have never actually known that she existed on the earth. Tonight she became real, when I became afraid that she was going to die."

He felt a faint breeze as she went past him. Shortly he heard her return. "She's sleeping," she said. They sat quietly and heard the clock strike in the sitting room. "It's late," he said, "very late." Absentmindedly he dried the pen on the front of his coat, as he was in the bad habit of doing, then turned his chair and faced her.

"There isn't much of me left," he said, "but I'm not so afraid now to show you the pieces. And I'm prepared now to learn something from you. Will you just tell me what meaning there is in the death of a boy like that. What does it mean, Marie?"

"Christian, do you think I can say anything that you don't know already?"

"Say? What does it mean to say?" he replied. "Perhaps that's the problem, that one always wishes that everything should be said and explained. I don't understand anything, but I believe you know more."

"Do you think it would be better if it were all easily and routinely explainable?"

"No, perhaps not," he answered. "No, when I think about our friend Pastor Nielsen and how simple everything seems to him, then I realize that easy explanations can be worse than none. But I can't be done with it; I can't wrench myself away from the question. What does it mean, that boy and all the other young life that we bury in the earth? Chaff that drifts away from the mad harvest floor of existence? What are they? Why do they come, why should they be taken that way? Nielsen could explain it easily, of course. Meaning? he would say, it's a test, a trial instituted by God. To be sure, from a theological perspective one can perhaps distinguish between the misfortune, which God does not have a part in, and the consequences of it in the mind of the misfortunate, where God's work begins. Doubtless, and yet, Marie, such thoughts belong in a high and rarified atmosphere. Ultimately, man must ask his question from within the perspective of human limitation. Why should those two out on the sandbank be tested so horribly rather than you and I? Did someone out there draw a blank in God's mad lottery? Should the Creator, who created, allow a child to drink himself to death in order to test two parents who have a hard enough time just scraping enough dry bread together? Test them in order that they can repent? And what if they don't? Little Jens Otto lies wasted in the grave. And what about Jens Otto himself, his life? Was his existence just a stroke of the ax aimed at his mother? I don't understand anything, but I do know that I'm a liar. You are a liar, Nielsen. You are liars all of you who teach that God plunges people into accident and wars in order to . . ."

"I'll stop now," he said.

"No, you shouldn't stop," she said.

He turned his back to her, and she saw that he was shaking.

"I learned much from that boy, all that I know," he said. "I've learned what my calling should really be. To give meaning to the meaningless. To bring something that is larger, richer, deeper than comfort and advice. But I've not learned to bring it. I come empty handed."

"Empty handed," said his wife after a pause. "I believe I can find something you can take out there. I'll pack a basket and some—"

"Out there?" he said. "When?"

"Now," she answered.

"No, Marie. And with a basket?"

"Yes," she said, "once you get out there with the basket, maybe you'll find more in it than I've packed."

"I can't go out there," he said, "what could I possibly do? I couldn't even straighten things out as much as our friend Nielsen. If I were he, I'd have been there and be back home, sound asleep in bed. I'd have gone in, shaken hands, looked them in the eye, spoken words of comfort, opened up the Testament to where a bookmark lay opportunely—oh, confound it. Marie, it's too much."

"I thought you were going out there," she said.

"Yes, I am going," he said, getting up.

She brought from the bedroom a pair of large sheets which she lay on his desk. "Maybe they don't have anything to lay him in," she said. "Where's your purse?"

"My purse?" he said, "yes, I wonder where . . ."

"Here it is in the drawer. A coffin has to be bought."

"Do we have enough for that?" he asked.

"It doesn't look like it," she replied, "but we have to do something, because they can't afford it. We'll have to see about it in the morning. The landowner will probably help."

She threw a cloak over her shoulders and went out into the garden. He took out his cassock and put it on; but then he took it off again and hung it away before she returned. Her arms were full of late fall flowers, dahlias and asters; their smell reminded him immediately of death. In the light she began to sort the wet flowers, many of them too old, rain beaten, beginning to decay.

So the priest went out to the sandbanks, past the well and the watering trough, and the damp night air cooled his forehead. But when he reached the third small house, he had to stop for a bit. Again the barrier rose up before him. I can't do it, he thought, it's a holy place and I've no right to come there. Would I want a stranger with me if one of mine—?

Then he discovered that he was standing before the door, and he didn't know how he had come there. But he felt that something indescribably strong had been, as it were, poured into his mind.

It was dark in the kitchen now. He saw a ray of light falling from the sitting room window, but this time he didn't look inside. No one answered his knock. Repeatedly he tried, but in vain. Then, raising the latch, he found the door was not bolted, and he stepped into the kitchen and knocked on the door of the sitting room. After an interval, the father opened it. He held a light in his hand and stood for a long time looking at the priest.

"Can you do it now?" he said.

"Where have you laid him?" asked the priest, and when the father heard that, he stepped aside and let him come in. The smaller children were sleeping now, in trundle beds and boxes. Only a larger girl sat half awake at the table. Over by the large bed a second little lamp was burning; the mother sat beside it. They had laid the boy in the middle of the parents' bed, and the priest saw that the linen he had brought would not be needed, for the boy lay wrapped in his father's only white shirt, the shirt he had been married in. It was much too large; even so, Jens Otto looked fine and handsome as he lay there in the bed where he had been conceived and born.

When the mother saw the priest, she turned her head away and wept, almost without a sound. But the father went over to

the bed, looked at his son, and said: "Can you bring him back
to life, priest?"

The priest looked into the eyes of the large, hard man and
answered: "If you can believe with me, then Jesus Christ will raise
him up."

The priest knelt down beside the bed. He took the hand of the
boy and was about to pray. The hand was ice cold. As he felt
this stiff, cold boy's hand with its rough, almost stony skin, as he
grasped it with his own soft, well-kept, useless hand, he was overwhelmed, his thoughts shattered so that he could not pray. Raising
again his smarting eyes toward the boy, he heard a terrible sound
come from the kitchen. Both the father and the mother had gone.
The priest went out there, and over by the hearth, pressed up
against the sooty wall, the man stood and wept, his wife standing
with him.

Then the priest knew that he had broken the barrier and
given the father the first, dreadful help, and he went back in to
be with the dead.

DANIEL

SHEEE-EWW, SHEEE-EWW.

The wind comes from the west, through the woods, down the ravine, and in over the bare fields. Shu-uuw. In over the low hills. In over the mouldy turf, in through the clattering thistles. Vi-iyoou, the red hawk glides with the wind, and the birds scream. Vi-iyoou it whistles in the oily hair of the Havnelev men. Then away it sweeps over gray acres, past Dead Man's Ridge, over the east parishes, out over the cliffs, away over the darkening bay.

The wind fills the ears of the Havnelev men so they can scarcely hear themselves. Perhaps it doesn't matter. What is there to say?

Six of the village men are tramping down the earth out here by the margins of Thorny Ridge where the sacrifices of misfortune belong. The others have plodded home with horses and scoops. In the dry ground sledge tracks can be seen, each pair gradually converging to a single track further down by the thistle patches and mugwort groves near Havnelev town.

The wind makes Jakob Jørn's eyes water. From his nose (which with the years is moving nearer to his chin, as if they were involved in an obstinate conspiracy) there hangs a drop of water, clear and light and containing a reflection of the visible world. But the other wind-tears which course down Jakob's face have a long trip before them and numerous ways from which to choose, so many vertical wrinkles he has; these are the wheel tracks of grief, the paths of resentment.

Kneeling, he presses earth around a little bush he has planted in the ground. A thorn bush. He snuffs in and wipes across his nose.

"D'ya think it'll grow?" asks his neighbor Kristian, a mast-tall man.

"It'll grow," says Jakob; "the plaguethorn grows when nothin' else will."

"Could be we should set up a cross and a tablet," says Kristian.

"Y'r crazy, you are."

"We could have your Daniel make letters on the tablet," says Kristian. "Methinks it should read: 'Valborg.' That last one of mine was called Valborg, she were a spring heifer."

"The poor man's joke, it don't last long," says Jakob.

"I just come to think on that with the tablet, it'd look right nice," says Kristian, staring at the large heap of earth in the middle of which they have planted the thorn. With a firm grasp, he takes a handful of his shirt in front and pulls it from side to side on his bony frame.

"We all be crazy," says Jakob. "Better dead for good and all than livin' always in fear and want."

The six men are through with their work. They stand with tools on their shoulders, looking at the pit which they have filled. On the little thorn branch, only a pair of small leaves remain, gold as the coins in the pockets of the overlords.

The year declines, it is fall. The fleet of clouds diminishes, while the great blue expanse, like a distant sea, gleams about heaven's white schooners. Over Fakse Bay to the south the sun stands majestic.

In the ground under the thorn lie the carcasses of sixty two oxen. Nourished by them, the thorn bush can grow until it raises itself like some black beast above the ridge. These are cattle taken by the plague. All of Jakob's have been struck down along with Valborg, Kristian's last remaining animal. None of the six men has any cows left.

And so they shuffle homeward, toward Havnelev town, which

lies there like a pile of cut brush with nettles growing up through it. A careworn countenance looks toward them, the gable in Jakob's house. Above everything rises the church tower.

"All right, y' shall say now what y'r meanin' to do," says Jakob.

"Well, one could wonder if you be goin' to do it yourself," answers Kristian.

"We be not the first," says Jakob. "If you've eyes to see, y' know there be now three deserted farms in Havnelev."

"It could be I've discovered that for myself," returns Kristian.

"One is either man or mouse," says Jakob, "but you seem not to know what y' wish or what y' dare."

"Could be I'll answer with a proverb," says Kristian. "When the crane makes promises to the wild goose, they go both astray."

"You be one of the weak-hearted," says Jakob Jørn. He is barely sixty but an old man to look at, shrunken, not much over half as tall as Kristian. His neck is bowed, his eyes triangular and red. Looking up at his companion he says: "Better to be a fool on unknown roads than a bound fool.* You've to choose now. This night I'm desertin' my farm, my father's farm."

There is a great crashing in the air far behind them. Black lightning falls over the burial pit. Ravens hang in the air over the plaguethorn. The atmosphere is disturbed. Around the paddock, tall ash trees stagger in the wind. If one stands in the courtyard and looks over the beast-like roof ridges up at these great protectors, they seem about to be flung dizzily into the heavens. But of course that doesn't happen. Dirt and chaff blow into the eyes of folks. The lusty wind jumps about the farmyard, dancing with straw and dried dung. How would the brittle farm withstand a real storm when it groans so in a little traveling wind?

It whistles also through the chinks into Daniel's room, but Daniel probably doesn't notice: he is reading. Sitting up in his black bed, he mumbles the words softly to himself. The book he

---

* In the period 1733–1788 Danish farmers were *stavnsbunden*, i.e. bound by law to remain on their acreages. The law was an attempt (unpopular and unsuccessful) to prevent widespread dislocation and resulting economic distress in the face of increasing agricultural failures and hard times for farmers.

is reading is large and heavy. It rests on the sour smelling quilt, and that in turn rests on two kale stocks, that is, on Daniel's thighs; only one person besides himself knows how thin they now are. But Daniel reads, muttering to himself, without even looking at the page of the chronicle on which his white hand is resting. And precisely as he comes to the bottom of the page and the end of the line, his white hand turns the leaf without his even looking, and his voice repeats distinctly the last word from the previous page, which is also the first word on the new page— it is printed in bold type. In such fashion his reading proceeds.

Occasionally he pauses and stares at the clay wall which inclines toward him from the foot end of the bed; so near it is that he can touch it simply by leaning forward a little. He looks at that clay wall as though there were a person there, he nods to the person—or perhaps one should say persons, he reads to them. And with his right hand, which is pale without being clean, yet luminous in this room where there is almost no light, he outlines something in the air before him, explains something to the clay wall with his hand.

Daniel has progressed in the art of reading to the point where he knows most of the chronicle by heart. Words have been gathered from the fields of the book, and they are planted anew as seed in Daniel's soil. In him they sprout and grow wonderfully. New lands are created in him, fields which are seven miles long, forests which are boundless. Silently the words of the book give birth to gardens and ships and cities in him, and to all of the people who belong with them. He knows all of these people as if he himself were related to them. They come in multitudes from the pages of the Bible or the chronicle, still he knows them all— and likes them all. Some are holy and gentle, others are dangerous; some are good, while others are evil. But even though he is content that the wicked are punished for their wickedness, as is fitting, he does not sit wishing the worst for them, for he likes them as well, so wonderfully do they live in the book and in his thoughts, and he continues to hope that with time they will repent.

He reads to the clay wall, which has not been plastered. It is

the backside of the baking oven, and like the belly of an ox it
swells from the chimney into his little room. The chimney walls
exude a close warmth which Daniel breathes, and that is a help
against his sickness. On that spot on the clay wall where his
fingers sometimes pause, three names have been scratched. Two
of them are complete. The top one is Niels, below it is Anders.
The lowest name is unfinished: Dan—.

Niels and Anders are Daniel's two brothers who preceded him
in turn in this bed and this room. Now only their names remain.
They could not do as Daniel does, they simply lay here and stared.
They ended by becoming large-eyed. They could not read. And
no one except Daniel, who was younger, came to tell them anything. There were so few words sown in them that they lay like
fallow fields in which only weeds grow. But Daniel came and told
them things, first to Niels, but at that time Daniel did not know
so much. When Anders replaced the dead brother, Daniel knew
much more; he saw everything in field and stable more sharply
now, for he must describe it all to Anders. And Daniel listened better. The stories of the old ones he carefully treasured up
and returned with them to Anders. But he had only just learned
to read when that brother was taken. Now Daniel is glad that
he can lie here and read to his brothers as well as to himself.

"Jannemund was young and strong," he reads. "The king had
a heart good and true, and he was a bold warrior. And so they
rode fiercely against each other, so that each was struck from his
steed. Whereupon they drew their swords and strove manfully for
a long hour. Never was such combat witnessed between two men.
At the last they had struck both shield and armor from each other."

Daniel does not notice the butterfly which flutters at the
windowpane, an exotic little Painted Lady which has hatched prematurely because of the oven's warmth. The butterfly thinks it is
spring. The windowpane is tiny, as if someone had stomped a hole
through the clay wall with his wooden shoe and then patched the
hole with a splinter of yellow glass.

Daniel can't think about all that, nor can he interrupt himself
at inappropriate places in his reading. For there is something
sacred about the printed word in a book, such that without a

sound it enters into and grows in a person. All writing is so.
Sometimes while he is reading, Daniel pulls himself together and
shakes, as if he were freezing. This happens when he stops to
think how wonderful it is to be able to read. Yes, this is his joy,
but sometimes it makes him almost afraid. Not that he believes
that what he reads of will suddenly come into being, with him in
the midst of it, but he is so close to believing this that he can
become fearful. And always there is something inconceivably
great behind it all, which a poor person cannot express but only
feel. It reminds him of what once as a boy he saw out in the
wild, how a large bird loosed its hold on the crown of an oak
and fell like a sack in order to swing out freely its powerful
wings—and it became an eagle.

"The king smote Jannemund on the right shoulder so that his
coat of mail was cleft in twain, and he badly wounded. Then said
Jannemund: 'You have a costly garland on your helm, he who
bound it there was not poor. And I see three stones on your helm.
While you wear it, there is none who can overcome you. Therefore, I shall seize your helmet!' And the king answered: 'With
God's help, I shall never relinquish it!' But Jannemund grasped
the strap and pulled the helm from the king's head. And then did
they struggle mightily to possess it."

The room is not larger than two strides on one side and three
on the other, little more than the size of a grave; but now, extended by imagination, it provides space not only for Jannemund
and Charlemagne the King but also for the millions of men who
are with them.

With his left hand which rests on the page, Daniel can feel the
heavy printed lines. But now he hears the clatter of iron from
within the chimney and a sharp, scolding voice. His sister is rak-
ing up the coals, his sister who always glares at him from the doorway when she surprises him in his reading. And so Daniel becomes self-conscious about his muttering, stops, can no longer remember his place, begins to cough deeply and finally must spit
up. But now he lifts the chronicle again and begins reading in a
whisper, just so that the weak sounds can be heard by the clay
wall.

"At that moment Roland appeared, bearing a broken spear in his hand. So small he was that the heathen Jannemund did not fear him. But as the king stood in great need, the faithful Roland stepped forth and smote Jannemund on the helm. But Jannemund marked it not and said: 'Unless you have a mighty god, neither of you shall go living from this place.' Once again Roland smote him, and this time Jannemund's sword flew from his right hand. Thus disarmed, Jannemund turned pale. Then Roland took up the sword and split Jannemund's head, so that blood came out of the mouth of him, and he fell dead to the earth. The king sat down to rest himself."

Daniel must rest, for he has been coughing again. He holds the bowl, into which he has spit, nearer to the window in order to look into it, nods, and leans back wearily, still with his hand on the book. He stares before him with a smile and dreaming eyes, which now in the darkening room are as large as his brothers' were at the last. He knows that it was worse for them, for they were impatient for so long and would not believe what was happening. They were poor; when they were alone they had only their pitiful fear. Daniel had come and sat with them and spoken God's word to them. Daniel is now only twenty years old, but he understands what lies ahead.

The day declines, the butterfly's colors die in the twilight, as perhaps it will die when it becomes still. Daniel cannot read now, and he is too faint to recall all that he could read well enough in the dark. Countries, cities, and mountains sink slowly and beautifully down in him, as if he were putting out to sea.

Later on he'll read again, for they have promised to bring the little candle in for him this evening before they leave. It is the last candle in the house, but Daniel will be able to keep it.

Though the wind rises as the darkness falls, he can hear the increasing activity in the house and courtyard. He can tell that they are pulling a wagon over the paving stones up to the door. The tramping hooves can be heard from the passageway; that means his brother has been out to the commons to fetch the draft horses as dusk falls. Let it be dark now, for there are people in the town who should not see what is happening. Talk has but a short distance to go before it reaches the deanery or the castle.

The porch door opens suddenly, screeching as the wind cracks it against the wall. "Did y' remember Martin Luther?" bawls an old-man voice. It is Daniel's father, Jakob Jørn.

The women answer. Daniel knows that picture is something they won't forget.

But will they remember the little candle? thinks Daniel, suddenly growing uneasy. Yes, they might forget, for they have so much to remember. He can hear his sister scouring the table in the kitchen. That's how she is: they're leaving everything, but it will be left orderly so that no one will question what kind of housekeeper was here.

It would be nice, Daniel had thought, to keep the picture of Martin Luther here, hanging above Niels and Anders. But it's better that the father take Luther with him, so he can hang him over the kitchen bench where they come—that is, if they find a place to sit. Luther is good to have along to strengthen and to comfort.

The latch of the chamber door rattles. Someone enters softly.

"Daniel, are y' sleeping?" she whispers.

"Maybe I was, a bit."

She sits at the other end of his short bed and is still for a while, Signe, his young sister-in-law. Yes, she is young, and she is heavy —the old bedstead creaks under her. As always, her coming makes Daniel feel a bit strange, his thought becomes narrowed and difficult. Only at these times does he feel a hopeless sorrow overspread his misery, such that he would gladly take a knife and plunge it into himself. He feels ugly. And he must smell bad too—he remembers how it was with his brothers.

"Daniel," she whispers.

"No, y' shall not do it," he whispers. But if only she will, he thinks.

"Yes," she says, and to make it worse, she begins to cry. She is weeping for Daniel, and as she does he breaks into a sweat and begins to cough. Quickly she moves forward to help him, supporting him with her arm behind his slender shoulders during the spasm. For a long time she has been the only one to come and help him. His brother and sister never come closer than the doorway, and his father storms out when he has been there but a moment. But Signe comes, and there is nothing she shrinks from helping Daniel with.

He has regained composure after the coughing, but suddenly she shakes him, she pulls him up firmly. "Daniel, y' must go with! I'll not leave without you!"

"Yes but Signe, it can't help at all, I've told it to you so many times."

"Y' sh'll go, Daniel. May be the others won't say anything, but I shall. For I just can't think that thought. Why will y' not go?"

"Y' still don't understand, do you, Signe. Let me say it again. Niels and Anders and I are stayin'. We're stayin'. There be some who must stay. That's just how it is."

"Daniel, little Daniel, y' can't stay here alone."

"I'm the only one who can stay here alone. And remember, I'm not alone."

"Yes, but what about tomorrow, Daniel, and the day after that?"

"It'll be all right, Signe, everything'll go as it must. And when they come, the sheriff and his men, and say that ye've deserted, I'll be here, and I'll say to them: With God's help, my father's family has not deserted, for I'm here, and where I am, there also are Niels and Anders, my brothers."

"Ah, little Daniel, do y' really think that matters?"

"Yes," he says, "yes."

For a time they are quiet, and she sits stroking his long hair.

"Are you afraid?" he asks. "It's sure to go well with all of you, I can tell it. You'll be happy again over there, I know you will."

"I wonder," she mutters. A pause. "Daniel!" she says, letting go of him, "y' know don't you, y' must've noticed . . . ?" and she falls silent. "Surely y' must've noticed?"

"Noticed?"

"That Hans and me are goin' to . . . oh, y' must have known it. We're goin' to have a little one, Daniel."

"What did y' say?"

"A child, a little child, Daniel."

"Well, think of it."

"And you must see the little one, y've got to see it."

"Yes." But then in a long breath: "No, I sh'll not see it. Surely y' must understand, Signe, that I'll not be able to see it. It's right this way."

"Signe!" calls a voice from out in the kitchen—it is the sister. Can it be that she'll come all the way to the bedside to say goodbye?

"Sig-ne!"

For a long time they sit quietly, even though the sister continues to call. She knows well enough where Signe is now, but she is probably ashamed to come herself. It is as if they have become more hostile to Daniel since they made the decision. Though they have not said so, he knows that they would try to take him with them if he asked. Yet he knows that they must cross the ocean—for waves erase tracks and dissolve the bonds which hold the fleeing farmers to their land—and he would only die on them in the boat. He knows that they are hostile to him because he wants what they really want, but what they will have a hard time forgetting afterward. Daniel understands them.

"Signe, when I know you're at sea, I'll read the Prayer for Folks at Sea."

"Yes, Daniel."

"Signe, I know the words of the prayer by heart. If I say it for you, will you understand that I mean it both for you and the others?"

Kristian from the next farm stands in his dark windswept passageway. And there likewise stands Jakob Jørn, the stronger of the two though an old man in appearance.

"Ja, there's something to that," says Kristian, and it's what he says each time the other tries to persuade him. Kristian has backed out, has refused to become serious about it. All along he's been saying maybe in the hope of not having to do more. Honestly, he can't get squared away, his wagon needs fixing and can't be counted on, his horses have run off the devil knows where, nor has he said a word to his wife—out of caution of course, one knows what her tongue is. No, tonight he simply can't.

"What sh'll I call ya?" says Jakob, "a dog, a cowardly dog? Ja, what?" The words hiss from Jakob's mouth like wind up in the eaves. Lacking expression for his scorn and frustration, the old one attacks in crooked fashion. Kristian tries to hold him off but cannot, Jakob kicks, he grabs up a swingletree in the dark and smashes it into his neighbor's face. Kristian groans. Then they reel and tumble about in the dark passageway, finally stumbling over a wagon tongue, struggling as they lie there, breathing heavily. Kristian's poodle comes now to join them, insinuating himself between the two combatants, yelping affectionately, for he knows them both. Then Jakob gets on his feet and walks away.

"Farewell, *dear* neighbor," comes his voice into the passageway after him.

It is later in the evening. The wagon clatters toward the courtyard gate. Jakob Jørn goes ahead to open it. He does not bother to close it after them; let the wind whistle through the black gate as it will. Nor does the bent-backed farmer open the outer passage gate carefully as is his wont. Rather he kicks the rotting boards so that pieces fly off in the dark, jerks at the dry-rotted bar so that it breaks off in the post slot, flings it from him with an oath. Then he walks ahead over the dark paddock with the storming ocean of trees around it, further on through the open field, his fists clenched. Not once does he look back. Those in the wagon all but lose sight of his light-colored sheepskin coat which seems almost to disappear far ahead of them.

With the seething trees behind them, they hear more emphatically now the howling wind from out in the fields, a long incomprehensible howling, like wolves in winter time. But without the trees it is somewhat lighter too, and out ahead they can see Jakob Jørn stalking steadily along.

The son Hans is driving the horses, his right hand resting on the rocking wagon box. He sits with bent neck and does not look at the women in the wagon behind him, Signe and the sister Marie. This is an hour Jakob's Hans has long anticipated. What if the authorities get wind of it before they've gotten away: they'll make him serve as a soldier for years, while the farm and his family

fall to pieces. But if he stays on the farm, this cattle plague will be
followed by a poverty he could never escape, by increased bond-
age, by endless debt and obligation to the overlords. That is, if he
manages to avoid the fate of Niels and Anders and Daniel. This
is, then, the great hour for him, the hour of freedom; he will
become a man. And yet with every step he feels guilt. The portal,
the field gate, and every step tell him what leaving means to his
father, who has always lived here, whose fathers have lived here, of
whom it is still remembered that they were among the first free-
holders. With every step ahead, the son gathers up the father's
bitter soul into himself. He is young and he is fleeing, but he is
aware just now that he is tearing up his root. This is the greatest
hour, and yet the deepest misery. Forward! He slaps the reins,
forward! And suddenly the wind takes them, whistles in the
horses tails, tears at the covers, then soars up over the desolate
fields. Hans straightens his shoulders, suddenly he feels like singing a ballad. But he stops himself; just behind them is a young
fellow who will follow them as far as the shore and drive the
horses back before morning. Doubtless he's thinking his own
thoughts—best not to disturb him.

Up in the wagon box, sheltered from the cold wind by the
feather quilts which are the family's most valuable possessions,
sit Signe and the sister. They are beyond the paddock now and
can see dimly the house behind the cabbage field. Signe sees the
faint spot of light in the wall. As they jolt along through the
stubble fields, she continues to stare at it until it dies out in the
distant darkness. She feels reassured by the sight, though she had
expected it to be hard to look at. It was Daniel's window; she had
remembered to bring him the candle.

Under a cluster of trees out toward the open land, another
wagon stands waiting. It is Ole Øster and his people. He too is
deserting. There had been three abandoned farms in the town,
now there are five. And more to come.

Ole brings out his stone jar and they pass it around as they wait
in the shelter of the swaying trees, thinking each moment they
hear in the creaking of the branches the sound of horsemen.

Each takes several pulls at the jar, including the women, but Signe thinks of her little one and drinks but a little. It warms them, bolsters them. They shout to each other in the wind, laugh, suddenly stop and listen, then shout again jovially. And then the wagons are again rocking and complaining over the fall fields. For some distance yet they dare not drive on the highways. The wagons jolt along in the night through a countryside which has suddenly become foreign and dangerous, even though these people belong here and must violate something inside themselves to flee. But in just this way hundreds of bound farmers throughout the entire land are deserting in the night, from exhausted soil, from fresh grave pits. Bump, bump, they rumble along. Hurry! screams the wind. Bump, bump, bump. Along toward the northeast. They can glimpse Jakob's coat out ahead of them. He is leading them beyond Havnelev's outermost ridges, around marshes and ponds, beyond grave pits and places where evil lives, beyond the country towns.

The wick has gotten too long, and Daniel must snuff it. But he has difficulty, he is not used to doing it since he almost never has light in his room. Drafts through the chinks make the little flame flutter, so that the walls are agitated and remind one of a stormy sky. Daniel looks about the room and smiles to himself. He looks at the candle, he could gaze at it without ceasing, for it is like a living being, a dancer, a small happy spirit. But light and reading belong together, and he bends over the book, whose letters are alive in the brightness like wildflowers in the spring wind. And he knows them all.

"To the chief Musician; a Psalm of David. There be many that say, Who will shew us any good? Lord, lift thou up the light of thy countenance upon us. Thou hast put gladness in my heart, more than in the time that their corn and their wine increased. I will both lay me down in peace, and sleep: for thou, Lord, only makest me dwell in safety."

Slowly the groaning wagons advance through the windy night, following rutted byways along the rocky coast. They are traveling

north to reach a wooded stretch along the shore. Jakob knows
people there who will carry them over the bay. And it ought to
be tonight, even though the sea is rising. Where are they going?
Surely they'll find some place, thousands before them have em-
barked; the city hides, as the saying goes.

They are all in the wagons now, exhausted. Here is Ole Øster
running alongside Jakob's wagon, and he is pleased: for they had
reached the bottom of his stone jar, but his thoughtful wife has
just brought out a mate to it. Now Jakob shall taste. And the old
farmer draws strength from it. He takes a little of the brandy in
his hand and rubs it on his face where the skin was bruised in
his bitter struggle with Kristian. He is holding the picture of
Martin Luther on his lap, anxious lest something happen to it.
The women are sleeping in the bottom of the jolting wagon, covered by the feather quilts. Through the thick darkness comes the
sound of waves breaking against the rocks. The wagons lumber
on.

How the old house sighs and moans in the wind. There is not
much left of the candle. Once again Daniel must snuff the wick,
and this time his luck is bad—the flame dies. He has nothing to
light it with, and so he sits there in the dark, solitary and peaceful.

Bless everything that travels and flies through the air at night.

Daniel knows that there are difficult hours ahead; he knows
what is coming. Without family to take care of him, he will not
last long. Helplessness and perhaps hunger will hurt at first.
Since his strength will be gone, he has by candlelight finished
carving his name under those of his brothers. Daniel, it reads.

The light has gone out, it is true, but he has light within himself, the images in the chronicle and the words of the holy scripture are engraved in his heavy book of memory. However much
the house may groan in the rough weather, it is not deserted;
and Daniel, who will rest now, is not alone. His fingers move
across the clay wall.

"Good night, Niels. Good night, Anders."

HAAVN

WHEN HAAVN AWOKE, it was dark and would be for
another three hours. Am I alive? he said to the darkness, the only
listener he was used to. Honestly now, he answered himself, if I
weren't, how would I know it. There had been heavy frost for a
long time, and Haavn had considered the possibility that some
night he might freeze to death.

Now he lay listening. It was terribly cold. Very often as he was
waking, he thought he heard footsteps just outside his door. The
footsteps of an old person. By the time he became clearheaded,
they were always gone. And still he lay there listening. There
wasn't a sound from the stable or any other part of the house.
Those thieves were quiet, and now they'd gotten away again,
that is, if they'd even been there. The footsteps of the old person
had nothing to do with the thieves. The first he heard very often,
the others were just something he assumed. Haavn had been
robbed one night over four years ago, and he expected the crime
to be repeated. So he left the door to his room unlatched and kept
an ax hanging on the wall by his bed.

Stillness dominated everything. That's how it should be at this
hour. As a rule, Haavn lay awake during the earlier part of the
night. The years had brought pains and troubles, and he had
become a fitful sleeper who killed the night hours by figuring
arithmetic problems in his head. Or he just lay and listened. There

was nothing wrong with his hearing, and earlier in the night there was always something to hear. He heard when the house-keeper in the house proper turned in her bed. She was like all the others in the continued succession of female outsiders in his house, she lay at night sighing and making noise. And there were the sounds from the stable. He could always tell which one of the animals was moving, or at least he thought he could. Formerly he had followed the activities of the mice and rats. They gnawed everywhere, especially here in the harness room where he lay. He had heard them when they were frantic and mating. Now they were quieter, for since the weasel came, there were only a few desperate rats left. He had never seen the weasel, but here and there he caught the scent of it. He remembered well the night when the weasel first came and how the little devils had screamed under the mud floor. Sometimes Haavn could give himself over to hallucinations, and for a while he had thought himself to be the weasel.

Often when he lay awake in the night, he could hear sounds that no one else would hear or understand. Sometimes he heard creaking in the old dress harness hanging there on the walls, as if the harness were out on a drive by itself. From the dust covered bells came a faint tinkling. And Haavn heard the tools, for his best tools were standing here in the harness room—a scoop shovel and a spade which he had put fifteen years of himself into, with the steel worn bright and sharp, the ash handles strong and shiny through use. They were tools he did not like to see in the hands of others. They were tools a man could wish to have with him in his coffin, and certainly no one would begrudge him that. From that shovel and spade he sometimes heard quiet talk, or sometimes music from far distant places, a wedding procession or something similar, far away and long ago.

And during the middle of the night, there was always something outside to be heard. Tonight Haavn had heard a creaking —a raven scratching in the frozen dunghill. The sparrows, who sat huddled up under the eaves, heard it. But their peeps, which remind one of falling drops, froze in their beaks, and the only noise they could make was with their feathers. Even though the

winter was hard, the year was well along towards spring, and the
raven hung about and complained.

Now and then Haavn heard even more, things he couldn't always explain to himself. Sometimes in the night he heard something moving around in the yard. Or else something heavy that
came and rubbed hard against the wall leading to the harness
room, as though there were an ox scratching itself out there. And
even when stillness returned, the dust could go on settling for a
long time. His neighbors were low-minded enough to irritate him
in this way, but it couldn't be them; they would be afraid to
come near his house at night. Besides that, he could never find
any tracks out there. That was too bad, for then Haavn could have
explained it. It was wartime, of course, there were enemies about,
and it would not have surprised him if they were out to get someone like himself. But there were never any tracks, and since
Haavn's stolid intellect could not function without explanations,
he wondered at times if he could be temporarily insane. Furthermore, sometimes when he lay dozing during the middle part of the
night, he was shot through the head—that was how it felt. Or he
was convulsed with a violent jerk in his chest which leaped through
all his nerves. When these sensations broke up, Haavn would lay
for an hour dizzy and afraid, thinking of the sudden death which
he hoped for. And yet he did not want death to come like a thief
when his senses were dulled and he unaware. He wanted to be
warned, wanted to face the antagonist. But something strange
was going on in him, and Haavn could only explain certain mysterious incidents as moments when he was a bit crazy.

He knew that in five minutes it would be three-thirty. In five
minutes he would get up, and as he did the knife would go into
him. It happened every day, and even though Haavn out of pride
desired a conscious death, he was always slightly disappointed to
wake up in the morning alive. But now he had five minutes
of freedom in which to prepare himself.

And so he lay there, listening. Everything was as it should be
now—completely still. No iron-shod hoof had scraped on the stone
floor, none of the animals in the stable was stirring. The sorrowful
raven had flown off. There was only that deathly calm which in

the course of a day rules in the hour just before the cock crows. Only this farmer's thoughts and pains were awake.

In the dark Haavn turned his head toward the alarm clock which sat invisibly ticking on a chair beside the bed. With the motion he began to rock, perhaps he was dizzy. He was aware of the vessel's slow movement in the swell, of a heavy sea running along the side. And that familiar sound, as if skin were being flayed off the ship. For a moment Haavn could feel the heavy vapor in the cabin. From far off came the sound of breaking glass —and he was clearheaded again. Just another horrible dream laden with bad memories. The dream usually forgotten in waking had turned at the threshold and seized him once more. Younger days. Accursed days.

With difficulty he pulled his right arm from under the feather quilt and tried to straighten it. Torture in the joints. Now he could tell how cold it was in the room (the skin on his face was numb). The cold was worse than it had been, but there were no drafts through the door; that meant there was no wind yet. In this way Haavn tried to think about something else as he straightened his arm with small jerks.

Extending two fingers, he touched the hands of the clock— there was no glass over the face of it. When Haavn read the clock this way, it was not because he had any doubts about what time it was. Many sleepless nights had sharpened his time perception until he had an extremely sensitive inner chronometer. Rather, touching the clock was a morning ceremony. And each time he determined that the alarm clock was wrong. Today it was four minutes slow.

Haavn said to the clock: We'll overlook it this time. Everything moves slower in this kind of cold, that's obvious.

As a rule, Haavn was tolerant of the clock's failures, and thus the ceremony was quietly upbuilding. But on occasion he would let himself go, he needed that satisfaction once in a while. In a superficial way the clock reminded him of the mindlessness of the times, of excesses in the world, of man's stupidity, lightmindedness, lawlessness. This alarm clock with its untrustworthy lead hands represented everything which Haavn detested.

Sometimes at this dark hour of the morning one caustic word could lead to another, and Haavn, cursing with his neck resting on the bed head, could grow suddenly afraid. For, having conjured up much of what he hated—neighbors and their cringing dogs, housekeepers, government, authorities, the foreigners in the country—all at once his words could seem too spindly, wholly inadequate. They might have shocked many, but for Haavn himself they were without bite or force. He felt disgusted with his verbal impotence. He was too clearheaded, not wrathful enough, in which state of mind his disgust betrayed him by allowing the intrusion of self-contempt. At that point his solid intellect deserted him and went over to the enemy; it was then that his traitorous reason lit the *ignus fatuus* inside him by the light of which he saw that he was nothing. Then Haavn the intelligent saw all his used up years floating like sticks in a pond. Just so much nonsense. He saw then that he was a paltry person. Slightly mad, sick, and paltry. A lonely blabberer, a complicated minus. And that was no good, one couldn't tolerate that. He knew what could happen next, and it was what he was so afraid of. It had never got to that point yet, but it could happen. If the nauseous yeast of humility once got into him, it could spread. He would begin to pity himself like that miserable Job in the scripture, warming his face with tears, comfortable in his blubbering. And if he became craven and modest like a dog fart, then people would accept him. Better to be dead.

Thus in these nightly encounters with the clock, if Haavn sensed pity emerging, he tried to nip it promptly. Sometimes he couldn't manage this without working himself into a rage. It was enough to evoke his enemies fiercely; immediately he could be furious with an almost holy rage that persisted for a long while. Out in the fields, for example, he might say to himself: you haven't been furious for seventeen days now! And if he happened to look at the weeds teeming up from the soil, it could occur to him that he needed to start raging again. Anger was a kind of grace that came over him, bringing strength and bliss to the weakling, making him a bright flame. Afterwards he could lie trembling like a pup, feeling strangely foolish. But the intoxication of wrath was a long-lasting defense against the worms of pity.

At the same time, Haavn was a little afraid of anger. For one who considered himself a brave man, there were more than a few things he feared. He explained this to himself by saying that he was too much of a thinker; it was his intellect with its hundred sharp eyes that made him fearful of so much. It was true that anger liberated him; it made a giant of him, gave him fierce words which sprang over fences like mad bulls. But afterwards he couldn't really say what had come over him, couldn't remember how he had smashed his knuckles. His reason was opposed to this ignorance. It made him fearful that one fine day he would lose his self-control in the presence of his enemies, and that wouldn't do at all unless his words could be translated into equally violent actions. But Haavn didn't think that could happen. His enemies hadn't enough fiber to be provoked to violence, and he would only look foolish.

As yet it hadn't happened. They were uneasy about Haavn because he was calm. His anger was like ravens mating. No one saw it. But it could be that some heard it. The forest has ears just as the field has eyes.

This morning Haavn's clock ceremony was peaceful, stimulating in a quiet way. His inscrutable perception of time gave him courage, and the result was a mild warmth that spread throughout his body. His corpse, he called it.

Haavn needed courage in the perfect stillness of the morning when only the farmer and his troubles are awake. It was he who must set life and day in motion. But he was a withered creator and thus could use all the excess arrogance the clock ceremony could provide. According to his inner chronometer, it was still two minutes before three-thirty. Meanwhile his body parts were waking to full anticipation of the pain about to come. Of course, the usual dull pains in his joints were always there; but for long periods they could lie outside his consciousness. Now they came. Haavn met them with his will, which was his real self; his body was merely a creation apart, many creations, many traitors. Cowardly companions who would tempt him to give up. His sensitive back, which had never been right since a fall long ago, became suddenly unbearable to lie on. Haavn bit his worthless teeth together—they creaked like a swinging door. And still he lay there. Now something in the joints blew life into the coals of rheumatism. Nor was his shameless bowel any better, jabbing him awake like a bayonet. At an auction he had bought a medicine chest, together with its old, dusty contents; from it he now and then took strong remedies to hold off the back and joint pains for a while. But they stopped him up with constipation. Sometimes to get some peace, the stomach attacked, and the exit from the bowel was torn apart. There were memories of the most deeply humiliating kind attached to those times, sitting out there behind the house trying to give birth to gray boulders, afraid that some would actually come, afraid one wouldn't survive if they did.

This was a typical day, beginning without compassion for Haavn. He knew that people wanted him to suffer, for the sake of his arrogant self-control as well as for other reasons. They knew his troubles, even though he tried to hide them, for as a rule he had a housekeeper. There had been many of them, one replacing another continually. Terrible women. All of them the same, concealing eyes that were always looking, always snooping. Except of course when he was in this room, for here the glances of those lascivious women did not dare to venture, here it was too dangerous for those superstitious pigeons. But otherwise they saw everything. Sometimes Haavn could be hit with a pain so jolting that for a long time he could do nothing but stand hanging onto something—that is, if he thought he was unobserved. But if he was aware of eyes, he would break out of that paralysis, strengthened by a kind of savagery, and depart suddenly from the spot with long, easy strides. And yet they saw it in spite of him, they understood it, rejoiced in it, and went out and gossiped about it with everyone. It rankled Haavn that they had this diabolical ability to see through him, that a man couldn't go around with the seeming indifference which Haavn considered his sacred right; and so he wanted to get back at them. Thus he pursued his little

revenges whenever he could, usually with tricks he considered
unworthy of himself. But he couldn't stop. His inability to understand fully his fear of their eyes made him petty and vengeful.
Of one fear, however, he was fully aware: that some day he
would collapse out in the field. It would be perfectly fine if he died
at once, they were bound to have respect for his corpse. But if
he didn't die and yet was so far out of it that he couldn't drag
himself home to the harness room where the loaded rifle was
hanging, then it would be bad. Then they'd come and carry him;
they'd help him, fetch the doctor, wash him, feed him, sit and
look at him with ugly expressions, with overbearing eyes, because
they were so pervertedly self-satisfied, because they were so glad
to help an enemy who was obviously washed up.

Now Haavn began the struggle with his limbs. Soon he must
get up, and the knife would plunge in. When you reach advanced
years, you needn't be ashamed if the wind brings tears to your
eyes. Perhaps it is even a mark of honor in an older person when
rheumatism makes his numbed nose a bit moist. Haavn rubbed
his perverse limbs to make them pliable. Well, no one sees a
damp horn in the dark. But it could be that a wet nose brings
memories, softens one up. Was solitude turning Haavn inside out?
God knew solitude was otherwise quite to his taste. If anything
in the world was right for him it was solitude and animals. They
belonged together, just as animals and stillness belong together.
The bellowing of a stag, the cry of the raven, the squeaking of a
bat only make the silence deeper. With animals Haavn was solitary
and at home. Among them, a steady person is master, their god
even. The thoughts of animals never reach up to the high, unreasonable world of man, but his thought descends to and com-
prehends theirs. That was enough for Haavn. But then solitude
turned its wrong side out, bringing back nonsense and much else
that once seemed good. Memories, nonsense. Something far away.
People from back then. Young man. Hot-tempered maybe. I'm
leaving all this, leaving it. Girls. Maybe one girl. Special. Just
once. That's how it is, eh? Goodbye, forgotten. Ship on the sea.
Drunk on shore. Goodbye. Hot-tempered person sees much, but

sees nothing. Continents, goodbye, forgotten. People once met, individuals, goodbye. Boat on the waves, waves on the sea, years that roll by like waves rolling on the sea. Goodbye.

Haavn hadn't counted the seconds. Now the time had come. The claw slammed into him. Abruptly Haavn sat up. Impossible to do it, yet he did it every morning. As he did, he let out a small cry, behind the teeth. Not a human cry, but as if from a cat giving birth. Only afterwards was he aware that he had meowed. And at this moment when Haavn rose in his bed, jerked up by Jehovah, waves of darkness and dizziness passed through him. Then consciousness returned. Sat there and listened, as if he would search out and strangle that traitorous little cry. But pain enveloped him. Usually it took Haavn about a quarter of an hour to get himself standing upright on the floor. First he must get his limbs extended by a series of small jerks. He broke into a sweat. Flattering, cursing, he attempted to persuade the cowards.

This morning it was more difficult than usual. Haavn reached only a half-sitting position. Something was pressing heavily against his chest: it was the feather quilt—though it felt more like the weight of a dead person. The upper part of it was frozen. Haavn tried to get hold of the cloth with his teeth, but it was like biting into an oak log. With an excruciating effort he managed to prop himself up against the head board, then reached up into the darkness. Something bumped against the wall, and his fingers stuck fast to the steel, but Haavn didn't swear. Quietly lifting the ax, he began to chop against the quilt so that it broke up inside the cover. Thus he managed to push back one end of it, as one would push back a trap-door. He had started to sweat from the exertion, and now the cold penetrated him. It was worse than ever. Haavn shivered, his head bouncing against the bedstead quite out of time with the ticking of the clock.

Haavn had forgotten how cold it could be. His recollections of weather grew stiff and died in this cold, his will became flabby. With his head shivering against the headboard, he couldn't hear if the animals were moaning over in the stable—and he almost didn't care. Now came the first of the morning's three temptations. Just when he began to feel that a sick, weak, half-naked man could not endure any longer, it occurred to him that soon it needn't be a problem any longer. He had only to let his will slip from that last notch, give in to apathy, and in two hours he would be frozen stiff as a log. He closed his eyes. Opened them. It was brightest when the lids were closed. He began to see pleasant things there. Already felt dull and tired.

In this way Haavn's thoughts acquired visible form out of shame and darkness. He saw himself standing out on the floor already in his pants, which were frozen stiff as armor from the thighs down. He buttoned the suspenders, no longer worrying what this devilish cold had done to the animals out in the stable.

Not until his clothes were on did the frugal Haavn light the stump of a candle which he had fixed in the rusted lantern. Then the gloomy room came into existence around him. The bed, built so that it could have borne the carcasses of several oxen, took up more than half the width. The cracked quilt stuck up from it, looking like a broad man sitting there. Along the walls hung the old harness, with cobwebs and hoarfrost between the straps. The vapor from Haavn and from the bed had created a miniature glacier which flowed over the window casing.

From a nail, Haavn took down a pelted cap. When he slung it over his head, the small, white, decent forehead disappeared—his light was out. What more was there to say of him now: he looked like a million other bearded, nondescript laborers. Except that his eyes were especially black and penetrating, even though his old military papers listed them as light blue.

He opened the door, but turned about momentarily with lantern raised. Already a rat was sitting in the middle of the floor, squinting at him. Then it ran up the chair leg, jumped into the bed, disappeared under the quilt. Haavn nodded and left.

A little creaking in the chestnut tree. Ice on the branches. Slight breeze from the southwest, so the frost will hold. Saltpeter in the stars. There's Charles's Wain up there; there's the North Star. Have read that it takes forty years to get down here. Figure out while milking how long it would take to walk to the North Star.

Haavn limped briskly along past the high snowdrifts in the

yard, opened the stable door, and stepped in with the lamp held
aloft. All of his animals were in this long, dark room. Both the
horses and cows were standing, that was unusual. The large animals had already turned their heads toward the door. Now there
was no movement in them, not an ear flickered. The light reflected
faintly from their dark, still eyes. Over the backs of the cows lay
a white covering; the muzzle hair of the horses was thick with
frost.

Haavn turned and held the lantern toward the wire netting
behind which the chickens were kept. The rooster and his eight
hens sat huddled together on the roost. Several of them inclined
their heads and blinked frivolously at the light, the others kept
their heads beneath their wings. None of them jumped down.

"Crow!" said Haavn. The rooster only ducked once beneath his
red comb.

"Go on and crow, you whoremonger!" roared Haavn; "now's the
time for it!"

But the rooster shut his eye, and the watch cry of the morning
did not sound.

None of the animals moved with Haavn's outcry, and the stillness in the stable seemed even more bizarre afterwards. It was as
cold inside as it was out, and there was no smell at all in the
room this morning.

Haavn said: "Which one of you little devils is dead?"

He limped along the stalls, holding the lantern above the dark
coats. Mournful eyes followed him. In the first stall beyond the
cows, four young pigs lay close together. They didn't move, but
each of them contemplated Haavn with a guilty look, as if stolen
goods were hidden in the straw beneath them. And in the next
space lay the sow, gaping. Foam was frozen at the corners of her
mouth. Haavn climbed into the pen, moaning softly as he dragged
his last leg over. The sow was ice-cold, hard enough to chop firewood on. It lay there like an overturned sofa, its legs erect.

"I don't like your manners," said Haavn, "but females are like
that."

He limped back, divided a sheaf of oats among the horses,
cleaned out the frozen dung behind the cows, took bucket and

stool and sat down to milk. The streams tinkled reluctantly in the
bucket without making any foam.

Haavn did not feel good at all as he sat there hunched over.
He mumbled: "Forty years then. Take off at three hundred
thousand kilometers an hour. No, three hundred thousand a
second. That would be—that would be—add a zero, three million
times six. Eighteen million per minute. That would be—would be
—add a zero and six times again. Hold still there, Valparaiso."

After Haavn had milked and knew how long it would take
him to get to the North Star, he fed the animals and went back
to the dead sow. He sat down on the big carcass, from which cold
quickly passed into him.

"Good thinking, little Florence," he said, running his hand over
the sow's stiff hair, "that's how one gets rid of a stiff neck, yes
indeed."

Haavn didn't know how he could manage now without the
sow, which unfortunately had not been insured. He had intended
to keep it until after Easter when the sale of the small pigs would
have helped him over settling day. Haavn made a practice of paying off his bills punctually, did it through a lawyer so that he himself didn't have to deal with creditors. But this would pinch.
Haavn was not well-off; he squeezed out all he could, but his
effort did not yield as much now. There was nothing for it but to
sell one of the other animals. Might have to ask for a postpone-
ment next time. But that he wouldn't do.

"I get the point, Florence," he said. " I should go with you."

There stood the lantern before him on the floor, and now the
second temptation approached cunningly, flickering above the
straw, dancing devilishly in the candle.

Haavn was, of course, a pessimist. He had always been skepti-
cal about mankind, a view which the war emphatically justified.
But there were many ways of being pessimistic, and one in particular appealed to Haavn as an inscrutable, if somewhat desperate,
game. His thoughts were so perceptive and clear that there was
something corrosive about them. His prophetic vision was never
light and friendly; rather when he considered the future of his
farm, the breeding of his cattle, sowing and harvesting, he al-

ways anticipated that things would go badly—that satisfied his twi-light mood. Yet Haavn was inconsistently opportunistic in that he tried to gain control of fate by means of his pessimism. He did not think so much as feel that if his prophecies were bleak enough, and wholly believed in, they would not come true. It was some-thing like exorcism. By thinking about and believing in misfor-tune continuously, he prevented it. With respect to the sow, Haavn's prophetic sensibility had long known that the beast would betray him by dying inopportunely. He had thought about this so often that he could scarcely imagine it otherwise. But behind these gray-black anticipations of misfortune sat his submerged awareness, calm and assured. Things would turn out right with the sow, after all. Belief in a saint could not have been more assuring. It had been so well-concealed that only now did he be-come conscious of it as it proved unfounded.

Haavn sat there on his dead sow, astonished that she really was dead, astonished that his acknowledged prophecy had actually come true. His amazement was such that it jarred loose some-thing massive deep within his mind. From where his childlike assurance had been there now rushed forth a new sense of ca-tastrophe to meet his normal anticipation of misfortune. They hastened to each other like bride and groom, inflamed with de-sire, gates were kicked open, footsteps echoed in the dark caves, scaly memories crept out of the corners, twisting and turning among themselves.

Haavn sat there by the lantern, smiling quietly. His shadow extended all the way to the North Star; walls and roof were to him nothing more than mist, sow and settling-day nothing but trivial foolishness. Suddenly he had become mighty; the possessor of enormous power. His prophetic thoughts had killed the sow. But that was only to see the insignificant side of it; his prophetic thoughts had descended from on high to ravish the virgin, that is to say, his naive faith. The former Haavn was destroyed, in his place sat an Almighty. Now truly he stared deeply into the essence of things. His thoughts killed. He was aware that the winter sur-rounding him, the cold, the war, the dying land were his work.

Thus Haavn understood all—even without his usual speculation, which, having initiated the process, now stood tame and trembling by his side. That speculation resembled a cowardly defendant in a paternity suit who would lie to avoid responsibility; it was frightened by its own offspring, that mighty, diabolical fantasy. Haavn was an unlimited spirit, a Satan, Night itself, swelling, blowing the cold breath of destruction into everything.

Haavn was probably not in this condition longer than it takes for lightning to flash across the sky; for no one could long tolerate to be so extended, so endless. Immediately he collapsed into loathing—he was a miserable person whose joints ached, a small shabby sacrifice to rheumatism. And he was almost frozen fast to the sow's carcass.

Haavn lifted the candle from the lantern. Before the temptation had really penetrated into his sluggish thoughts his stiff hand closed around it. Haavn held a straw over the flame, it flared up, grew slender and black, the stump of it fell to the floor and lay glowing among the other straws. Haavn sat the candle down in the middle of that straw.

"Heat!" he said, "let's have some proper heat." Then shouting: "For once let's have it really warm! Don't you agree, you little devils? Do little devils like us even exist without heat?"

Haavn was a man with imagination, and it sprang up: In a minute when the fire takes hold, open the door a little. That will feed the flames. Up they spring, into the hayloft. Then it really gets going. The bitch over there in her bed, she has a chance, a good chance. An old house rustles as it burns, sounds like waves in the wind. Of course. She only has to listen. And if she doesn't, what does it matter?

Haavn could see himself going back and forth between the stalls as the fire flickered above them. He was the man, the animals were his charges, he had to calm them: Easy now! Just take it easy, you ignorant little devils. You have to understand this. Warmth is good. It will only last a short time. Just be calm, now, you'll soon by happy. Just be quiet, you innocent beasts. You'll be glad before long, you'll be in your paradise, in the heaven for horses, the heaven for milkcows and calves, the heaven for chickens and pigs. And then you'll see the sow again—she's ahead of you. Just so. Goodbye, pleasant journey. Yes, maybe you can have the farmer along in your heavens. Which of them should he choose? He might like being a little beast, a bullock perhaps, or an old rooster, then he could go along. But does he know what he wants? He just knows that he doesn't want to remember. Let him lie in good clay soil without remembering. But be happy all of you!

The fire was slow. One straw after another lit its neighbor but died out before a sufficient number could get hot enough to flame up. Haavn forgot what else he intended to say in delivering his fireside admonition and farewell to the animals. He sat there looking into the light, and he saw something in it: a ruthless countenance.

The little tallow candle was one of the last he had, even though he had used them sparingly. In a mouldy old chest he had found a bunch of these candles that were older than he was. Since the rationing they had come in very handy. They had been dipped by his grandmother, she who once reigned here in this house. She had been dead for many years, but it was her countenance he saw in the flame.

"Oh, yah! That's what you think, you confounded old witch!" he said.

"You're still a blockhead!" she said from the flame.

"Well, and what of it?" answered Haavn. "What business is it of yours? I'm running things here now, get that through your head, you're all finished. Get out of my life, witch!" he suddenly screamed, pounding the sow, "your time is past!"

He sat there glaring at the light. Haavn regarded his grandmother with an emotion that was worse than hate. No one else knew how Haavn felt about his grandmother, he scarcely admitted it to himself. He took good care of the things he had inherited from her; for him there was an obscure kind of revenge in that. Didn't entirely understand it himself. From the time he was fifteen there had been enmity between them, and in life they never saw each other again. She was a strong woman, hard, maybe Haavn was like her. But there was something in his grandmother's will which he did not understand; in fact, much of what he didn't

understand seemed to originate with her. He was aware of her
everywhere, even though she had been dead for so long. Behind
all of his sneaking enemies, he caught glimpses of his grandmother's form. There in a fine mist she stood, driving them toward
him. She was a gray fog and a gray cat, and a keyhole was her
eye. When Haavn lost lawsuits against his neighbors and the civil
authorities, he knew it was she pulling the strings. But he had his
revenge by keeping her awake and unable to find peace. Yes, it
was her he heard in the night, her shuffling footsteps, her weight
against the wall. She was the exhausted rat which stole into his
bed. Haavn knew this was true, though he scarcely dared admit it
to himself.

Now she was there.

"Think of your father," she said. "What would he say to this!"

"He was a fool," answered Haavn, "soft as butter on a hot po-
tato. You drained the life out of him. But you'll not get me!"

"Put it out, you ass!" she said from the light.

"Oh, what the hell," muttered Haavn. Immediately he stood up
and stamped out the weak fire. And he didn't look any more at
the candle flame. Shame was a force in nature, it came over him
now, and he didn't understand it. Impossible now to raise his
glance and look at his animals as they stood there munching in-
dolently. He heard law asserting itself in him. Man provides for
animals, they are with him, they belong to him. Over them he has
dominion, he brings the cow to the bull, he castrates the young
boar pigs, he slaughters the heifer. There is law throughout all
nature, and even man is subordinate to it. For if a horse crazy with
fear rears against his halter in a burning stable, the man does not
remain outside overcome with tears and pity as if unable either to
kill or help the animal. He goes in after it, either to come out
with it or to remain with it. That law was the law for Haavn. He
arose, stood there on trembling knees, and looked about. "That
was bad," he muttered. "Now what?"

Shortly thereafter Haavn went to work. He fetched saw and
ax, cut the legs off the dead sow, and bound a rope around its
snout. Then he harnessed the two long-hoofed horses to a swingletree and drove them around behind the stable. They pulled the

sow out through the door. As the carcass slipped free of the door casing, the horses bolted suddenly forward, plowing through snow drifts in the yard with the sow and Haavn in tow. He said nothing to them, but let them tire in the deep snow, after which they drew the sow more sedately until it lay before the main door. A strange sight to greet the dawn.

Next Haavn entered the house. He cleared his throat several times and waited a minute before he opened the door to the sitting room and stepped inside. Vaporous heat struck his face, causing his eyes to water, and with blurred vision he saw Johanne the housekeeper. She raised her tousled head from the pillow—she had moved her bed into the sitting room where, for the time being, she kept the stove red around the clock. She was a very indifferent woman, came from somewhere else; whether widow, divorcee, or maid—Haavn didn't know. It was so warm in the room that the feather quilt no more than half covered her, and his wet eyes observed various white superfluities. Johanne didn't care.

"You'd better get up," he said; "she's lying out there and she'll have to be quartered."

"Who'll have to what?" said Johanne, laying a naked arm under her neck and looking at Haavn with sleepy eyes.

"The sow!" he answered. "Frozen to death. She has to be quartered. You can begin after you've given me breakfast."

"Would you mind handing me the sugar bowl," said Johanne. Haavn gave it to her. It was all right with him, since she used her own stamps.

"If I remember correctly, Haagensen," she said, her cheek bulging slightly with sugar, "you can't, according to our contract, require me to do outside work."

"That's true enough," said Haavn. "But it doesn't matter; I'll quarter it and carry it in. Then you can boil it, that's inside work."

"Boil it? What on earth for?" she asked. The sugar was eaten. She stuck her round, white legs out of the bed and reached for cigarettes.

"You boil a dead sow to make soap."

"How much soap do you expect to get?"

"Three hundred and fifty pounds."

Johanne glanced at Haavn's face, then at his hands. "Think that'll be enough?"

But Haavn was occupied with his own thoughts: "Didn't you say folks are complaining they haven't enough soap stamps?"

For answer she pinched her eyes together and gave a little snort through shiny pale lips. That irritated Haavn some, but he said: "In the old days, folks helped each other in bad times. One should think about that."

"You intend to give the soap away then?"

"That can be decided later."

"But you don't have any soapstone," said Johanne, "and you can't get any; no one can get to town with the roads the way they are."

"We'll see about that," answered Haavn, "but first there has to be some breakfast. And then you can get ready for the boiling."

"That's indoor work all right," she said, "but there's nothing of that kind here I intend to boil. It's against the law, and I don't want anything to do with it, Haagensen. It's forbidden to make soap at home, and even animals that die naturally must be delivered to the authorities. I read it in the paper. Don't you know that?"

"It's reassuring to know that a woman refuses to break the law," said Haavn, "but aside from the fact that they make harebrained laws, I don't happen to know that law. Never heard of it. A law you don't know isn't a law. That's the end of it."

"Oh yes, Haagensen, you know it now because I told you about it."

Haavn wanted to reply with something poisonous, but he controlled himself. And it was easy—so easy it surprised him. Of course Haavn usually was able to curb himself; doubtless it was precisely this deliberate calm which so unsettled his enemies. But his control on this day derived from another source: benevolence moved him. "You can sleep as long as you wish," he said to her. "There's nothing to worry about just now. I'll manage the boiling myself. And I'll have to get the soapstone. But first there must be something to keep alive on, a hunk of bread, a herring, and a bit of yesterday's pudding. I'll take care of it."

The housekeeper sat up with a jerk, covered her superfluities, and straightened her nightgown below. "Oh yes, sure you will!" she grumbled, getting out of bed quickly and drawing a blanket around her.

Haavn turned his back to her amiably and sat down at the table. The indifferent Johanne stuck out her tongue at him, then hurriedly put on her clothes. Was this some kind of trap he had laid for her? For a moment she had expected a different ending. Haavn had stood there staring greedily at her, his hands twitching. And she would have been glad enough to thaw the ogre out. But she'd not stand for him to make a fool of her.

"Besides, it wouldn't do any good!" said Haavn, preaching to her as she left the room. "It wouldn't do a bit of good to notify the authorities. No car could get through these roads!"

"No, of course not," came her response as she disappeared.

Haavn sat there at the table, his hand under his bearded chin. Not bad to say that about the car and the roads. It hadn't occurred to him before. Such an objection would have carried no weight at all with Haavn in his usual frame of mind. But now he observed that these words had acquired a certain gravity through being understood by another. Even this frivolous feminine intelligence gave them weight. Everyone would agree. Truth with substance.

Haavn was not glad to hear it was against the law. Ordinarily he observed the laws scrupulously. Not that he considered the present laws good, on the contrary. But he despised the sneaking attempts folks made to evade them. In that way they became the slaves of bad laws. Haavn, on the other hand, made himself a free man and greater than the laws by observing them strictly.

That was his usual view. Had it happened yesterday, he might have moved heaven and earth to deliver the sow and fulfill that foolish law. Now everything was changed. He needed the sow for his generous purpose. It was strange that a good thought should immediately bring him in conflict with the law. Let that be as it may. And now he could say—and all would agree and say with him: the law could not be observed under the conditions.

Thus Haavn rationalized, picking up his steel-rimmed glasses.

They were old, he had found them tucked away in a drawer once after he began to be farsighted; they weren't quite right for him, but he got by. Maybe they had been his grandmother's. Haavn was almost touched by that thought as he sat there polishing the lenses with the housekeeper's tepid nightgown. Next he took math books and scratch paper from the corner cupboard. Haavn's math books were spotted with grease because he often worked problems as he ate. These were the books he hung over in the evenings until a little before eight when he left the parlor and retired to the harness room. The continually changing housekeepers also had to be in the sitting room, but Haavn seldom noticed them. He would sit there figuring, mumbling to himself —it sounded like low growling. And it usually got on their nerves —the wind outside, the winter sounds in old house, the man's growling, his stiff, dark countenance—before long they were ready to climb the walls. Johanne, though, was devil-may-care. She would sit there knitting, chattering fast and loose all the while, paying no attention to him. She had told her life's history many times, detailed the plot of this winter's serialized novel, and Haavn scarcely heard any of it. He had thought that her eternal jabbering would disturb him. But her endurance compelled his brusque respect. He had responded by strengthening his concentration, and now her chattering was actually a pleasant household noise. If she were away for an evening, he'd get so mentally scattered that he could forget a logarithm he had just taken from the table before he could get it onto the paper.

With moistened pencil, Haavn quickly checked to see if his mental calculation out in the stable had been correct. It was. If you walked five kilometers an hour steadily, day and night, the trip to the North Star would take a good eight and a half billion years. But this morning he was too impatient to occupy himself with mathematics. He blew out the lamp and sat drumming on the table with his fingers. Dawn was coming on. Through the broad portal out there, the earth looked deep blue and desolate.

The careless woman came with his breakfast. Haavn spooned diligently at the mild, lumpy pudding, and he devoured a very large Icelandic salt herring, shiny with brine. He had reason to believe it would not agree with his stomach, but for now—as always—it had a very animating effect.

Haavn wiped his mouth on his sleeve and said: "You may find one thing or another new coming from this quarter, Johanne. An old stiffneck like me may have to take another tack. I've been thinking it over."

He limped quickly to the door and threw it open. The housekeeper stood there dumb. Never before had he called her by name or referred to himself with the pronoun I. His words shook her, and in her confusion she didn't know what to make of them.

He would be home again in six, at most seven, hours, he declared, and the door banged shut behind him. Johanne stood behind the checkered curtains and watched him hobbling along in his great coat, leading the old mare Frisko until he disappeared through the gate.

It was twelve kilometers to town. Frisko was balky and only reluctantly let herself be dragged through snowdrifts, over fences and cloddy, windswept fields, but even so he traveled two kilometers before he cursed the animal for the first time.

The going was too hard for him to ride the horse, and when they had laid another half mile behind, Haavn was fully aware that he had ventured upon a fool's errand. Frisko's weariness and his own good sense warned him. For a somewhat older mare without spirit and a somewhat older man with sick joints, the only reasonable thing to do was turn back.

They had now passed the first small forest. The salt herring began to feel unpleasant in his stomach just as they came fully out into the open. Here the wind rushed freely over an endless plain, grain-covered in summer, now a white wilderness of death. As yet the wind was not fierce, though the dry snow whirled about. But it went through Haavn as if he hadn't a thread on. Nor did it help that he had worn his father's ancient greatcoat, which an arrow could scarcely penetrate. Haavn could not remember that it had ever been so cold.

He was not an imprudent man. He was thoughtful enough to be afraid as he stared, with the wind in his face, forward over these punishing fields. Had he been younger, as strong as he had been just ten years ago, he would have found such a jaunt good fun. But a weakling stood here now, he knew that well enough. And he noticed that the mare had not gotten warm with the exertion but stood with hanging head, its will to live dangerously weakened. The horse would be a burden to Haavn; he would have to support its spirit with his own will. He had done that before, through long nights, with sick animals. A horse gives up before a man does, and weak animals will lean on one for support. Haavn looked into himself, taking stock of his defects: they rose up like a beseeching chorus. If he were to get through, his pains would be the worse for it afterward. But Haavn wasn't sure he could slip through. Probably it was that that settled the matter.

He discovered that his nose was numb. Let it fall off! But he took the feedbag and tied it around the head of the mare to protect its muzzle. Frisko snorted into the fodder; chaff flew up and was carried away by the wind. She ate nothing, simply stood there quietly with head against Haavn's chest as he fastened the jaw strap of the bag. He noticed that the horse's eyelashes were frozen together, they looked like scabs moving over the eyes. Haavn's own eyes watered in the wind, and he could feel the tears freeze.

He took snow in his mittens and rubbed his face.

"Come on, little Frisko!" he shouted.

Slowly they crept along over the passable spots in this lonely land of death. The only sign of life was smoke rising from the chimney of an occasional house. It was a remote district where none of the roads had been cleared after the heavy snowfall. But in one spot, where some withered mugwort stuck out of the snow in the lee of a drift, sat a pair of partridges. Haavn and the horse came so close he almost could have touched them. They did not fly but simply turned their heads and looked up at him with defiance in their eyes. Haavn liked them for that.

"Well, what do you think, Frisko!" shouted Haavn to the sluggish mare as he pulled her along, "what do you think of our hellish errand? Why are the partridges sitting in twos when its so damnably cold?"

They were more than five hours getting to town. When Haavn

finally found a place where they had soapstone, he bought a
hundred pounds. By himself he loaded the heavy sack on the back
of the mare, who stood there crookedly in the freezing street.
The wind lifted the hair on the animal's back and spread the tail
about the quivering hocks. Getting the sack up was almost more
than Haavn could manage. The effort cost him some blood in his
pants, but that had happened before. Here and there the frost
had melted partially from the icy window panes, and when Haavn
realized there were eyes behind them, he stepped around the
horse and bit so hard on his mittens that he could feel the skin
break underneath.

They lost almost an hour in town, even though Haavn did nothing else but buy a loaf of rye bread. He devoured one corner of it
as they passed the last of the houses.

The trip home extended far into the night, perhaps thirteen
hours, but at the last Haavn was no longer keeping track—his
chronometer simply stopped. It seemed that they crept along for
an eternity in the dark. They had not come very far from town
when the light began to fade. Whether that eased the mare's mind
or whether she merely understood they were going home, she
found a reserve of energy, quickened her pace, and got her head
out in front of the painfully limping Haavn. With that he jerked
her hard to a stop and glared straight into her ice-sharpened eyes.
"It will be said, Frisko," said Haavn, "it will be said that I was
led home in the night like a drunken pig by my horse. You stay
behind me, is that clear!"

It was drifting now as this procession wandered on. And then
in the forest not far from Haavn's farm they got lost. He knew that
forest in and out from the time he was a child, and he never lost
faith in that knowledge while he and the horse floundered about
in the deep snow beneath the trees. He stumbled forward into
drifts, breaking through the ice crust of them. The horse sank
down and groaned, then plunged up again, driven by Haavn's
cries, while the man himself fell further forward in the snow at
the end of the tight line. He did not give the disheartened animal a moment's peace but jerked it forward with the rope and

pulled it up with his hoarse roaring. In this way they sailed sedately around in the forest. And then Haavn was happy, for he
had stumbled onto a track. Someone had passed through earlier,
repeatedly falling forward. Here were the outlines of many dead
men who had fallen, had left their images compressed in the
snow, and were taken off again. It was a good trail for a sailing
man and his horse, and Haavn gladly sailed that course. Suddenly they were actually out of the forest. Their rambling there,
over the brittle, clattering ice of hidden brooks, over dead
branches breaking beneath the snow, seemed to him now to have
lasted five minutes, though they had been there six hours. At
length they were home, where no one saw exhaustion's madness
written in the eyes of these two creatures, for all was dark and
still. Haavn remembered to take the sack and the harness from
the horse, he broke up the ice on the trough to give her water,
which she didn't touch. He put grain in the manger and reached
out in the dark to pat the horse, but his hand found nothing—
she was already lying down in the stall. He didn't notice that the
evening's milk stood in the milkcan. He was aware of so little
that, when he fell over something large and rockhard lying in the
middle of the yard, he simply lay there and said aloud without
anger: "What is it folks leave lying in the yard, so other folks come
and stumble over it?"

In the harness room he saw by the light of the candle that food,
cups, and a coffeepot (wrapped in sheepskin but now ice cold)
stood on the chair by his bed. With an easy movement, he swept
them all onto the floor. The alarm clock likewise toppled, but it
had stopped long ago. And when Haavn discovered under his
feather tick a hot water can still mildly warm, he flipped it likewise onto the floor and then crept in where its warmth could
still be felt.

As day broke, Johanne was wakened in the warm sitting room
by noise from the cook house. It appeared to her that the frost
was less sharp, for the heat from the stove had almost completely
subdued the ice flowers on the panes. Then she became aware of
smoke from green firewood, and she knew he had taken it from the

wrong pile. She got up and went out there. Haavn was just coming through the entry with something monstrous in his grasp —the black head of the sow. He had a good fire going under the hearth kettle; the water was already steaming, in spite of the green wood.

"What's going on here, Haagensen?"

He didn't hear her, but he nodded. She stood there wrapped in a blanket, holding her nose. The sow's head filled much of the kettle. If the whole carcass had to be boiled, the kettle would have to be filled at least four times.

"Is your tongue frozen too?" shouted Haavn.

"I can't get over how it looks and smells here. And then you going around with fever, Haagensen."

"Who has fever? Go back and go to bed!"

"You have, Haagensen. You're all too shiny and smooth in the face. And look at your eyes. Let's hope you haven't caught your death."

"Is that how you tell fever?"

Johanne stepped up to him, laid her hand gently on his cheek, then on his brow. "You've got fever all right, you're sick. It's bad enough I could cry over it. I won't stand for you to be up any longer. If you insist on having this messy business finished, I'll have to do it, even though it's the most repulsive thing I've ever seen. Now get you in and lie down in my warm bed, I can take care of you there and get you well. Do you hear!"

Haavn stepped back a little. He looked her up and down. For a long time. With that old penetrating stare. It frightened Johanne. She had made a mistake; she thought that she had gotten the upper hand and that he, miserable as he was, would give up in that sweet way that many a brusque man has done after he has first shown how unbelievably brusque he is. And it hurt her more than a little.

"Go back inside and take care of your own business!" he snarled. And then he called after her: "If this is what fever is like, one ought to have it all the time!"

It is true that he shivered and trembled from time to time, but he could scarcely feel the rheumatism, or the weariness from yes-

terday's journey. It had been easy to get up this morning. No problem at all. He had big things going now.

Soon Haavn had the kettle boiling briskly—Johanne had
shown him the box containing dry wood. Vapor rose in waves up
to the beams. Warm fog pressed through the passageway out into
the frosty air. The cook house, the passageway, the whole yard
smelled of it. It steamed rawly, merrily. There was much glad
wildness and drive in it, as if Haavn were boiling spring itself up
out of the ice world.

He went through the steamy passageway and threw open the
parlor door.

"Come out here!" he bellowed, standing like a warrior in the
midst of his own smoking gunpowder. "Just take it easy now! One
talks a lot of nonsense sometimes. But listen, it's boiling like
crazy now!"

Haavn sniffed deeply and looked at her with sparkling eyes.
The housekeeper followed, humbly glad. Like one subject to a
loving tyranny, she admired the rumbling kettle, from which a
terrible stench was rising. Haavn slapped her roundly on the
buttocks. She turned away from him, with downcast eyes.

It was later in the morning. Haavn was out in the yard, down
on his knees sawing at the sow. He was shiny with grease. It was
still cold enough for iron to stick to the skin, but the sun up
there made the frost haze golden. As Haavn stood up, he became
aware of a woman in black standing between him and the gate.
Her head was wrapped in woolens to the point where only her
eyes were visible.

It startled Haavn a little. "In any case, it's not a vision," he said,
mostly to himself.

The woman unwrapped the scarf from the indispensable mouth.
Haavn recognized her as one of the pluckiest women on the commons, one who had never been afraid to argue with him. She
wore a pinched smile and stared pallidly at the air beside Haavn.
He rose up on trembling legs, prepared to defend himself. This is
a clever woman, he said to himself, remember now, she's clever.

"Magnificent weather, eh?" he shouted, "really fine, spring, eh?"

Yes, of course, but she thought it was terribly cold. Her voice was very small, thinner and colder than the air. Like a martyr's complaint. All the while she stared calmly and searchingly at Haavn.

Pain and death, he thought, but remember now that this is a clever woman. "Froze to death," he said; "she'll be resurrected as soap."

"Yes, so they say," answered the woman, holding his eye as though he were a fish she was reeling in. "They say you'll sell soap to us. How much do you think you can spare?"

"No need to be close-fisted about it. Fifteen, maybe twenty pounds for every house on the commons, there ought to be enough for that. Those with small children can have a little more."

"I see. And how much do you expect it will cost?"

"Oh, we can come back to that later. No need to worry about it. There's been something laid out for the soapstone. One could figure the sow is worth something, but we won't worry too much about that. If one were to figure it out, it might come to a little half hundred øre a pound."

"That's a high price, isn't it? Because your soap isn't likely to be too good. I just mention that."

"By all means, mention it," answered Haavn, "but no one is talking here about selling. That was only figuring. In any case you'll get yours gratis. That way you'll keep your mouth shut."

When the woman had gone and Haavn had entered the passageway, the housekeeper was standing behind the door. "That was not as bad as it might have been, Haagensen," she said, "but it was not so good either."

"What's that supposed to mean?"

"I think I know why she came," said Johanne, "and that was why I didn't come out. But she had another witness all the same; I saw someone out by the gate."

"Now don't go and get all flustered just because she's always been thought the most poisonous hag in the district," said Haavn. "She has her sharp edges of course, but she's good with her animals. Everything considered, she's a good woman. One can't blame her if she tries to protect herself. One is just curious to know how she found out about it."

"Take a guess."

"Ah ha! so that's it. Had to let it out, eh?" Haavn had fire in his eye, and he gripped her soft arm so fiercely that it left red dents.

The housekeeper walked into the parlor. Without turning toward him she said: "If anything should happen, Haagensen, remember that it was with good intentions."

"Nothing will happen," answered Haavn.

Several hours later Haavn became aware that something was blocking the light from the main door. A large man in a fine coat with velvet collar stood there looking in. It was Oluf, the most influential farmer in the district. He was exactly Haavn's age, but still handsome. Johanne had shot out to meet him before Haavn emerged from the steam. Something going on between them, thought Haavn grimly.

"Well, something's happening here!" said Oluf.

"Yeh, something's happening here," answered Haavn. He stepped forward now and walked with the tall, friendly guest out into the yard.

"One could hardly avoid seeing something as one came in. You're not concealing a thing," said the habitually soft-spoken Oluf. His art in speaking was such that he could transform the gruesome remains of the quartered sow into simply "something."

"You can see what's going on here. Was there something you wanted?"

"They say you mean to charge a high price. I'm not ready to believe that."

"It's as free as rain from our Lord. When it's ready you'll get your portion too."

"Good words to hear," said Oluf, "I know your goodwill as much as anyone does. It's partly therefore that I've come to warn you, for old friendship's sake."

"The devil take that old friendship," said Haavn. All the while it seemed to him that the smiling Oluf stood there glancing over his head toward Johanne, who had become quite radiant. "Good words again," added Haavn, "nothing particular meant by them."

"No, of course not. We two had a lot in common as boys."

"Quite," said Haavn, "and you ended up with all of it. Since then you've drawn the long straw. You got the girl, and with her you got a comb for your handsome hair. But good words again!"

"Yes, good words again," answered the imperturbable Oluf. "But look here, folks around here have gotten angry at you. It's hard to understand why, but it must be this business with the sow."

"Bulls will have calves before the rabble says thanks," said Haavn, and then he added: "Now don't mind me running off at the mouth. One can understand them well enough if they think they'll have to pay barefaced prices. Go and tell them that they'll get the soap for nothing."

"I'm almost afraid that folks won't take your soap in any case," answered Oluf. "They say they won't have any part of lawbreaking. I don't understand it, but they claim you're trying to get them in trouble."

"Of course," said Haavn.

"There's a lot of bad palaver," continued Oluf, "I can't remember anything like it. That's why I came. Of course there've been some bagatelles between you and the others in the past. The fact, for example, that you demanded your share of the rationed tobacco, though you don't smoke, they can't forget that."

"Quite so," answered Haavn, "that wasn't too bright of me. One should rather have done like those who drive into town on dark evenings to sell their wheat illegally. They don't lack for good cigars. Wasn't thinking of anyone in particular."

"Of course not," said Oluf. "But I'm relieved that you're taking all this so calmly. I just hope now that you'll be equally composed when they come. It would be too bad for all of us in the parish if anything of this got into the newspaper. But they're pretty worked up about it all. And they can't be too far away now, that's why I came. The thing is, someone telephoned the authorities yesterday and said you have a sow to be delivered, and now they've shoveled and pushed the commune's car through the roads over the commons. They can't be more than seventy-five yards from your gate now."

"To be sure. And who called the authorities?"

"It was me that did!" cried a voice behind him. Haavn turned to face Johanne, who stood with arms folded, staring at him. She was trembling.

"Yes, to be sure," muttered Haavn.

"We can see what they have to say, can't we?" said Oluf. "Just promise me now that you'll be reasonable about it! I'm not happy about it either."

Haavn had nothing to say. With jaw askew he stood staring at the gloomy remains of the sow. Johanne watched him. Against the blue calcimined wall she looked yellow. Oluf walked back and forth in the yard with hands in his pockets, sending Johanne a soft glance as he turned at the one end, stretching his neck benevolently toward the gateway as he turned at the other. In this way a good hour passed.

Then a truck appeared outside the yard, with chains on the tires and snow packed around the wheels. A leather-coated driver got out. As he came through the portal, other men popped out behind him, nine or ten of them, goosestepping, with shovels in their hands.

The broad-shouldered driver nodded to Oluf, then made over to Haavn: "I've been sent to pick up a sow."

"There just might be one by the doorway," answered Haavn.

As Haavn raised his head and looked at them, the men came slowly forward and spread out around him. There seemed to be something fearful in Haavn's glance. His eyes were clouded, like someone used to wearing strong glasses who has lost them. He didn't look fierce, as they remembered him and had expected to see him. His clothes and hands were covered with the work he'd been interrupted in. A filthy little weakling with knobby rheumatic hands. They came closer.

"There's no cause to play games with me," said the driver, "I'm here on official business. We were notified yesterday, and I'm here accordingly. When can we get it loaded?"

"Whenever you wish," answered Haavn.

"Lovely to hear him back down," said one of the others, "but then you really weren't expecting us, eh Haavn?"

One of them stepped close to Oluf and asked: "Was he difficult?"

Without losing his smile, Oluf snapped at him: "Now let's just take things easy. You can hear, can't you, that everything's in order."

"He doesn't need to think he's going to get off as easy as Oluf would have it sound," said one, "he's not going to slip out of it. He wanted to sell unlawfully and implicate us all. He's got to answer for that. We have both our wives and the housekeeper as witnesses."

"You certainly can't count on me!" shouted Johanne, her head held high.

"What do you expect from one like her? She can't afford to be thrown out."

"I hope to God you finish boiling your soap, Haagensen!" said Johanne.

"Enough! Let him get it loaded!" shouted one.

"Yes, let him get started!"

Haavn bent down slowly, in small jerks, for he had gotten stiff —they may have heard him grunt several times. Like one who is nearsighted, he groped around among the remnants of the carcass.

Oluf saw what he was reaching for, and he went quickly over to him, bent over and said: "Pay no attention to what she and the others say. Remember what you promised. We don't want this to end badly."

"Move aside, Oluf Jensen," said Haavn, "one gets sick of such good people."

"We'll give him one minute to get started!" someone shouted.

Haavn straightened up slowly, he had the long-handled ax in his hands. "Come and get started, boy!" he said.

Oluf had drawn back. His smile jumped around uneasily on his face, and he said in a loud voice. "Don't do anything rash, you mustn't! We'll all come to regret it!"

Haavn leaned forward over the sow. "Well, who's coming? Well, who wants to get started?"

A younger man stepped forward with shovel lifted: "It's wrong of you to try to shame us. I have wife and children, and you have none."

"No," said Haavn, "but you are young, and a shovel is longer than an ax." He stepped toward him and the man retreated.

Haavn said: "If there was one real man among the bunch of you, there could be something to tell at Thorup market. As it is, Haavn, as you call him, is going to have things the way he wants them. A herd of cowardly sheep, that's what you are and that's what you'll always be. But one get's sick of the sight of you. Get off my place! Clear out!"

"Gladly," said the driver, "this row is none of my affair." He walked away first, the others followed sidewise after.

"This'll be reported to the police," shouted one.

"You'd better hurry," said Haavn, "or someone'll beat you to it."

He followed them all the way to the portal and stood there with the ax over his arm, whistling. As he came back he turned into the harness room, for he had suddenly remembered the alarm clock which lay stopped on the floor. He found his bed made, the room straightened and swept. The clock itself stood ticking on the chair. It showed seven minutes before twelve.

"Minute and a half fast," said Haavn, "that's typical! But it's nothing to make a big issue about either."

Inside the passage the housekeeper stood waiting. "I expect you want me to leave now," she said.

"Haven't any opinion about it. You haven't broken the contract."

"I went yesterday to telephone the authorities while you were gone."

"There's nothing about that in the contract. The law says it's your duty. You could have mentioned it though."

"Yes," she said, "but I didn't know anything about what they tried to do. I just knew they were after you. And so I called and said it was a message from you. That way you'd done what you could. And I thought everything would be all right."

"Well thought," said Haavn.

"You think then I should go," she said.

"Don't have any opinion about it."

"I'll go then, unless you ask me to stay!" she said.

"No one is going to ask anybody anything," answered Haavn, stepping into the passageway.

"I'm leaving then," she said, "I'll go just as soon as I finish fixing your dinner."

"How long will it take you to finish it?" he asked over his shoulder.

"Maybe half an hour."

"Forget about dinner then," said Haavn, "it's better if we consider your services terminated exactly now. It's almost twelve o'clock. This way we can figure your wages from and with the first day until today's date at twelve o'clock. If one has to add on twenty minutes, it gets to be a matter of øre and decimal points."

Haavn calculated the wages in less time than it took Johanne to get ready, and he had the fire blazing under the kettle again when she came out to the cook house in dark cape and silk stockings, elegant and a bit red-eyed. Haavn watched out of the corner of his eye as she powdered her face.

"I'll send for my trunk and suitcases."

"After all, it's not necessary to drop everything if someone runs off unexpectedly."

"Oh for God's sake," she said, "you don't . . . why are you boiling that again?"

"Something a wise woman wouldn't have to ask. It isn't finished yet."

"But they'll send the police out here."

"Well, then things will be taken care of when they come."

"Now listen, Haagensen, listen!" she said. "Be serious now. I mean in the other way. What you thought of doing yesterday can't be done now. What you believed . . . God almighty, now it's boiling over . . . !"

"One thing at a time," said Haavn. "You follow a wild goose a long time before you find an ostrich feather. I should have known that. But do you think spinelessness can ever change stiffneckedness?"

"If one only knew . . . ," she said.

"Exactly," answered Haavn, "but maybe it should be otherwise.

Who knows, maybe Frisko and me have had a taste of something.
It's just possible some folks are waking up. If you run into any
of them, you might mention Haavn and Frisko."

"Yes," she said. They were silent. Haavn poked in the stove,
she powdered herself again.

"Listen now!" she said, ". . . hmm, what was it I meant to say?"

"How should somebody else know that?"

"Goodbye!" she said.

MARCH NIGHT

A CREATURE of some sort, probably a sparrow, chirps once up in the willow branches. It is cold, sighs the creature, it is dark.

The day's wind has fallen to rest in the darkness. Here by my side, the old willow tree stands completely still. She is like a troll woman, this whispering willow, always full of the night's gossip, but good enough in her dry-rotted insides, good enough up in her black head where creatures live in her mouth. A creature once made a speech up there, sitting there and reading the Nordic history of the world to the people. He looked down on them like a second Simon Søjlehelgen, looked down on the earth and saw all the nations wandering there under the pinnacle of his wisdom. But he came down to the earth again ever so long ago, and I wonder if the willow would now even know such a one as he. For many years now when I've come, I've simply given the tree a quick glance and thought: more dry-rotted and hopeless, it will fall soon. Now we are to be parted, and the willow woman is silent.

The lapwing cries from the meadow, from down where the field disappears in the darkness of the hollow. Come again in a month by night and all the voices down there will have you believing that you stand at the borders of your lost Eden. Dear ones, calls the darkness, I am here. You have but to stand and listen.

Now only the lapwing cries from the meadow. I haven't heard you till now, have only today come from the city, riding through Sjaelland against the wind, foot by foot, straw by straw. Too late, too late, said every straw.

Lapwing, you mean to say no doubt that I should be happy. Come soon and see my young, you cry. But your meaning and your voice are incongruous; you seem rather to be crying: my little ones are murdered, my little ones are dead. Yes, one knows there is something strange about the fields here. They look peaceful, but one can get morbid contemplating them.

Silence. Then from the marsh comes the wild hen's call. It sounds but once, yet that screech evokes something sanguinary, and it seems as if a presence had arisen out of the marsh and is staring at me. Did I know that presence better once, in distant days, in darkly distant time? But he who is lying in the parlor no longer hears the partridge in the evening as he heard it spring after spring, as his father before him heard it, and his father, and all tillers of the earth before them, as a sign of the rhythms of birds and seasons. And now the last and only one who can hear it does not plow with a plow.

Let me cut a finger-thick branch from the willow tree as so often before, make a scratch on it and tap on the cold bark with the knife handle. No, the bark will not loosen from the white wood. The sap has come up only partly into the old tree, and I will never again be able to cut a whistle from it as once he taught me to do.

My fingers wander over the gnarled bark of the willow trunk, a text as full of curiosities as the Old Testament. Once I cried here over a misdeed, with my forehead pressed so hard against the tree that afterwards I actually bore a mark of Cain. But standing there unhappily, staring at the gray bark, it had occurred to me that it must appear just this way to God when he bends down over the earth and brings his eyes close to the Alpland or some other mountainous region. I saw ants and small mites traveling in the mighty mountains of the willow bark, and it was good for the heart. My father didn't laugh when I hesitatingly shared my vision with him. He leaned against the tree and told about avalanches, glaciers, and tunnels. He had not been in foreign lands, but he had read and thought.

My hand travels along the mountain ranges and valleys of the bark down to the willow tree's roots; and down here where one can't see, the fingers meet rough and wormlike sprouts. These are the aspiring hops, who want to rise in the world. And here is a tender goat-weed, smelling like the Sjaelland summer. I can tell also that there are violets near, but violets are like darkness itself, and they are not now where they were—more than twenty years ago.

Out into the field—let me try a clod in my hand. Yes, it crumbles easily into fine particles, a good omen for the whole field. And the smell—it is that sweet smell for which captives long in exile. What will you do, soldier, when rain is falling on the camp and the terrible earth inside the barbed wire smells like that of the homeland?

I could tell him now that the wind has made the soil workable. In the fallow earth I can see dim traces left by his wooden shoes. They are from yesterday. Tomorrow they will be gone, and a stranger will come to sow. The earth spins on, and the sun will not stand still in Gibeon. Here by the fence stands a forgotten fork, its shiny handle cold and damp. I should take it in. No, let it stand here with me in the night.

Within the courtyard one can see light faintly around the edges of the blackout curtains, and one pauses to question oneself a little. Is there any point now in perceiving the smell of violets or the cry of a lapwing, in feeling a clod of earth, when the cold is rising out of a coffin, when people drown in horror, when the monster oppresses the land, when—yes, all of those things we're aware of?

Be still, and listen to what is happening high up in the darkness. The light is coming. Spring has never had more vigor. High, high above, its messengers travel on rushing wings. A great flock moves northward through the chapel of the night.

In the parlor, lights are burning. Through the long winter, those two in the house have had to see by a small, wretched light. Tonight two beautiful large candles burn for the one who has no use for seeing any more. And the draft from the door makes the flames jump from each wick like young lambs testing their tether.

All is silent. The clock strikes, it is late, but one does not notice time passing. Now the flame points rise straight from the tapers, hissing softly, and trembling so that the shadows in the corner are never still, so that life's subtle flux seems still to transcend the sleeping features of the dead one.

They are one now, the man in the flower-covered coffin and the man who came too late. Thirty years ago, also on a March night, he who is dead had watched over the other, and he too had come late. Time is inexorable, and there have been throughout the generations meetings like this, two men together at night, one dead and one living, one the witness of birth, the other witness of death. The father lies silently, but when the day breaks, his words lie heavy on the son.

If this son had come in time, if he had stood in the room and met the dying man's eyes, what would he then have done, what said? —The winter seed is coming up better here than where I've been. And the father would smile a little: —You had a head wind coming? —Yes, but it's the kind of wind that dries things out.

What else could these two talk about before the great threshold. Earth and weather. Any other topic would be awkward. They are like strangers, but strangers they always were if one of them began to speak of the unspeakable, of that which a woman can say to her husband, or he to her when he is weak. According to a strict unspoken law, between father and son there is no word for fear, none for consolation, none for faith, none for shared happiness. The fully living language, emotional, vigorous, tender, is one's mother tongue. His father's secrets hide themselves like marrow in the bones.

But as they meet this last time at night, the one laid in Charon's barge, the other standing there and seeing him as never before, they are free with each other. Cradles and coffins loosen things; beside them there is refuge from the law. Now we can almost be as we were then when you sat the small boy on your shoulders and became a runaway horse.

And now that bearer is helpless. Another 'shall decide for him, choose the day, choose the grave. His course is in the hands of survivors, and he can correct nothing, explain nothing, add nothing. Gone is what he thought, there remains only what others think. When he died, he traveled abruptly back through all his ages and took with him into the unknown the personal perspective which makes every memory shiver in expectation that once more it can be given flesh and blood.

The large and the small in life's course seem to lie naked to the watcher's view. But when Death, that great mystery, raises another fulfilled destiny up before him to be judged, the watcher perceives in his bone and marrow that he himself shall be judged. The helpless one in the coffin is powerful; it is rather the living survivor who is weighed in the balance.

There is a sound in the quiet house. She turns in her bed, sleepless perhaps, the one who woke last night when it happened and was left alone. Let sleep come, and with it a vision of forty years ago, of the first meeting with the young farmhand who plucked a barley straw and bit into it as he pondered what he might say to her.

Tonight he looks young, even though furrowed and gray. Looks drawn out and tall, larger than in life. The broad chest stretches the white athletic shirt which in youth he wore when his team, in distant parishes, won a new pennant for the color staff. Yes, handsome he lies as he is ferried over.

Yet over his face run roads and paths. Furrows, signs of a kind heart, lines of pure character. They remind one of the roads and paths of the country which he knew so well. If he had been there but once in youth, he never lost the way in later years, whether by night or day. Remarkable how roads loved him, indulged him, twisted themselves in whichever way he desired, even on first acquaintance. And he contemplated whatever they had to offer. There was no road so dismal or insignificant that he didn't take time to stop here and there. He had an eye for the conditions of the poor, but he never saw poor nature, for no land was poor to him. What lay beyond his own island he saw but once, but then he measured it step by step. Heavily armed, he walked over Fyn and Jylland with a defending army. Every path, every field, every church tower was written on the foot soldier's map of memories.

Why should the parlor windows be blacked out the last night you are in the house? Shall the enemy have power to prevent your death candles shining over field and path? You and your father and his father and his father all bore weapons to prevent that which has occurred. Then we were free, and as a free man you shall lie here this last night. Take the black from the windows. You will not be here to see peace return, but field and road shall see light shining from your house.

Outside the darkness seems thicker now. I wonder if the lapwing is still crying. Fresh, cold air enters through the open door, and the flames of the candles are diminished. But I pause as I step over the threshold, for I remember hearing in the previous moment a slight clearing of the throat, and I turn abruptly in the door and look back. No, of course not. It had occurred to me to say something about the wild geese I had earlier heard passing over, and, I realize now, it was I who cleared my throat. That male clearing of the throat I remembered from when I was a child.

I walk some distance out into the field. The lights can be seen from a long way off in the great, deep night. The lapwing cries less often now, and only a single flight of birds passes overhead, eastward along the shore. Or am I mistaken? Now and then one hears waves running up into the shallow water along the shore.

One comes back into the parlor from the fresh night air, more aware of its briskness.

Yes, I thought I'd tell you that the sap is running in the trees now. I saw one today where it was running out of a sawcut. And the ground is workable, it can be sown before Easter. I wanted to tell you that I heard a large flock flying north this evening, it must have been geese. Once when I was a boy, I remember, we two lay in the snow behind kale stocks and watched the gray geese resting on the marsh. There was heavy frost, but we lay there for a stiff hour.

But you don't hear the geese passing overhead, nor do you

hear me. And so I'll not tell you these things. Rather I'll ask: who are you, and who am I?

Earlier I was caught by a childish little expectation which emerged from below my rational mind—I thought you cleared your throat. Ah, at last, it seemed to say. And I had not then really understood. Now I ought to sit quietly here and let the cold from your blind, deaf, and dumb body run through me and freeze the violets and other small herbs of sentiment which hide the world's horrors under their blossoms.

My throat clearing is yours, I am you as I walk. Are these resemblances found only in the mortal flesh? Is there in spite of them a wall between the living souls? And is there ocean and darkness between the living and the dead?

A good man's life—a good man's death. The seed harvested. The dead elements beautified for parting with flowers and linen and light that shines freely over the field, as is fitting for this man. An honest man, who did not shrink from settling his account—one day judges the day before, and the last judges them all. It does not do him justice to speak simply of flowers. The trembling candles illuminate the beauty of death. Light and meaningful is the peace of death, for this human life was full of significance. But behind the head of the coffin stands the deep, black shadow. There under the dark bow of the ferry one can see that which has made Charon's eyes smart.

From the meaningful death, one's thought turns to the meaningless, as his so often did, to Europe's immense harvest of youthful corpses, piled in heaps, burned on ashen mounds, to the pits of Maidanek, to all the horrors one is aware of. And let us not deceive ourselves that we have thoughts, theories, or ideas strong enough to keep us on our feet when the question storms over us: where and what is the meaning in all this?

Drive the demagogue from you, dismiss the exegete. They supply ready answers, fly them from every mast, lay them out everywhere, but their answers are like cobwebs when the question comes. Rather, your learning place is here—you stand in the pits, the ashes, the piles of corpses, which shall freeze you and contaminate you until you know. You learn through the heart's horror, with the heart you can comprehend.

One thing is certain: the moslem's scooped-out remains and the tenderly prepared body lying here have come down to the same thing—the physical matter in which putrefaction occurs. The flesh's truth. Your dearest one is dead, whom you caressed as child, woman, or man. You touch him or her for the last time, and you go out and wash your hands, for they are poisoned.

Is that then all? Yes, they say, that is all. Call to the dead! Call, and call again.

No answer. Perhaps it is as they say. Don't try to hide the facts of the flesh under the tender hypocrisy of flowers, under a violet faith in the loved one's restful sleep in the earth, under a flowering lyric's consolation: of the elements' fertile transformation and the body's resurrection in a rose on the grave. Nature has no fine feelings. First come the worms.

On humanity's raw coffin boards one lays a bouquet of flowers. Spring will come again and again, without end, the lapwing will continue to sit on its eggs, the violet will exude its fragrance, and the earth will become green in the light, even when we are gone, when all of us are gone. Is nature's consolation strong enough for you? Yes, perhaps for yourself, in a mood of manly resignation. But how adequate is it when you perceive the stench of the rotting bodies of murdered children?

Is that all then—that you and I are upright animals, and as cadavers we are nothing? The consolation of nature adds insult to injury. Nature loves the living animal exactly as much as the cadaver. The child and the scorpion which stings it are equally dear. The good mother and the mad executioner are equally dear. Nature makes no distinctions.

Are we then in any position to judge? If that which in an earlier, simpler age we considered to be fixed and eternal—the spirit we called it—is only a fever in the blossoming flesh, with what confidence can we judge and be judged. Nobility becomes then not simply rare but an unhealthy trait, that is, if naturalness is determined in the abyss. The upright, spiteful animal—hairless, awkward, foul-smelling—which is the terror of its fellow animals, cannot judge. It can only retaliate. Nor can it be judged and exalted. It can only be tortured and slain. Maidanek is its nature.

And thus one must in honesty say to him who is already laid in the barge of death: I had hoped that you could give me understanding before you were laid away. I thought that your life and your death were meaningful, complementary. I had to believe that the nobility of a mind is a light in darkness. Therefore, with your worth as a beacon, I turned my thoughts toward meaninglessness in the hope that in spite of everything I might glimpse some meaning in it. But if that faint odor—tomorrow it will be more noticeable—already blended with the smell of flowers is the final and eternal truth about man, then the meaninglessness of Maidanek overshadows your life as well.

The candles have burned short. In the middle of the flame's blue portal stands a little black man with bent neck and bright face—it is the wick.

Where is one's knowledge? Vanished with the candles. When I entered this room, knowledge remained standing on the step outside. Experience stopped at the threshold. Ignorance is deep and great, greater than a child's and different. For a child's ignorance is free of responsibility, but this ignorance only increases its weight.

The candles burn shorter, and gleam and shadow do not fall now as they did earlier. The quiet, resting figure seems more plastic and alive now, a semblance of life which in fact could startle, or again provoke a wild, illusory expectation. But if cold fact has penetrated the observer, he can watch in cheerless but quiet serenity as the quivering light vivifies the stiffening features, and anticipate what can still occur, that the immoveable countenance can again become mobile, that the form of the dead one can arise and step into the mind's familiar environment where one can see him walking, working, deep in thought, peering at the clouds to see what tomorrow's weather will be.

Is that all then? One can call—there is no answer. But if one in his responsible ignorance calls inwardly, doesn't one hear an answer? Yes, remarkably near, as if just behind one's back, surprisingly assured. Listen in your ignorance, and you hear the weight of the answer. The defendant calls, and the jurymen answer.

But can you make this experience valid for others? Won't they say that the answer is probably the echo of your own cry?

Proofs for, proofs against—all cobwebs. But one does have the right to let ignorance ask. And it does not ask: is it possible to go on living? It asks rather: is it possible to die?

How do we know death? The dead do not move, do not breathe, do not eat; the body decays. These are the signs, and they do not deceive. But they are external signs. Life has corresponding external signs, opposite and positive; they apply equally to a Plato and to an earthworm. But in our inner being we have stronger, mightier, worthier signs of life. Here everything lives. Here the signs and the experiences of death are inferior. Even the concept of death is whirled along with other concepts in the stream of living thought. Thus dogmas of death, fear of death, longing for death—all are subordinate to life.

Would you prove the existence of the living dead, would you borrow wings to find them, flying out over that dark sea where Dante and Theresa flew in spirit? Would you seek them in that place from which Maeterlinck returned with a feeble knowledge written on a table that shattered against the earth? Or there from where they return with a straw or a lump of mud in their beaks, miserable answers from the spirits indeed? No, the timber from which that bridge is made which swings over the abyss is not constituted of such proofs. But when you call, the jurymen answer that they have reached that bridge.

Somewhere in the deep of the night, late becomes early. It must be early now. When I open the door, fresh air streams in, and the flames leap against their tether. The darkness is graying. In a little I'll hear the birds, who now are stealing their last slumber.

From the distance a bell peals—four times, or was it three? I didn't count. But there were bells. First they will ring on earth, and then above. Easter. He is risen.

Maidanek. Be merciful to a sinner. Among one's thoughts are many tormentors.

A large flock of birds is flying over. There is a rushing up there in the dawn. Without having turned, I know that he is standing there and hears it. His hands are in his pockets, as always the hat is down over the brows, and he looks up.

—They were geese.

—And they're flying north.

—Then the time is getting close.

Part Three

EASTER BELLS

Easter MORNING. The sound of bells.

The day is fresh and cool as water from a well. The air is still, and the sound carries a long way. It follows its invisible path through wet hedges where red willows show their plump, light-colored catkins, where on the sunny side violets are growing. Were one to sit by such a hedge, it might seem that the delicate pealing came from the willows and the violets and all the small shining water drops on the branches. And the sound glides like bluebirds over the plowed fields, where here and there the crusty surface—soon ready for the harrow—would crumble between the fingers. It flies over meadows, making the roots of the grass itch and tingle, over meadows where partridges are mating among the tufts. It calls up the dozing larks, and they arise like small clerics to sing an invocation. The fields are a dead green, dark in the low hollows, reddish where the plowed layer has dried. And as the soft morning sun kisses the bare trees, it is apparent that the bark is not merely dark like raw silver or light like polished silver but has many color values. The sky itself is clear as a fisherman's pale eyes freshened by sea mist. Yet the Easter morning seems yellow, though one might find it difficult to say why. Perhaps it is the yellow of all the small flowers so noticeable to the eye. But the pealing of the bells is a slender, sparkling blue.

It can be heard in every room in the country village. Heads

rise from pillows and listen. Eyes brighten, as if glances were turned inward for a moment. It's lovely, a strangely jubilant sound. It enters like a singing child through the open door of the ears, into the dim rooms of the mind, creating unrest in the secret depths of memory. And not merely heads and bodies rise up with the sound. In the twilight of the soul there awake small flowerlike beings—or sluggish, amphibious creatures who creep out on clammy, dark stone. Some minds are offended by the sound.

An old man who has lived longer than is good for him lies listening. His heavy arms hug the feather quilt tightly, as if he were clinging to an icefloe in order not to sink. And now his veiny hands grow restless, even though they appear to be hands of one who has long been a corpse. He had been dozing and had forgotten everything, but now he is restless. His decrepit thoughts stand in a circle about the bed and shout at each other, as if hard of hearing. There is nothing good left in those senile thoughts. There is nothing in them but old resentment, stench, and corruption. There is just one kind of love left in them, and even that is but a caricature of love. His worldly goods—that is what preoccupies his agitated mind. What will happen to his worldly goods when his heirs lay hands on them? Of course they covet that wealth, desire his death, and attempt often to take his life, but they still don't understand what the inheritance is worth. In his bank book the figure is almost forty thousand, and that doesn't include the house and garden. They have it all figured out in kroner and øre—they think. But what it is actually worth they don't grasp. And sometimes it vexes him that their greed is not stronger, that they don't more intently desire and attempt to bring about his death. He always tastes the first spoonful of food carefully, or sees if the cat will touch it. But he is old, and sometimes he forgets to be cautious when he eats. There has never been poison in the food at such times. Apparently, then, they don't try every day, and at bottom that exasperates him, that they aren't willing to take even that much trouble.

And what will they do with his place? With sluggish, corneous eyes he peers around the low, dark room. His bed is as large as a sailing ship, a galley, but full of holes—he hears the woodborers working in it every night. Everything here is peasant-old-fashioned. Now it all smells like him, feels like him, and like him it thinks only about the book in which the last figure is almost forty thousand. If you opened a drawer of the old bureau or lifted the lid on the heavy chest, maybe you could smell faintly lavender, linen, and balsam. But those faint smells and everything associated with them are nothing to him now, not worth a thing.

They will quarrel and bicker and wrangle over every piece in the place. It is not that that vexes him; on the contrary, to think about that is a pleasure. The inheritance will increase the jealousy and resentment among them still more, and that pleases him. No, the exasperating thing is that when they are unable to agree on anything, they will break up the old domicile, so that each of them ends up with a couple of pieces of antique junk which they will throw up in their attics where no one will get any money out of any of it. If they weren't so stupid, they'd sell it all in one package and get money out of it. Because it's worth money.

The figure in the book is almost forty thousand. If he hadn't had that book to think about day and night, he'd have been dead long ago. A remarkable power emanates from that book. Every krone added to it extends his life by a day. Or is it perhaps his irritation over the costs of burial that prevents him from dying? If you count the food they'll eat afterwards, the whole thing will probably add up to six hundred kroner. Those hypocrite heirs will make a big show of it on his money, because of course he's the oldest one in the family. He doesn't want that. There's no one who really knows him. And it vexes him more that they will probably waste a couple of hundred kroner for a stone to set over him. Who the devil would want to see that stone, he thinks. To waste all that money on the worthless corpse that is left behind. If only one could sell the body like some do. Worse than all this, though, is the huge bite the greedy government will take, the inheritance tax. With this thought he begins to hiss until his bearded chin is wet.

And now comes the worst thought of all. (Damn that chiming,

which has reminded him of the expensive burial and all the rest of it.) Now comes the worst. For when he has thought of the burial and the stone and the inheritance tax, there is no way to avoid wondering how the heirs will spend the rest of it. Here he breaks into a cold sweat, his as-yet-living body trembles violently, and he dares not even think.

That damned chiming. It is the spear point thrust into the trembling body of the dragon. And the dragon writhes over his precious treasure.

The sound of bells.

It vibrates intensely in the school which lies so near the church. It reverberates in the ears of the first teacher who, seated alone at the breakfast table, has just spread the napkin over his knees and is about to plunge his spoon into the oatmeal. He lays the spoon down and nervously jerks out his pocket watch. Horrible how that sound pierces one! he thinks. And then he looks up at his wife, who can't do a thing about it but nevertheless ought to take responsibility for it.

She stands by the opposite side of the table, buttering rolls for the two sons who are home on holiday and so spoiled that they have their morning tea in bed, thereby escaping the oatmeal. And the first teacher is irritated still more at the sight of his emburdened wife. Now this is simply impossible! he thinks. Absolutely impossible, absolutely! Meanwhile she stands there looking lost, peering out the window without seeing anything, with only that stupid, faraway look on her face which he had once found captivating but which now is torture for him to see, worse all the time as she gets more wrinkled.

"It does bring back memories," she says.

He doesn't answer, just drums nervously with his fingers on the tablecloth—and she doesn't even notice. Absolutely impossible! he thinks, all absolutely ridiculous!

"It was an Easter morning like this," she says. "We'd finished milking, and the bells began to chime."

Yes, nothing more than that. And yet there is a lot contained in that distant little moment. That Easter morning when she stepped out of the door with the milk, and the bells began to peal. There she had stood in all of her youth, with all the weeping in her which had not yet been wept.

She smiles at her husband, and he answers with a smile that freezes hers. Yes of course, he's right. A milkmaid she was, and that's all she'll ever be. She has a duty to be something else, something more, and she has struggled so hard to be it. But now, tired and growing older, she lapses so easily into the milkmaid, and she loves that identity secretly and tenderly.

"So it's begun already! It's later than I thought!" says the first teacher severely. The lean, graying man wishes he could bring himself to use much harsher words. Another day ruined.

"But Father, there's still plenty of time!" she says.

He stares at her, and she knows she had better be silent and act as if she didn't exist at all. If only things will go a little better for him as the day progresses. If only he can meet someone or other who will gladden him and lighten his mind.

There is still a long time until the service, and the first teacher needn't worry about being late. But he had assumed that his breakfast would be finished before the bells began to chime. He pushes the dish of oatmeal away and drums nervously with his fingers on the cloth. She knows it will be better if she goes, and so she gathers up the buttered rolls and leaves the room. Once she has turned her back to him, he is largely out of her mind. For he has worn too much on her, has worn himself out of her. And now she is only aware of the sound.

"Easter morning," she says to herself. "We'd finished milking. And then . . ."

On the floor above, the second teacher wakes and raises his tousled head.

"This won't do, love. Up and make the coffee!"

"Uh!" says a voice, and another head appears, a charming head it seems to him. She's playacting, he thinks, she's been awake for a while, I can see she's been playing possum.

"Ooh, it's cold out there, Per. You'll be sweet and put the water on, won't you?"

"And then fix the coffee and fix everything else too, heh? I know your type of aristocratic female!"

"Per, it's so lovely to lie here with eyes closed listening to the bells."

"Simply atavism!" he says.

"How can you say that, Per? The little one here likes to hear the bells too."

"The devil you say!" he replies, springing out of bed. "Under the covers and inside your stomach the little tyke can hear it, eh? Oh, he's going to be gifted!"

"Why do you keep insisting it's a boy?"

"I take that for granted. Good morning, love!"

"Good mor—. . . no kissing, Per!"

"What is it? Seems to me the lady looks so melancholy just now."

"That's not so, Per. I am happy. But maybe one can be a little melancholy out of happiness, don't you know."

"Does the lady wish to have two or three rolls with her morning coffee? She's a very dainty lady and wishes only two small ones, but when she gets going she'll gladly eat four!"

In his pajamas the second teacher prances out to his wife's sparkling kitchen. He makes a lot of noise with the dishes, he curses—when he isn't whistling—and he anticipates with pleasure how, after the service is over, he'll provoke a little argument with the first teacher about the tempo of the hymns. The first teacher likes to sing them at a droning pace, and just to tease him, his young colleague sometimes attacks the sedate old church organ at such a tempo that the singer falls several beats behind.

No, the Easter bells evoke nothing dark or bitter for the second teacher. But his young wife snuggles under the blanket with fingers in her ears. Now suddenly I can't stand it, she thinks. I can't let it make me . . . I won't think about . . . I do care for Per! I care a lot for him! But Hans, Hans! Why, Hans? Why? Yes, I must whisper, I must watch my thoughts, for there is another with me now that I must think of. It's Per's child, Hans. But why couldn't we two have . . .

"Per! Per!"

"What the devil? Shall I get the midwife?"

"Come back, Per! You forgot to kiss me good morning!"

The sound of bells.

Church sexton Johansen has climbed up in the tower to witness Saddlemaker Olsen's artistic performance. It's a fine place to
be. Sunlight and fresh morning air enter through the open port-
holes, and the light reveals every detail in the mighty timbers
which bear the heavy bells. It is Johansen's business to keep an
eye on things. He stands there rubbing his newly shaved red
chin, thoughtfully observing the bell at which Olsen is hammer-
ing away. Sweat shines on the saddlemaker's yellow, shrunken
face, for it takes all a man has to ring these bells.

Johansen is a heavy man. He stands solid and erect on his legs,
without at all looking stiff. He is wearing his sexton's clothes,
newly pressed blue serge suit, stiff white collar, and round-
crowned black hat.

The sexton is doubtless aware that he is no longer particularly
welcome in the tower. But after all, he is the church caretaker and
can come if he pleases. Now he stands lost in thought, watching
the large, pealing bell and paying no attention to the sour faced
bellringer, who refuses to look at him.

They had been friends from youth, and before Johansen rose
in the world by becoming caretaker, they had often had pleasant
times in the tower when he would come up and give Olsen a
hand with the ropes, bringing along a couple of beers in his pocket.
But that's changed now. Since he became sexton, the devil has
gotten into the man. Pompous and fussy! The look he gets in his
eyes when he climbs up here. He doesn't crawl up to the belfry
now, he ascends to it. You'd think it was his belfry, that he
owned the tower. And how he can ruin the pleasure here for
anyone else. It used to be nice to come here, but now one always
thinks: Am I going to meet that man again? Yes, little by little he
has made Olsen downright afraid. The bellringer is not so strong
now, everyone with eyes can see that, and for that reason he must
sometimes send his half-grown sons up to ring for him. But pups
will be pups, a little irresponsible, and if they arrive in the tower

a bit late, not over a minute even, there stands the caretaker with watch in hand. He doesn't say anything, he just stands there with his watch. And it can happen with Olsen himself. It can happen morning or evening, weekday or Sunday. One can never be sure. This morning, for example, when Olsen came groaning up the ladder, the man was naturally standing here. He nodded good morning and acted friendly, but though he turned his back as he did it and didn't mean to be seen, Olsen could not help catching a glimpse of the watch. And that hurt Olsen as never before, for today he was punctual and he knew it. No, that man makes him afraid. The sexton has not said anything directly, but Olsen is not too dull to add two and two. More than a few times Johansen has commiserated with him over his increasing weakness; it isn't easy for a person to keep going when something inside is tearing him up, the sexton has remarked. Clear enough to see what the drift of that is, isn't it? The atheist wants a new bellringer. And what he'll try to get is a socialist bellringer. And naturally an atheist like himself. No one will dare to say that Olsen belongs among the black sheep. But if both the sexton and the bellringer should be atheists, the end wouldn't be far off. The end isn't far off for Olsen, and when that something inside finishes tearing him up, it will be all over with the belfry and the church.

The mission-minded and the high churchers should have thought about that when they were fighting over who should be sexton, when the reds saw their chance and put Johansen in. The devil himself helped. But the man had kept pretty quiet about it. Of course he'd always been an atheist; Olsen had known it well enough back when Johansen used to come with beer in his pocket and give a hand with the ropes, but he had always kept it to himself. Yet no sooner had they chosen him as sexton than he stood up in the parish council and told the priest and the others to their faces that he was an atheist and as caretaker would conduct himself accordingly.

Indignation and sorrow strengthen the bellringer's strokes, even though his arms are very tired. And suddenly there comes something shrill and impure in the chiming. Probably it can't be heard outside the belfry, and doubtless there are many whose ears are

not sensitive enough to hear it anyway. But Olsen can hear it.
That shrillness in the chiming pains him, and he alters his stroke.
But now he has fallen entirely out of rhythm, and upset as he is,
he cannot find the tone again. It's all that man's fault. One ought
to be alone for this. Bellringing is an art, and only Olsen understands it. That big bell, which can talk if he simply rubs his hand
along it, is more sensitive than most people. But the stone must
strike the brass at just the right spot, with just the right force,
with just the right rhythm if there is to be really beautiful chiming. Yes, at times it seems to Olsen that his bells are closer to him
than any person. At such times he belong to the bells, and he
belongs to that invisible society of bellringers and artists of whom
he is sometimes aware here in the tower—when that man is not
here, mind you—those who in a long line of succession have
been the masters of those bells for many hundreds of years. Yes,
if folks only knew what a bellringer thinks as his bony hand
slides gently over the heavy brass and it answers him from its
inner core, yes, if they only knew what can come to a man when
alone and in peace he plays on the bells, making them ring out
over the town, as if he had opened the portals of heaven a little
so its music could be heard below.

I am the last real bellringer, and now they're going to get rid of
me, thinks the weary, sick man, and he is actually near to tears.
But listen, now he has become an artist again! Listen!

The sexton is a journeyman mason, a capable and steady craftsman. From that perspective he enjoys the sight of the bell gallows,
reared of massive Pomeranian oak timbers. And the church
building itself gives him a similar pleasure. It was built in its
time by working people, and although here and there the crafts-
manship is primitive, his professional attitude is more than tolerant, he is capable of admiring the primitive, even the faults, in it.
He has a special weakness for those places in the walls of the
chancel and the nave where the medieval handworkers omitted
the bond, forgot to use a level, or broke the pattern with rough
field stones. When he thinks about how unadvanced the common people were in feudal times, it doesn't seem so badly done.

At the same time there are many fine details in the building, the arches and the vaulted ceilings for example, which present-day craftsmen would have to admire, so well they are wrought. There are things here which we couldn't do better, he often thinks. And the more time he spends about the church, the more fascinated he becomes with details in the architecture. On a given Sunday, he might stand and look at a cornice for a good hour, picturing in his mind how the medieval mason moved and what his thoughts were as he placed the stones. At home the sexton has a steadily increasing number of books standing on the shelf, histories. He reads quite a bit, a knowledgeable man, though he doesn't talk about it.

But the use to which the church is put does not set well with the sexton. A confirmed atheist, he maintains that many base their beliefs largely on sentimentality. But that will change with the rising level of information. As far as religion and tradition are concerned, his positions have been clear and consistent since his youth when he read a lot on the subject and adopted radical views. Even though he didn't talk much about it, he scandalized more than a few at that time, just as now some are scandalized at his being sexton. His anticipations of a happier future for individuals and for mankind presuppose the eventual extinction of religion. And he can easily demonstrate that this view is not in conflict with his responsible position as sexton, as some folks have asserted. The whole population, nonbelievers as well as believers, supports the church through taxes. The believers cannot, then, demand exclusive rights in the management of these properties. From Johansen's point of view, the nonbelievers, who are in step with the future, ought to be interested in seeing that the properties are suitably maintained for posterity. The sexton is obviously clever in argument, but first and foremost he is a champion of justice and freedom. Religion must eventually yield to historical inevitability, but one ought not to hasten that defeat by unworthy means. One might come to rue that. Johansen believes he can serve the good cause best by never misusing his authority. And in fact, the church could scarcely have a better sexton. No one could surpass his quiet, dedicated care for the house and the landscaped graves of the churchyard.

On his days off and on holy days, he often spends many hours at the church. The first to come, the last to leave. But he does not attend holy services or other church ceremonies. He likes to slip inside just before the services begin, feel the radiators, even though the bellringer has felt them already, make sure the required lights are on, even though Olsen has just checked them. He looks to the organ. The second teacher and the bellows-treader are in their places. He glances at the chair in the choir. No, the first teacher is not yet where he should be. Yes, there he pops up beside the chair. The poor nervous man had just dropped something or other. Finally the sexton turns his sober, steady glance toward the altar, toward the altar candles. They have still a third of their length remaining, but he will nevertheless insist that new ones be bought soon. It doesn't look good if they are too short; besides, he doesn't want anyone to say that the sexton is petty, imposing poor conditions on the congregation. Moreover, it seems to him that the large altar candles are handsome to see. Of all the things he has under his care, there is perhaps nothing he prefers more to look at than the large altar candles. Especially when they're lit. But though he is much about the church, it's a rare day he sees them lit, for the custom here is to light them first during the service itself. The sexton has now and then thought about buying such a candelabrum to have at home in his living room. He could light the candles there himself. But that's impossible. Everyone would misunderstand it. They'd think there was something religious behind it. But that wouldn't be true for the sexton. He just happens to find the candles beautiful.

Thus he stands typically a moment in the aisle beside the door. A quiet man, but solid, not without authority and influence. His short visit is not intended to menace anyone, but it may be a gentle reminder that there is strength in his convictions. It is enough that he can be tolerant and attentive. And so the sexton goes out again. He leaves the door slightly ajar and listens as the organist begins the prelude. That way he can help belated church-comers with the door, which tends to creak if one isn't careful. He oils it repeatedly, but oiling doesn't always help. Standing there, he is often amazed that certain ones among the believers can be so unpunctual. But as the invocation commences, he closes the door, quietly, without creaking, but firmly.

Now it is Easter morning. Olsen is chiming. And the sexton is lost in thought about the bells. What shall we do with the bells when that time comes? he asks himself. Naturally it won't be to-day or tomorrow, but the time will come. To what use will the future put those bells? There's valuable metal in them, some silver even, but we're not likely to be short of metal. Ought they to be melted down for statues and the like? The sexton doesn't care for that thought. He would prefer they remain here to be rung in times of peace and happiness over the good land. But isn't there a danger that the chiming of the bells could tempt many to re-action and relapse? And on what occasions should they be rung?

And it chimes steadily out into the blue and yellow morning.

They hear it in the bedroom at Lindegaard where the middle-aged couple is getting dressed. The farmer's wife, stern and bony, sits in a mauve slip, her stockings hanging down about her thick ankles, combing her wispy gray hair in front of the mirror. A broad face, ravaged and corroded. Corroded from within, by the mind. She meets her own raw, hard look in the mirror, and she sits for a long time staring hatefully at her image, listening, without moving the comb through the wisps, without stirring at all.

Then she rises and walks to a window overlooking the garden. She opens it and leans against the casing. A burning feeling comes into her cheeks, and she knows that a pair of red spots have appeared on them, that her neck and her chest will likewise be covered with red blotches. Her eyes smart. She holds them wide open, she forces them not to blink, forces them until the hot, smarting eyeballs seem ready to spring out of their sockets. The woman will not yield. And yet that is what she wishes most to do. What almost never happens, the chiming bells cause now to

happen: for a moment she is not in control of herself. The hard
shell surrounding her being opens, and she sees and hears. The
vision is clear and deep, as if originating in a heart which has
been through everything, understood everything, and has not
shuddered. Now everything out there changes before her eyes,
the spring flowers, the grass, the trees. The earth is stirring. And
her eyes are bathed in something that seems to her worse than
acid: damnable tears. But though she resists this emotion, light
and sound are too strong for her. Her sight is not external now,
but inward. There within herself she recognizes a little yellow-
haired being. God in heaven, does that memory still exist? Is it
alive in spite of the heavy, bony body with its hideous distribu-
tion of boniness and flabby fat, with its unclean smells? She stands
there freezing in her doomed flesh while the little yellow-haired
girl in her looks out over the window casing with open, smiling
mouth. For the bells are ringing.

"That's making quite a little draft, don't you think?" asks the
man who, newly-shaved and red-cheeked, shuffles around in shirt-
sleeves behind her.

"I want to go to church today."

"All right, we can well enough."

She stands again before the mirror, combing her gray, loose
hair. The man's pacing about irritates and depresses her, and she
allows the image of the child to sink, indeed she forces it down.
Now she looks at herself in the mirror, calmly, mercilessly eval-
uating herself as a woman. She evaluates herself as a sexual being,
an examination she makes over and over, time and time again,
though she hates it. It is not that she hates the merciless judgment
which each time she must pronounce. She simply longs for the
judgment to be final, decisive, so that she will never more have to
think about it. But regardless of how harshly she judges her body,
that judgment will not yet give her peace.

Now she smiles at her mirror image. It is not a pleasant smile.
Almost diabolically she rejoices in her ugliness. Lasciviously she
ridicules her body. She is not more than fifty, but she has worn
badly. She does not owe her decline to sickness, she is still strong
as a cow. Rather it is the mind which has eaten through from

within and disfigured her. For almost twenty years now she has
thus perversely rejoiced at every new sign of decline in the mirror.
For almost twenty years she has striven thus to grow ugly and die
out, and she cannot be far from the goal now. Her husband she
put aside almost twenty years ago. He had meant nothing to her.
Their relationship was bad before, and it has remained so. But in a
year or two she might very well win. Until then, she will dress
in a manner corresponding to her repulsive exterior, in poor materials unfashionably cut. When she has achieved peace, she will
begin to dress in expensive, splendid dresses made of heavy, rich
materials.

The husband paces about behind her, humming. Deliberately
she is taking a long time combing and dressing. He would like
to get to the mirror so he can set his collar in place and slip into
the warm sitting room. But he dares not disturb her. She smiles
cruelly. For twenty-seven years he has had to walk behind her
and like it. Like the boy that he is. Sometimes gross curiosity has
plagued her; how has it been for him since she turned him away?
He has tried several times over the years to approach her, but
timidly and half-heartedly. Yet she has never had reason to suspect him of being unfaithful. Not that she'd want him to die in
sin, but she does rather scorn him for his willingness to accept
the situation. Could he be hiding something? He is more wily
than one would think. No, he is a thing merely, a thing to be
moved about at will. She has controlled him not merely since
they were married but even before he had seriously thought about
her. She manipulated families and parents until she could take
him. She knew that he was weak in character, and for that reason
she wanted him. She didn't dare consider a man whose strength
was equal to her own. In spite of her pride, she feared that the
right man would prove unmanageable. And so she had taken
this man together with his limitations. Because he was physically
strong and handsome, with so many girls swarming about him,
she had not guessed that he'd be impotent. They were strict
about morals in her home, and she herself had been so with him
until they were properly bound. The old custom allowing intimacy
with engagement was condemned. Thus there was no way for her

to know how he was. Subsequently it had been a nightmare for them both. But could it be he was impotent only with her? She knows, of course, that he has always been afraid of her.

In some ways they have suited each other. Owing to her he has become a capable man whose property has increased. He is vigorous in his work, shrewd in his accounts, a crowing cock and jovial when she is not around. And she is quite aware that her ugliness gives him a kind of self-satisfaction, for he could almost pass for her son. He and their daughter are like brother and sister; actually he is like a younger, boyish brother, for he knows next to nothing about the girl's adventures.

"You'll break the backs of your shoes walking that way, Christian!"

"Well, yes, that's true enough," he answers cheerfully, straightening the shoes.

"We'll look in on the old one. Did he say anything in particular yesterday?"

"No, he just lay there muttering about poisoned food and the forty thousand."

"It would be best if he could get it over with."

"Yes, of course."

"Did you remember the business about the Barnholmer clock? Ingrid is determined to have the old thing. I don't know what to think of the ideas young people have now. They collect old junk. She wants his Barnholmer for herself."

"Uh huh, we'll have to remember that."

"There's no one else who'd even want it."

"There probably will be when they hear Ingrid wants it."

"Well, they can hardly expect it. It's us who've looked after him most."

The bells continue to peal. For a moment the sound seems to come from closer by, from down in the farmyard. But it is just someone banging buckets.

That's Johan! she thinks. He's home today. And suddenly she wrenches her glance from the mirror. For an instant a strangeness appears in her eyes, as if she would spit at the mirror, as if she might flay herself in the face and throw herself screaming onto the floor. No, she would never do that! Not even in private would she scream or throw herself down. Never. She just thinks about it. That's Johan down there. That's what the right man might have looked like, the one who could have saved her. Not that there has been anything between her and Johan. Only grim watchfulness. But they understand each other perfectly well, and if there had come a hired man like him twenty years ago, even ten years ago, everything might have been different, she thinks.

She knows what Johan is and what he wants. He is calculating, covetous, selfish. He has his eye on the farm, and accordingly on Ingrid. The housewife is aware of everything. She knows that something could happen very soon. Again she smiles cruelly. All the other hands have the day off. The two of us will be in church. He'll be alone here with Ingrid, and she's been waiting for him a long time. The girl wonders what he's waiting for. But Johan is shrewder than those she'd dallied with before.

"What would you think about having Johan as a son-in-law, Christian?"

"Who? . . . Johan here? How could that be?"

"Wait and see, he'll take her."

"Take, Marie, take? You just don't come and take!"

"That shows how much you know about it."

"Yes, but we must . . . And our Ingrid, what about her? I thought she was aiming . . . a bit higher. She's interested in piano playing, and she rides and plays tennis and studies languages and all that."

"She just might get more interested in Johan."

"But, Marie, he doesn't have a krone to his name!"

"It doesn't matter, not for someone like him. For that matter, he has saved a bit. But that's of no importance. Just as he is, he's worth more than a fellow with fifty thousand."

"I can't quite see that."

"Whether you like it or not, it's true."

"Let me tell you about something, Marie, that I haven't mentioned before. Johan has cheated us a couple of times when we've had him sell cattle!"

"But didn't he get us a good price for them?"

"That's no excuse!"

"You could hardly give him a better recommendation, Christian. I've known about it all along. And you've kept your mouth shut about it because you were satisfied with the sales."

"No, seems to me we'd be throwing our girl away, Marie!"

"Ingrid?" she says, laughing cynically, "I think it's for the best she be bridled now. I haven't any idea how many she's given herself to already, but they'd add up."

"What are you saying?"

"Are you blind? Yes, you certainly are. You're like a newly confirmed boy who doesn't see anything. It began some years ago. The first time I flailed her with a dog whip here in this bedroom where I bore her, here in this room where I've suffered so much. You didn't hear a thing. And I'll have to admit, she's not one to scream. She's not one to listen either. But she's smart, so I let her alone. I didn't approve, but what good did that do? The young have to have a 'past' now, otherwise they're not interesting. No, she didn't stop with playing tennis, riding, reading languages, going to town, and all that. One after the other, they've had her."

She smiles at her image in the mirror, and it is quiet. The man doesn't move. But in the mirror she sees him suddenly standing behind her, his face drained of color, his teeth clenched. Suddenly he is a man, and he shakes her so hard that she can see nothing at all in the mirror. Perhaps never in all their miserable life together has he seemed so strong to her as now.

"Aren't you ashamed, . . . you . . . you . . . !" he stammers.

"What are you trying to say, Christian?"

"Watch out, woman . . . just watch out!" he whispers. But then he releases her and staggers over to the bed. Sitting with his back to her, he looks slack and old. Everything within him is in turmoil. He was not prepared for this, and if need be, a man can be allowed to cry over some things. His wife stares at him with caustic sympathy.

Johan, the farm foreman, has a head full of calculations. He is working in the large barn at that brisk pace which is natural for him. His daily work is in the fields rather than the barn, but the cattlemaster has the day off and Johan is filling in—the sort of thing he's willingly done since he came to the farm. He is almost through with the morning chores, though it's an hour and a half before the cattlemaster usually finishes. In the process he has also swept out the cobwebs, straightened up the corners, and given the cattle a more thorough currying than usual. The backs of the milk cows are shining now like ripe plums. The cattleman is a rather slack fellow whom Johan would send packing if it were up to him. Not that he expects others to accomplish as much as himself; he's never met anyone who could. Even so, Johan has made enemies everywhere, for a number of reasons but most often because he is such a hard worker. Few are as willing as he to lend a hand, yet he is always blamed for trying to make others look bad. More than a few have found this sufficient reason to hate him. Johan has another standard than most. As he toils in field or barn, no matter where or with whom, his thoughts are different. He proceeds with one basic assumption: that his present activity is just a game leading up to the real thing. And when the real thing comes, he won't have time for tools and physical work. For then he won't be following men, but ordering them about. It will be worth a great deal to him then to understand all this, to know the physical work inside and out. And yet Johan is still uncertain which way to power he will finally choose. One thing is certain: he is determined to have a voice that is listened to. He is convinced that others will likewise benefit if his voice is heard, for he will exercise his power thoughtfully. He is interested not in ideologies but in realities. Still it has not been easy for him to choose between two alternative ways to power. The first way is through them who have only their hands, and its appeal is strong in him. In his background Johan is closely tied to the working class. To a strong fellow such as he, one who has never been slow to give the overburdened a hand, the thought of using his strength for the benefit of them who have only hands is enticing. Their politics must be of the most radical kind, and that suits his purpose. But he intends to command others, and just there lies a snag: some hypocrisy will be necessary, for it must appear that he is their servant whom they command. He doesn't like that.

There is, of course, the second way, the way through them who have more than their hands. If he chooses that way, he may openly command those who are willing to serve him. With these, who have more than their hands, Johan has likewise much in common—the desire for ownership, business, land. It's good to have a solid place to stand if one will seize power. But there is something else that motivates him, something driving in him, something mysterious and important which he cannot explain even to himself. He does not want property simply to possess it. No, he must have a large stake lying before him on the table when the real game begins.

Johan is just a hired man on a farm. There are certain of his old school friends in his far distant home town who inquire after him when they come back to visit. He was always the natural leader among them. They never see him, but they always ask about him. Some of them have gotten more education and now have fine positions. They are amazed when they hear that Johan is still nothing more than a rural hired hand. Maybe deep down it even pleases them. Johan just smiles at that. In good time they'll envy him again. They may have studied, but they haven't that most important knowledge which he has acquired, the knowledge of how one bends others according to his will. He has not wasted his time. When once he is ready to spring, there will be weight enough in him to make the ground tremble wherever he lands.

Now it appears that the way has been determined. Johan has chosen something lesser in order to gain something greater. Last fall he left a good position as manager of a farm where, though he had been there only fourteen days, the widow was already interested in him. She was not so old, and both she and the farm would have been good enough. But he left to take a job as foreman here. That summer at a ball he had danced once with Ingrid. And though she was there in the company of a smooth fellow who seemed to know her well, and though she displayed not the slightest interest in Johan, the matter was decided for him after just one dance. Johan would take Ingrid and Lindegaard. It was a better farm than the widow's, and Ingrid was a lot better than the widow.

Though he was but a foreman, Johan did not think it strange

that he should be quietly interested in the girl's reading, music, and theater-going. Nor did he resent her pleasure-seeking, even though it meant she ran off now with one fashionable fellow, now with another. With a sharp eye he followed it all, though he disclosed his interest to no one. It would all serve his purpose. He was well aware that in that world he meant to subdue he would have need of the "finer things" which he hadn't learned. For that he could use a woman like Ingrid. Her assured manner would be an asset to him. In no way did he feel reduced or threatened by her superiority in such matters. On the contrary, he worried some that she might be inadequate. He kept his eye on realities, and he perceived that there was character in her, a certain firmness, yet at the same time he saw that in many ways she was a confused girl who played roles and fancied a lot of things which she somehow could not bring herself completely to believe in. She had lofty notions about the fashionable world but at the same time had her reservations. Johan felt certain that she was not as credulous as she had been. Everything indicated that the fashionable life about which she had dreamed so much now disappointed her. But he didn't want her to give up being fashionable. That could be used. It would be worth much when he was ready to launch himself.

It was true that she had had her amorous adventures, but her inner being had not been touched, he felt. If she had played fast and loose, at least she had never sunk to affairs with men of Johan's social class. That was immensely satisfying to him. If he wished it, he could no doubt now become the exception. But he wanted more. Not even the sons from very good farms had gotten anywhere with her. She had amused herself exclusively with fancy outsiders. Many of them surely must have wanted to get more, for she was a rich girl. But they discovered that they got nowhere, even though they went to bed with her.

The inner core of her is intact, thinks Johan. She appears to be absolutely indifferent about the farm, but she has the family's instincts in her. She resembles more the mother, though, and the old madman with the poison and the forty thousand. She's waiting for the man who is right both for her and for the farm. And she knows now where he is.

Johan moves alongside the large, black bull. As he begins to
curry the animal, his thoughts race. The farm has one hundred
twenty acres of fine land. It isn't badly worked right now, but he
is just the man to increase the yield a good ten percent. The dairy
herd is good, but by breeding with better stock and enlarging
the herd—which the farm will support—he could up the milk
production by twenty-five percent. And the farm is almost debt
free. Ingrid is the only child. And there is another inheritance
expected in the family.

But is that good enough? thinks Johan. He lays his elbow on
the bull's back, rests his jaw on the broad hand, and smiles. Is
that good enough?

Johan knows precisely what he is up to. The fruit is ripe. If
he has subdued her, it is because he has subdued himself. He is a
conqueror, it is in his nature to take what he wants by assault,
and in these months he has had a violent urge to do so. Doubtless she would have welcomed him. For some time she has disclosed with subtle signs that she wouldn't mind playing around a
little. But he knows that where it matters she is strong and
cold. So all along he has gone about here as if he scarcely noticed
her. He changed nothing in his manner when he discovered after
Christmas that she had stopped amusing herself with others. But at
the same time she stopped dropping those playful little invitations.
From that point she has gone about as if she weren't aware of him.
It was hard then for Johan to control himself, for he now saw her
as a woman, and he too ceased to go after others.

For that reason he has worked harder than ever, almost until
the sinews snapped from the bones. It isn't always easy to keep
himself in hand, and that is one reason he loves hard, physical
labor. He is no giant, though tall and strong, but there is often
something dangerous inside him which he must work off.

But is she good enough, he wonders, as the bull's back shudders
nervously under his elbow. Is she good enough? Now that it's so
easy to pluck the fruit he's no longer certain. Yes, she is exactly
what he should have. She has the right instincts in her. Physically
and otherwise she's a desirable girl, and as luck would have it,
she's experienced. He has not met anyone better suited for him.

But is she good enough? Surely Johan can't be having moral scruples? He's the right one—but not the first; is that the problem? Would he prefer to have an untouched innocent who didn't suit him at all?

Is the whole thing absolutely crazy? he wonders now. And there arises a great unrest in him, something ungovernable, so that he is ready to gnash his teeth, so that there is a ringing in his ears. Yet that which he can hear doesn't come from his own blood; it originates from without. Bells chiming. And he has heard them for some time without being aware of it.

Thoughtfully he draws the curry comb down over the bull's shoulder. Too late he is aware of a wound there, and the beast thrusts its body against him. Johan is pinned between the bull and the wall. He can't free his arms, can't even move.

"He's abused it," he thinks more than says, for he can't get his breath. The bull rams seventeen hundred pounds against him, against his rib cage, kicking and snorting. Luckily it can't reach him with the horns.

"You can't . . . do it . . . my friend!" puffs Johan. No, this time it does not manage to smash him. But it will try again.

The bull straightens up and eases off him a little. But Johan remains there.

"Come on when you're ready," he says, and smiles. And the beast comes. Bull's and man's bodies are once again strained against each other. I wonder if he likes this as much as I do? thinks Johan.

The bull straightens up again slowly, as if disappointed. It shakes itself, and the coat looks even blacker, for the hairs bristle.

"That wasn't a fair contest, my friend," he says. "You were tied. You ought to have been loose, eh? You have your horns, and I could have a knife six or seven inches long and a couple across, sharpened on both sides. What would you think of that, my friend?"

Rubbing the bull's flank carefully, Johan discovers several other small wounds there. The cattlemaster has obviously been setting something sharp, something or other resembling a spear, between the bull and the wall when he curries it.

"He didn't say a thing about this," thinks Johan, "He'd be glad enough to see me trampled to death."

He walks along the row of cows. They shine like ripe plums. A window stands ajar, and as he passes it the chiming sound seems much closer. He ducks his head, as if avoiding a blow. What about it then? Is it good enough? Is she good enough? What if you were to leave now, just as things are? There's war in the world, Johan—in China, and in Spain!

He turns, goes back, and stands a long while looking at the bull, which returns the gaze through bloodshot eyeballs.

Finally all is still in the churchtower, though the bells continue to vibrate ever so softly. Then they are through, and everything in the tower is dead. Olsen sits hunched up and tired on a floor beam. He resembles a sack from which the contents have run out. Everything that was in him the bells have drained. Now he is nothing, nothing that is except one who has a tearing inside him. But he won't think of anything now, will just hang on here until bent Severin and the boys come to help him with the ropes when all of the bells must be rung at once for high mass. That man over there seldom helps with the ropes anymore. He's too afraid of soiling his fine sexton's clothes. And the beer? You don't see it any more either. It is true, of course, that the man persuaded them to give Severin and the boys a little more when they help with the ropes and the graves. But that was only to be expected; after all, he's a red. For the moment Olsen is not so angry with Johansen. He has been chiming, and that takes everything out of him. Right now he doesn't care. He slumps further down, consumed by weariness and the tearing inside. But suddenly he is startled to attention.

It's the sexton. For a long while Johansen has been standing up on the little ladder looking out of the porthole, out over the village, down on the churchyard. But now an exclamation bursts from him up there, a word, a name, not clear, half bitten off in his mouth. The bellringer sees that the sexton is about to lose his balance on the ladder. He must seize the casement with his heavy mason's hand, and as he leans against the wall to right himself, his clothes—about which he is always so fussy—are smudged with whitewash. He clamors down, passes the staring Olsen without a word, climbs down the belfry ladder, and disappears on the winding stairs.

There in the narrow staircase, where ordinarily he is most careful of his clothes, the sexton stops and breathes deeply. He is alone there, and he can seize his forehead with strong fingers, pressing his eyes as if to blot the sight from them. It can't be. It's ridiculous! I was mistaken. An optical illusion.

As Johansen draws his breath, a weak, hoarse sound comes from his throat. In the narrow staircase it is amplified to a strange rattle. Then he descends briskly and steps out into the churchyard. The sun is shining, and among the graves he sees several old ladies who have come early to place flowers above those who came even earlier. There is no one else. The sexton stares for a long time at one spot in particular. But there is no one at all.

There must have been someone or other who . . . yes, of course! Of course! he thinks as he brushes the dust and chalk from his clothes. No, I made no mistake! There's no one else it could have been.

And the sexton pays no more heed to his clothes. The rest of the chalk will be allowed to remain as he walks along. A solid and calm man from all appearances. Yes, but only on the outside!

He looks about him and calls softly. Not that he calls by using a name, that is not something the sexton could do here.

"It's me!" he calls softly, looking all around him. Listens. He can hear no one. He walks to the other side of the tower and looks about.

"It's me!" he calls in a quiet voice. No answer, no one. No, naturally not. Naturally. But he walks further. By the corner of the chancel he stops and again looks about him.

"It is me," he calls.

And he steps back a pace, for something is rising up behind a large gravestone. But it is only an older woman who stares at him strangely. The sexton says nothing, just turns and walks away. He doesn't call anymore, he just walks around. His eyes are downcast, and yet he is looking about him. Not a bush, not a stone, not a tree escapes his notice. There is nothing. One place he scrutinizes with particular attention, but without stopping. No, nothing there.

"I must be going now, your grace! I'll have just time to run through a couple of melodies."

"Per, I think maybe I'll go to church today!"

"Well, well, such a pious wife you're becoming! Pious, strong women who are . . ."

"No, don't tease, Per! Yes, I will go. Besides, it's your work, and I'd really like to know you when you're working. I'm almost ashamed that I've only been to hear you that one time."

"I was quite sure you'd had enough!"

"Hymn melodies do sound lovely in the church."

"In spite of colic in the organ?"

"Don't you want me to go, Per?"

"Don't I want you to, love? Yes, of course I do. You and the little tyke shall hear Dad in all his brilliance. I just hope the tiny gentleman doesn't develop complexes from it. But there'll be some pauses in between. You might take along a novel to read during the sermon. Hemingway maybe? I'm off, love!"

And now the bells are pealing. With the first time, folks on the outskirts of the parish leave home. And now they ring again. At the outer edges of the villages people step out of their doors. But those who live nearest like to come at the last moment. Some folks cycle, some walk to church. It would be too much to say that they come in a stream, but the pews will be filled, and then some. It's Easter Sunday, and many will take communion.

The sexton is standing on a chair in the sacristy watching the arriving churchgoers through a vent below the ceiling. He is waiting for them to thin out so that he can slip out unnoticed. Naturally as the sexton he can come and go everywhere, but out of tact he seldom enters the sacristy, the priest's chamber. This time, however, he was virtually forced in here.

He had been walking out there in the churchyard, saying to

himself: "It was obviously an optical illusion. Obviously, obviously!" But then he saw the churchgoers coming down the road. He knew that they would want to walk around a little among the graves at first, and it had seemed to him that he needed to find a spot where he could be alone. So he had gone into the church. But where in there could he go? The sexton had looked about him in the nave which his craftsman's eyes understood in a way completely different from the others. A handsome room. Amazing that they could have made it thus so long ago. But where in there could he be? Just himself?

The sexton had felt himself an outlaw there. He could come into the nave just before services to make sure everything was properly prepared. But he couldn't be there as people began to come. Why? Their thoughts made him an outlaw. They might imagine something that wasn't true, and so he couldn't stay.

At that point no one had come. But there were voices out in the churchyard, and the door might have creaked at any moment. It was certainly not the place the sexton should have chosen. But where then? Olsen and the others had been in the tower. His wife had doubtless been sitting at home, and he would only have made it worse for her if he had gone there this way. There had been no place for him to go. A man is an outlaw.

And even if he could have been alone in the church, where could he have gone and felt right about it? Pious people would choose to be near the altar, up in the chancel. For that reason alone it wouldn't have been right for him to go there, even though the chancel—for completely different reasons—drew him most strongly. It was romanesque, the oldest part of the church, and it was in the walls of the chancel that he had found the thought-provoking mistakes made by the old masons for which he has a particular weakness.

And then there were the altar candles. They were beautiful. He would so much have liked to see such candles lit, but it wouldn't do at all to have altar candles at home, and it was so terribly seldom that he got to see them lit in the church. He was always the first to remind the council when new candles needed to be bought; thus through his tolerance he showed the strength of his own convictions. But he himself almost never saw them burning. The last time had been some years ago, on a definite occasion. In remembering it, he had suddenly thought that he might just light the two large candles. No, that would never do. Even if he had been certain that he wouldn't be seen, he couldn't have brought himself to do it. He was an outlaw.

Then he had heard steps and whistling in the church porch. And suddenly the sexton had behaved like an outlaw, almost running along the mats and up into the chancel where, breathing heavily, he had placed himself behind a pillar beside the clerk's chair. He hadn't understood what came over him, and he'd felt heavy and old and tired because he couldn't comprehend it.

It was the second teacher and the half-grown boy who treads the bellows. The second teacher had whistled steadily as he opened up Berggren's collection of popular songs. The sexton recognized the whistled melody; it was from a musical revue, and he had heard it on the radio. Then the teacher ran through a few bars of it on the organ. The sexton had stood there preoccupied, playing with the first teacher's large heavy psalmbook which lay on the chair just before him. He had a good opinion of the young teacher, who had visited him several times. The young fellow had a keen, quick head on his shoulders, he was politically awake, and naturally much better read than the sexton. They had in common an admiration for the teachings of the great Karl Marx. Understandably enough, the young man was more radical in his views than the stolid sexton. He was keen, consistent, and systematic. He might even be a revolutionary, though he hadn't come right out and said so. That he found the sexton's political position too easy-going was clear. But since he was still a young man, that seemed to Johansen only as it should be.

But he had not liked to hear that melody there in the church. That the organist amused himself by playing it there was not, as the young man may have supposed, evidence of strong conviction. At least to the sexton it hadn't seemed so.

No, the sexton didn't like it. His displeasure was not, of course, based on religious considerations, nor was it merely a concern for others' feelings. The young fellow ought to have considered that over this floor all the dead are borne, regardless of their beliefs. The dead are brought here, young man. Sorrow comes here. There is nothing amusing about carrying a loved one over this floor.

So the sexton couldn't stay there, and he had slipped into the sacristy. It is a damp and cool place, it chills him a little. He stands here quietly, absently—until he begins to wonder how he is going to get out again. He can't leave through the church, for others have come in now, the door has creaked. They would be amazed to see the sexton stepping out of the sacristy. The same danger exists if he uses the door leading directly from the sacristy into the churchyard. On the path just outside, churchgoers are steadily passing. Nor can he remain. Before long the priest will be coming, and he will enter the sacristy immediately. There is no enmity between them, but they don't entirely understand each other. Meeting the priest here . . . it mustn't happen.

The sexton is an outlaw caught in a trap. As this dawns on him, he is filled with a peculiar sorrow-laden calm, and he ceases to think about it. He stands a long time on the chair looking out through the hole in the wall. The humiliation which may await him seems insignificant compared to the other thing weighing on his mind. But it will all come right once he ceases to fear it. Now there is nothing to be heard outside. He opens the door and steps out. There is no one.

Nor is there anything. But the light is blinding, and he is again intensely conscious of what he has seen this day. With hands behind his back and eyes cast down, he walks along, glancing obliquely at every tree, every bush, every stone, but failing to notice two people whom he meets.

"Did you see the look on his face?" says the woman over her shoulder.

"I never pay any attention to him," answers the man who walks diffidently behind her.

"He was better looking when he was young," she says.

"Could be," he answers indifferently. If he were naturally in-considerate, he might have suggested cuttingly that others too had once looked better.

"He doesn't even speak to me now!" she says, though apparently without resentment.

"He's an intolerable ass! When trash rises in the world . . ."

"Ah, are you calling *him* trash?"

"I don't speak to his kind."

Ordinarily Christian does speak to Johansen, for the sexton has a decided forcefulness and could assemble backers whenever he might wish. Apparently fresh sorrow and indignation have made Christian harsh so that he intends never to greet the sexton again. Today he had not spoken, nor had the sexton.

"You can be glad he was only a mason back then!" says the wife with an acrid smile. She would be glad to hurt him.

"Damned if I can think why I should be."

That one landed.

The bells are ringing for the last time, the priest is now in the sacristy, and the organist has begun the prelude. With hands behind his back, the sexton idles along the graveled path outside. That he keeps a sharp eye on the gravel is further evidence of his watchfulness as caretaker. Recently he has had gravel spread on the paths so that spring mud doesn't damage folks' shoes. But it is not that which occupies his thought at the moment. He sees now what he has not really noticed since he was a boy, that the gravel consists largely of small colored stones. Especially in the shadows, where it is damp, there are many clear colors. There is a gladness in this gravel, and it occurs to him that all these small, colored stones must have been gathered by a happy, little boy who thought: They shall have some of every kind.

Hurried steps. It is the first teacher, who comes running out of the church.

"Tell me . . . do you have my psalmbook?"

"Your psalmbook?" says the stolid sexton. "No, why would I have it?"

"Someone saw you . . . the boy who treads the bellows . . . in my things," says the nervous, trembling first teacher, ". . . it seems odd, it's undeniably presumptu—"

"What are you suggesting?" asks the sexton, straightening up a little.

"By heaven, you do have my psalmbook there in your pocket!" exclaims the first teacher, turning completely pale. "What does this mean? Did you hope I'd get up there and . . . and . . . not be able to read the invocation. Was that your intention?"

"After thirty years, one would think you'd know the prayer by heart," answers the sexton, handing him the psalmbook with some embarrassment.

"Are you reproaching me?" says the first teacher, now even paler, "one is bound by the text . . . always bound by . . . May I ask what business it is of yours? In heaven's name, what concern is it of yours?"

Inside they are waiting for the first teacher, but he has virtually forgotten the service.

"That was not my intention, of course," answers the sexton.

"Oh no? Oh no? . . . But tell me, why are you always sniffing about here? Unceasingly? May we anticipate some happy result from your . . . sniffing? . . . Like this, for instance! You were in there sniffing in my things."

"To be sure, but there was no thought of interfering."

"Oh wasn't there, wasn't there?"

Stragglers walk past them with stiff masks. Well, well, the sexton being dressed down! Isn't that something, it will be worth telling about!

"It wasn't, eh? I wonder if you don't have exaggerated notions of your . . . importance! What is a sexton? What is a sexton in reality, I ask. He is in reality nothing at all. He has nothing to say . . . an insignificant occupation of officious people . . ."

The sexton takes out his watch and looks at it. Then he raises his eyes to the church tower and lets them linger there. Thus he gains the upper hand. All too easily. The trembling first teacher must hurry in to his place. The sexton did it too easily. Actually he was and remains the culprit. The psalmbook was in his pocket. He has done something which he can't excuse himself, something which puts his cause in a bad light. And he has been caught and exposed. But he walks on, not forgetting it, but with slow, calm steps. Walks about among the graves. Pauses and studies them. He inspects the dead. But there is one spot at which he does not stop, a spot he does not even approach.

Johan is showering, the soap lather runs from him. But he hasn't had enough of the cold, biting water, and soaping himself from top to toe once more, he steps into it again and begins to sing. When he finds the room's tone—it lies deep—he holds it until the walls vibrate. The door opening on the courtyard is ajar, and the thin sunlight penetrates through it. He stands in the light as he towels himself. His face and neck are brown, weather-toughened, but the long, lean, muscular body is shining white. He rubs briskly, so that the skin is flushed. Because he is lean and has difficulty holding warmth, gooseflesh appears, but he is robust and loves the feel of cold cutting him.

Now he hears something just outside and turns toward it. She is standing there. Just like that! he thinks, flashing a toothy smile. In a way he had expected her, yet he is not particularly pleased. He feels a certain dissatisfaction in being thus naked. Not that there is any fault with him, he is more than adequate. But nakedness has its proper time when there is power in it. Now, gripped by cold, he feels light. He doesn't care to be on exhibit just now.

"There's breakfast on the table," she says uncertainly, "I didn't know . . ."

"Thanks," he says, looking at her with sharp and questioning eyes. He doesn't know exactly where he stands with her. Yes, when it comes right down to it, he knows well enough. Still there is something confusing in just this. Maybe she did come by the door deliberately to see him. As a sign perhaps? Maybe the waiting has become unendurable for her, she must be at a high pitch now. On the other hand, maybe she came to secure herself against him. If so, thinks Johan, she could not have found a better way to do it. This meeting could very well—in some way or other which he cannot explain—weaken the drive in both of them; their force could be discharged into the ground. Between two people who desire each other, intimacy must not be too great before they touch each other. Nonsense! he thinks. He is actually confused, though it doesn't show outwardly. Maybe she really is surprised, maybe she actually came without any suspicion he was standing here this way.

A large, well-built girl she is in any case. Usually she runs around in long pants, but today she is wearing a red-checked dress with a full skirt. It makes her look new and untouched. Maybe she knows more about his submerged feelings than he does. There is something unsophisticated, pure, and shy about this dress and its style, and maybe a woman changes according to the clothes she has on. There really is something shy and soft and confused about her as she stands there. He smiles. Quite a pair just now! But he understands her. If the dress had actually made her what she appears, naturally she would have run away blushing. But Ingrid is a bold, open woman.

"You look very good," she says.

"I'll pass muster," he answers with a laugh. He stands tall and shows his white teeth. The strange, laming confusion is gone now and likewise the clean, hard chill; the blood is vigorous in him.

Exploding with laughter she turns and runs. If he sprang after her now the matter would be settled. But again he is most inclined to postpone it a little. It will be good for her to understand clearly that he is strong and used to his own way. Naturally he will take her, he doesn't intend to insult her. And I'll be glad to have her, he thinks, a month, two, three months! But the rest of my life? Is this the most I can get?

He turns the shower on again, he wants more cold chilling water pounding him. But he shuts it off immediately. It will dull and weaken him, and she deserves better than that.

Johan enters his own room and takes out clean, light underwear. He chooses a red-checked shirt which matches her dress, and sharply creased light trousers. After all, it is spring now. Then, thinking he hears a slight movement, he goes out into the hall and opens the door of the next room.

Borge, the cattlemaster, is lying on his bed fully dressed reading a magazine. He is a large, dark, handsome fellow.

"What are you doing here? You have the day off?"

"Where is there to go?" says Borge.

"It's fine weather," says Johan. He doesn't understand this cattleman. If he himself had remained on the farm on a day off, he'd have given a hand to those working. That fellow lying there wouldn't think of it. But there must be something else.

"What have you been doing with the bull? He tried to crush me."

"Me too. I had to set something in between."

"How do you manage when you take him out?"

"When I have a couple others help with rods, we can handle him."

"Kindness will get you further with a gentleman like him," says Johan. "If I had him I'd see that he learned some manners."

"Yes, you're so much better at it than the rest of us."

"What's that supposed to mean?"

"That you're better than the rest of us, of course!"

Well, the peevish pup is up to something! thinks Johan. Borge has never liked him, but there is something more here than his usual cringing, crawling ill will. Some kind of hate is working in him that makes him actually bold. He must have heard and understood what is going on. Did he stay home to disturb? Well, well! Maybe the right thing is to make him angry, get him outside, and then call her out as a spectator. But only for a moment is Johan tempted to fight him. The play would be too unequal. Borge is as tall as he and heavier, but against Johan he would be nothing.

"I'll have some food brought over to you."

"I don't expect anything of anyone today," says the other, smirking sarcastically.

"Nonsense!" replies Johan gruffly. "And from now on you can leave the bull alone. I'll take charge of him."

"Anything you like."

The door slams after Johan. Borge's handsome face contorts in a grimace, and he rips the magazine with the naked girls in two. That that devil should surprise him with it. He in particular, and precisely now. After all, Borge has decidedly different and finer taste in reading than that braggart.

He flings the pieces into the wastebasket. The cattleman has in fact not merely a wastebasket but a beautiful desk and an excellent book shelf. And he sends many a long letter, pregnant with feeling, east and west to girls throughout the country, yes, even to several outside the country. He gets their names through a correspondence bureau. To one girl friend he is a college-trained agriculturist, to another he is a forester's assistant, to yet another a substitute teacher. And so on. He has letters sent to him *poste restante.* He has discovered that a little mysteriousness stimulates interest. The farm is no more than a place where the gifted melancholic lodges. He spells well, he expresses himself well, even delightfully and grandly when he writes about his bitter loneliness, and that is what he always writes about. Gradually the distant girls come to desire the melancholy young man in the attractive photograph—his dark hair, handsome features, deep eyes. And then the crisis which he both fears and desires approaches rapidly. When one of them becomes so enamored that something must give, he sends her many pages of sentimental evasiveness at the end of which comes a touching admission: he is a cripple, he has only one leg. With bitter pleasure he proves that this cools most of them. He weighs them and finds them wanting, they prefer a leg to a soul. But occasionally there is a girl among them so good that she wishes to meet him in spite of the leg. And that shakes him. Not because his deceit will be revealed with the discovery that he has two good legs, but because the claims of the letters must be made good. Sometimes he has had to leave job and parish and save himself with flight.

Yes, he has a great heart, he is victimized by his incredible sensitivity, and he has a feeling that something is going to happen today, some criminal resolution. It paralyzes him so that he cannot bring himself to leave the farm, even though he would gladly flee. Is it because he wants the daughter for himself? He is repelled

by and at the same time drawn to her. He can scarcely stand to
see her. Even less can he stand to see anything between her and
Johan. What do they see in that lean devil who is neither dark nor
light but something nearer gray? He's tedious, annoying. What
do they see in him? A painful and hate-filled agitation develops
in this Borge who so bitterly loves defeat, who so perversely loves
to see young women turn away from him when he admits that
he has but one leg. What makes them do it? It's their disgusting
bestiality. That's why this Johan has power over them. He makes
Ingrid unfaithful; he makes all women unfaithful.

The second teacher's young wife hurries down the stairs. Naturally she is late in leaving home, for she is so easily preoccupied
with one thing and another these days. Now she must hurry to
get to church.

As she crosses the courtyard, she sees that the kitchen window
is open. Inside stands Fru Nielsen, the first teacher's wife, peeling
potatoes. It will hardly do to run by without saying something.

"Good morning! Aren't you afraid you'll catch cold, Fru Nielsen?"

"Good morning. It's so lovely to stand here by the open window. You can hear the bells ringing."

"Wouldn't you like to come along to church, Fru Nielsen?"

"Oh, I just haven't time. Not at all now the boys are home."

Is that what I have to look forward to? thinks the young woman.
The first teacher's wife has rough, red, ruined hands; she looks
worn, prematurely aged, and—sad to say—a bit slovenly as she
stands there over the large kettle of potatoes which she must
peel in good time for the large family. No one helps her with
anything. Is that my future? thinks the young wife? Dear little
one, she says to the new being growing inside her, perhaps one
day you too will be a big, strong son who gives not the slightest
thought to his mother's toil. Ah, no! with us and with your father
things will be different!

The thought of the little one causes her to cast a sidelong
glance at the first teacher's wife. Has she been wondering? Does
she know how far along Per and I are? The young wife knows

how much older women think about such things, their eyes ever
alert for signs. But Fru Nielsen has such a naive look today. A
touching, simple look.

"It's very pleasant here just now," says the older woman, "I'm
so glad it's spring. When the bells ring, I hear them. And when
they aren't ringing I listen to the lark. It brings back so many
memories."

"I really must be on my way now!"

She walks quickly. But the older woman calls to her. And now
Fru Nielsen appears both anxious and embarrassed.

"I hope you won't mind if . . . I hope it's all right," she says,
"but I happened to think that you . . . You are a fine, sweet girl,
I know . . ."

"Can I do something for you?" asks the young woman, dis-
regarding the confused compliment.

"It's about Father, my husband . . . Nielsen that is. You know
that he can be difficult?"

That is no secret of course. Fru Nielsen has spoken thus about
him before. For the young wife it is hard to understand that she
can speak of her husband in this way to a stranger, and in a voice
so indifferent.

"You must have heard at times how he shouts," says Fru
Nielsen. "His nerves are so terribly strained. It's money and so
much else. The boys must be sent to school, you know, and he
ponders day and night where the money shall come from. Gradually he's gotten so he can't tolerate anything."

"Maybe your husband needs a real vacation."

"I don't know any more what he needs. No, he doesn't really
want a vacation. He couldn't make the time to go. Simply couldn't.
He can't stand his work, the students get on his nerves. But he
can't stand time off either. God knows it's hard." Her tone of voice
seems to say that she could scarcely care less.

"It must be terrible for you as well as for him, Fru Nielsen."

"Things just go crazy, like they did today before he got off
to church. I'm afraid of what might happen there. And I'm afraid
of what will happen when he comes home. His singing at the
church has become just like a sickness for him. It really has!"

"Aah, now I understand . . ."

"My dear, it's not that I . . . I can understand so well that a young, healthy, joyous husband like yours would feel the hymns should be sung a little faster . . ."

"Listen, I'll speak to my husband about it, I promise you."

"There's something else," says the first teacher's wife. "Could you go up to my husband sometime and tell him that he has a nice voice. Would you mind that? He's very vain, I'm afraid. But I do think it's a nice voice, even though it isn't what it was. He dreamed about singing once, you know; I mean really singing. And now there's never anyone who says anything to him. Would you do that? I know he likes you. You're so sweet and fine."

And the first teacher's wife smiles a broad and gentle smile when the younger woman nods and turns to go. But then she calls after her again: "He should have had one like you, not this old flounder!" And now the younger woman doesn't like her smile. There is something coarse and wild in it. So much sorrow there is in the world, so much suffering, she thinks as she hurries on her way.

Johan had not gone directly into the house. As he came out into the yard from his room, the bells began to chime together for the last time, and he had stopped. Sensuality and its fantasies disappeared, and that incomprehensible unrest came over him again. He had sauntered past the large farm house and out through the portal, knowing that a woman's ears followed his footsteps. What of it?

Now he leans against a lime tree where the short lane opens into village street. Everything is still. Several stragglers can be seen further along, hurrying toward the church.

The sun above the quiet town smiles with promise. Picket fences, branches, flowers, and stones have tiny mirrors which shine in the early morning light. Small suns everywhere. A little way off he sees a shining star, a little sun, brighter than the others, and he wonders what it is that lies there sparkling so.

Soft footsteps. He sees only the feet and shoes as they go by. It must be a young girl. Now she stops and turns toward him.

"Could you tell me please . . . were the bells ringing for the last time? . . . Our clock had stopped!"

Our clock, she says. She must be married then! thinks Johan. Damn, I'm too late then, I won't be able to . . . Lovely little woman, I want you!

"Yes, that was the last time!" he answers, and she goes on her way smiling, her neck bent slightly.

So, that was doubtless the new teacher's wife. Actually Johan needn't have been too late there. Actually there is no such thing as too late—if a man wills. And the way she for a moment looked at him! No, he thinks, suddenly weary of it, let it alone! That wasn't what she had in mind, and it wasn't what you thought when you looked in her eyes. You only thought: too late, too late.

He strolls along toward that which lies sparkling in the street. Well, the star is just a piece of glass! But he sticks it away in his pocket and goes slowly back to win possessions for himself through the power of his loins.

Through the door of the sacristy the priest enters, passes along the altar rail, and finally stands waiting with eyes lifted up toward the image of the Crucified. The second teacher repeats the prelude, and now finally the first teacher appears with his recovered book. Loudly, nervously he clears his throat.

"He's really out of it this morning!" whispers the second teacher to his young wife, who has just sat down half hidden behind him. She shakes her head.

The organ falls silent, the priest kneels, and the first teacher steps forward in the chancel and reads the prayer: "Lord, I have come into this thy house to hear . . ."

The invocation is an old, involuted text. The young wife remembers how this prayer and other old, involuted texts occasioned a bad conscience for her when in earlier years she went to church with her parents. It was not that she didn't understand the texts. Most of them she understood well enough. But it pained her conscience that she hadn't sufficient strength of will to follow inwardly the words in all their irregular meanderings. They had sounded to her like nonsense verse, so will-less and indolent she felt. That had pained her, and so she had ceased to go. It is long since she has been in a church. The last time she came here with Per had likewise been meaningless. She had watched the churchgoers, these people among whom she was to live, feeling responsibility toward them because she was Per's wife, even though she had as yet no definite conception of what her responsibility was.

Nor does she now follow the text word for word. She is not at all engaged by its literal surface. But it doesn't pain her anymore. Her uprightness disarms the words; they cannot accuse her in the same way as before. Is she simply more corrupted now? Since she was a large child going to church with her parents she has seen and done much that is bad—one thing especially she hates to remember—but she knows that is not the explanation. She is simply mature enough now to understand in another way. That she doesn't follow the words in all their involutions is not wrong. Their conventions, their ornamentation, and even the literal content in them resemble the baroque carvings on the altarpiece. Only that which lies behind them has significance.

And today she feels she understands this. Not that she could offer even a single word by way of explanation. But it is there nonetheless.

It is the first teacher's voice and everything about him of which she is aware that makes it simple and accessible for her now. His voice is not pleasing. It is the sad worn-out remnant of a good voice which yet believes, must and will believe, that it possesses still something of beauty from happier days. It wheezes and whines like a loose concertina. She can imagine how affected it will be when once it begins to sing, for it is that even now while speaking, tottering along like a drunken man through the in-voluted passages of the text.

All this would be repulsive to her and make the old prayer hollow and disgusting if she didn't know as much as she does. She can hear that the voice is dead tired. It tastes the words, it is doomed to it and cannot do otherwise. It is affected, and that is its curse. It is an old dirty harlot of a voice, and it knows it.

If she wishes to do something kind for this worn-out, tor-

mented man, she must certainly not praise his voice, for that is
his loathing and his horror. It is the ruin in which all his new
bitterness, exhaustion, and misfortune dwell. Where once he bore
beauty, there remains only ugliness from which he cannot escape.
If she would help him, it must be done in a completely different
way. She must become the good friend of this aging, nervous
man, his confidante. And one day as they sit talking easily and
about nothing in particular—as people often do when it really
means something to be talking with each other—then she will
say: "You can't imagine how painful it is for me to hear myself
play and sing. It sounds so inadequate, so wretched, I shouldn't
even try." And he would look at her and protest strongly, and
after a bit he would break down, and he would talk and talk,
acknowledge, complain, lament, curse, talk and talk. In that way
she could help him a little.

As he reads the prayer his voice is a confession of shame, of
ruin, of all his suffering. His sick thoughts lie exposed before her.
And now she is aware of something behind the text which she
had never noticed there before, something living which she perceives but of which he is unaware. I must help him, she thinks.

And she looks at her young husband, whose long, slender,
straight back is half turned toward her. His eyes are directed
toward the chancel, resting on the hoarsely declaiming first
teacher, while his trim hands move playfully over the keyboard.
She doesn't know what Per is thinking of now. Were she to touch
him, surely he'd respond with this or that boyish witticism. But
Per is really not so dryly detached as he'd have you think. And he
is fair. If she talks to him about the ruined man down there, he'll
not tease him anymore.

Per is not watching her, and she suddenly folds her hands. She
has not done that for many years, and a shiver passes through her
—from a sense of shame perhaps? Perhaps she is not so much
ashamed for her young husband's sake as for something unknown,
something she daren't find a name for. And can she pray? What
should she pray for? What words should she use? There is no
word, no phrase she'd dare to say. Several names she might possibly mention, father's and mother's. Names of the dead. And

maybe one other name? No, she dares not say it, she must not. She will think neither words nor names but simply for a moment incline herself toward that peace which she approached when her hands strangely, secretly folded themselves.

In a pew on the men's side sits Christian of Lindegaard farm, hands resting on his knees. Nor is he listening to the words themselves, but they have moved him nonetheless, and suddenly there are tears in his eyes. He dares not nurse his wrath any longer, dares not sustain it; to do so will only make him ridiculous. At home in the bedroom when his anger had been fresh, he'd felt full of power. He would show that shrew Marie that indignation and sorrow made him more than a match for her. He had felt like crushing something and had looked about him in the bedroom. There was the clock! No, it was too valuable to smash. He'd looked at the dome of the lamp. No, he hadn't brought himself to smash it either. He'd looked at the medicine bottle on the nightstand. No, not that either. He had known he'd only be ashamed afterwards. As it turned out, he hadn't been able to smash anything.

Christian cannot live in wrath, for if he cannot bring himself to smash something, wrath will become a corrosive acid in him. Already it has completely exhausted him. He is as soft now as a rotten apple, there are tears in his eyes. Let Johan take Ingrid then, let him take the farm and her both, let Ingrid then be . . . no, he'll stop thinking about it altogether. For he's old now. Suddenly he's become an old man. It's time to give up. And he longs now for the easy comforts of the old, wants only to drift with the current, to glide along with old age. Lord, how old and weak he is.

Just then the man beside him jostles him a little. Christian turns, nods, smiles a ruddy smile. But that stiff feeling in the back as he turns evokes for him a blue and charming vision—the hussar. The hussar! He pulls himself up straight. Devil take it, suppose he is getting old, his back is still strong, his thighs tight. Once he was a blue hussar. And he turns and looks over at the women with a blue, audacious eye, this hussar.

Across the aisle sits Marie, stiffly, grimly erect. With her sharp heron eyes she glares at the clerk, whose windy peroration seems to her only empty noise. Harshly she contemplates everything about her. The women seated here, for example, their thoughts are full of vanity and malice, of concern for Sunday's dinner, or indulgence in stuffy emotion. Marie's mind is like a stony husk hiding that vision of the morning hour, that little yellow-haired creature she had seen. Perhaps she'd like to have that husk pulled back, but it is more than she herself can do, it would require too much. It would shatter her if it were to happen.

"Amen," mutters the first teacher and steps backward, dropping his glasses of course, bending down to retrieve them and coming up again with a fierce look.

The second teacher's foot rests lightly over the pedals, his fingers are poised above the keys ready to release the birds of melody from the pipes. His eyes rest on the priest who remains kneeling at the altar for a moment yet. Then slowly he rises, and there is form and style in the movement. Immediately the tones burst forth under the second teacher's hands.

"Yes, I hit that just right, of course!" he thinks. "And there's no denying I'm an important person here in this theater. The tones are pulsing through their nerves now, making them sentimental, making them receptive. It doesn't matter that I don't give a damn about any of it. Well, maybe it does embarrass me just a little; but they'll see my heels when the five years I agreed to are over. Isn't it that way with any position, and after all, I have to live, have to provide for her and the little one. Meanwhile, by heaven, I'll make those sentimental minds tingle; I can do it with the music. An important supernumerary, that's me. It is theater after all! We have direction, cues, and the principal role. And the principal actor down there in the costume, what goes through his head while he's on his knees at the altar? Does he seriously enter into it? His priestly style, his practiced movements when he rises as he's doing now, his measured steps, his placid gestures—doesn't he see that it's all theater? If only these priests were spontaneous, direct, if only they acted like real people, if only they'd deliver it straight from the shoulder!"

A motley colored butterfly, a Colored Lady, flutters in the sunny window above the pulpit. It flutters awkwardly against the pane according to its nature. A flying starling hurls past the window like a stone from a sling, and a sparrow swings through the air in the same direction, but in gentle arcs, as if amusing itself in childish fashion by passing imagined obstacles. Butterfly, starling, and sparrow, each possessing its own nature, each its own art. And out there with the starling and the sparrow is the sexton, walking thoughtfully with hands behind his back. In another age, or in another part of the world, a man thinking his thoughts would seize his clothing by the seams and tear it to pieces, thread by thread, would sink to the earth, would fill his hands with gravel and cascade the small rocks over himself as he howled out his lamentation. Sorrow has its own theater, and in the cold, harsh lands the drama seems stern and stiff.

Perhaps the second teacher's thoughts are not altogether unfamiliar to the priest. He is not so old, though somewhat older than the organist, and he has been through his own skepticism. He is not too old for the memory of doubt to be fresh, it can in fact be strong. Nor does he seek to forget it, though it sits like a thorn in him, though it awakens anxiety in him lest this ritual should actually become empty habit.

But theater? Yes, it is theater. That is precisely his personal view of it. The worship service is a drama, the oldest, the most genuine, and all good theater derives from it. A drama in which One who is not seen participates. And he in the vestment is merely a vicar.

His mind has absorbed the ceremoniousness of church and congregation, and his thought centers on that which should now occur. He is servant and proxy, as such he seeks to immerse himself as he kneels at the altar, and as he rises his movements are not mannered for him but natural. Nature and art? A man's natural movements before a shaving mirror and a luncheon table, would they be natural here? If they were, the altar would necessarily be a luncheon table, the altarpiece a shaving mirror. There would be no altar. The butterfly has its art, which is nature, the starling and the sparrow each have theirs, a seeking and sorrowing man must adhere to stern forms—and the altar has its nature and its form.

Immediate, direct talk, straight from the shoulder? Is not the young priest precisely he who has thought most often, most intensely of it? Once he was so radical that he wanted only that, direct talk, straight from the shoulder! And the altar had answered him: Be that way if you will, but if you will be so honestly and sincerely, naturally you must take an axe and hack me to bits and pieces, for if only that matters, I am nothing but a grotesque old box. Then you must scrape off the frescoes, smash the carved woodwork, extirpate the psalms and hymns. And the house here must be leveled to the ground so that you stand with the terrible naked earth beneath you and the naked heaven above you. And will that be enough? What do you mean with those words? The direct and the straightforward set no boundaries for themselves. Only drunkenness is completely direct, only madness is completely straightforward.

It is the well and the water in it which matter ultimately. But shouldn't there be ceremony as it is drawn and poured?

Not that he is unaware of the dangers of form. He has the reputation of being a trifle poetic, and just there he feels a defect in himself. If it can be said of some of his turns of phrase that they are poetic, that is an indication that they fall short. It means that God's reality, God's poetry, God's truth, is not in them. It means he has not succeeded in transforming the ceremony into the drama of life.

Yet for some he does succeed in spite of every limitation in himself. As he turns now toward the congregation, this young man of forty, this face like a million others, he becomes the true vicar for those few who are just now a church within themselves.

Up beside the organ sits a young wife, watching him intently.

The hymn rings out over the churchyard. It is almost as though it rises up from the earth itself, as if the buried dead had raised their voices. The church floor now lies lower than the ground outside. For centuries the churchyard has been gradually raised by the dust of the dead, as if therewith they were attempting to build a new tower of Babel. The mountain of the church lifts itself toward heaven.

Out there a man walks with hands behind his back. He cannot hear the words, just the melody, but it is enough.

> As the golden sun breaks forth
> Through the threatening clouds
> And spreads its radiant beams
> So that gloom and darkness flee:
> So my saviour from his shroud
> From the dark depths of the tomb
> Rose triumphant over Death
> In Easter morning's joyous dawn.

Yes, thinks the sexton, you learn it by heart in school, and whether you want to or not, you can never forget it. Sometimes you worry that it might overcome you in old age and that in the end all you'll know are hymns. Does that mean that one day you turn your back on your convictions simply because you get old? Do you give up just because you lose all your teeth? Old age won't get me that way, I won't let it. Better to drop over cold while one is still a man, still honest and true to himself.

The sexton continues to walk slowly along the narrow paths. Whenever he passes a pauper's grave he nods. At least the poor folks have better places here now, don't have to put up with lying off in the corner. That's a step forward, and he knows who's to thank for it. Rich and poor lie side by side with equally ample elbow room. And what if the stones aren't equally large, a man's honor doesn't depend necessarily on the dimensions of his monument.

Many farmers are buried here, that class with whom the sexton has had sharp encounters. Yet even though he holds the belief that property above a certain size easily corrupts a man, as sexton he has become reconciled with all the dead and is the protector of all, regardless of class.

But between the church and the gate opening onto the street is a sunlit area which can be surveyed from the houses of the town. In the middle of it is a grave at which the sexton never pauses, over which all the nearby windows seem to watch.

Johan rises from the table, and she slips up next to him, drawing his arm around her waist. She had been sitting close to him as he ate, as though she had never witnessed anything so interesting.

"Why don't we take a walk?" he asks.

These aren't the first words that have passed between them since that bizarre encounter by the shower; here at the table words have been spoken, but they have been wild and crazy and incoherent.

Johan looks down into her eyes. He's glad enough to be with her now. Perhaps in spite of everything he doesn't know very much about Ingrid, even though things have gone as expected. Short and wild, like the meeting of two swans on turbulent water. A meeting in broad daylight so blind and out of hand that the memory of it already is becoming strangely dim as he withdraws his arm from her waist.

"Don't you want a jacket on? It is cool."

"No, it's spring now."

"All right, I won't wear anything over my dress either."

They go out, and as they pass the barn, he picks up a measuring stick and hangs it over his shoulder. It resembles a giant letter A.

"What are you going to do with that?"

"We'll have to measure the estate," he laughs, looking her directly in the eyes.

"Johan, do you mean . . ."

"What would you say?"

"Is it the farm or me, Johan?"

"Both! The woman and the land belong together. And you know that!"

"I'm not sure any longer . . ." she answers.

Tossing back her blonde hair, she takes his arm again and looks at him with a little smile that trembles slightly at the edges.

"Johan!" she whispers, "I think someone is watching."
"Nonsense!" he replies and kisses her. And they walk farther
out in the open field.

The darkly handsome Borge stands at the window watching them
go. Everything seems dark to him now, his thoughts are black as
the grave. That couple out there, they're destroying him. Not that
he could ever get her for himself, though he is something of a
gifted person. He is too much afraid. He has written numerous
long letters to her—they lie neatly piled in his drawer, never sent.

Look at them, a pair of felons walking out there! She in a red-
checked dress, he in a red-checked shirt, as if bleeding in the thin
sunshine. It's too late now, and that awareness pierces his head,
shrill, ringing.

For whosoever hath, to him shall be given, but whosoever
hath not, from him shall be taken away . . .

His head pounding, suddenly he is aware of the telephone
ringing down the hall. He hurries toward it, glad for any kind
of distraction!

"So, you're home alone," says the voice, "that's too bad."
"There's sure to be someone back before noon," answers the
cattlemaster, "but that's of no consequence. I can easily handle
him alone."

"Well, it'd be best right now," says the neighbor, "because the
cow's ready. She's been running around the field without stopping. So if you think you can . . ."

"Don't worry about that," answers Borge, assuming a slightly
pompous tone, "it doesn't matter in the slightest. Come right on
over. I can easily take him out alone, I do it all the time."

He replaces the receiver, rings off, and moves in front of a
mirror in the sitting room. At first he can scarcely tolerate his
reflected image, so gray it is. But then he is fascinated: something
terrible, something evil lurks there, and he feels some great
happening is imminent.

"They don't know what they're doing," he says aloud. "They
don't know they can drive a person too far, even to death. Why did
that bastard tell me to leave the bull alone? Because now I have

to do it, don't I? Yes, now I have to. And by God, I will, that's sure. Whatever's going to happen, let it happen!"

And he stares steadily into the mirror, peers into his own eyes —as he often does, as he loves to do. He can look so tragic, so remarkably pathetic. No doubt he could have been a great actor, so moving is his expression.

"I shall die!" he exclaims, almost shouting it, at the same time throwing out his arms and casting up his eyes; in the mirror his image is great and terrible. "I'm doomed. With someone like me, it cannot be otherwise. But let them beware, those felons, let them beware! Who knows what could happen to two people dressed in red!"

A sudden inclination seizes him, and he steals softly through the dead house, up the staircase, and stands before the door of Ingrid's room. He takes the handle in his hand, but stops. "My God, man, what are you doing!" he groans. "You can't do that! What's come over you!"

He bounds down the stairs and back to his own room.

As yet they have not gotten around to any measuring. The measuring stick lies at the end of the field where Johan has dropped it. He is a bold fellow, and he calls her to follow him into a toolshed which stands adjacent to a hedge. No one can approach them from the rear, but they seem quite unconcerned that someone might see them entering the shed together.

Johan spreads sacks out on the earth floor and over them a blanket which smells strongly of horses. Ingrid stands a little apart, leaning against a seeder, staring at her shoes.

"Come!" he says softly.

"Johan . . ."

"Yes?"

"Give me a moment . . . just give me a little time."

"Time? Why, take as much time as you like."

"You don't understand, Johan."

"Ah, but I do!"

"I'm not the right one for you."

"No? Just wait, you'll see."

"I don't regret anything, Johan. But still . . . if I had known before, some things could have been . .."

"It would still have come to this, my friend."

"Johan, will you be a good friend to me?"

"Yes, and then some."

"I mean . . . talk with me a little?"

"Come and lie here beside me, and we'll talk for a while."

"Oh, Johan, this is nice. Now I can have a really good look at you. And you must tell me more about yourself."

"There isn't much. It's all straight down the highway."

"Come on, my friend, just tell me!"

"I'd rather talk about what I have in mind for the future."

"That I'd love to hear."

From the epistle of Paul the Apostle:

"Purge out therefore the old leaven, that ye may be a new lump, as ye are unleavened. For even Christ our passover is sacrificed for us: therefore let us keep the feast, not with old leaven of malice and wickedness; but with the unleavened bread of sincerity and truth."

I don't understand very much yet, thinks the young wife beside the organ, but it will come little by little.

Her husband turns toward her with a slight smile, nodding roguishly toward her waist. So it was another he was acknowledging. Then his fingers attack the keyboard, the hymn begins again, and she sits there thinking. Her complexion reddens ever so slightly as she glances down at herself—surely one can't see any sign yet! But the way he behaves, the whole town will know about it.

Is it on account of the little one that she has become so thoughtful? Maybe it isn't healthy for him. Or could it be that it is actually he who brings these thoughts and whispers so much to her? Little one, dearest—by what name shall I call you—is it you who gives me so much to reflect on? As if you didn't give me enough to think about without all the rest of this! Ah, my little one, do you think your father is right when he says I should only have diapers, food, house, and such in my head and not think about anything else? There are two kinds of thinking, he says; the one doesn't amount to anything, and the other is the province of men! He's a fool, don't you think? For that matter, my dear, he contradicts his high-flown socialist opinions, according to which there can't be any differences between women and men! Foolish, right?

If one simply uses his reason and begins at the beginning, proceeding a step at a time, he won't get himself messed up! So says the great and self-important Per. But listen, Per, are you aware that if I were satisfied to think in that way, things would go badly for us two? And it wouldn't take long, Per. If we're to make it, Per, I'll have to think in the other manner. Yes, I'll have to think and learn that way, my boy, if it's to work out for us. It's got to work! Dear Per, you aren't even aware that in love there is duty, that I have a duty to love you, that I want to love you wholly, and that somehow I shall!

It's the little one who forces me to reflect on this. Now that he's growing in me, now that I'm aware of him, the game has become serious. I have to remember that, Per, I have to know it unconsciously even.

Per, I like you a lot. I am fond of you, I'm fonder of you now than I was, and yet it is only now I realize this isn't enough. I'm deceiving you, I'm demeaning you by just being fond. It isn't enough. You aren't the real thing for me, Per. You just aren't a deeply serious matter for me. And only now do I know it fully, now when we two are to have a child together. The child is seriously real for me, and you should be seriously real. But you aren't, Per. Not yet.

If you could hear these thoughts, probably you'd remark that I seem to you a very serious lady, and that gradually I've become all too serious. I'm snappy, I'm easily irritated, I'm often unreasonable, I withdraw too much into myself.

All perfectly true, my friend. I am insufferable. But if I weren't like this, and if I couldn't be like this, well, I'd get deadly serious, and I'd go my own way. Immediately. Goodbye. And all this isn't just something caused by changes taking place in my body, Per, normal mental disruptions. That's what you think, I can see it in your eyes. So now she's crazy again in that sweet, natural way; it's the boy's fault, of course! That's what you think. And when I see that you think that, it makes me fond of you. But at the same time I'm very far away from you. For that's not the explanation. No, the explanation is that now when we're going to have a child, I ought to love you. Now you ought to be a man, Per. But you aren't. Not yet. You are just a somewhat larger, lovable boy of mine.

Per, I'm not afraid of you. I see plainly that you are self-important and have an exaggerated notion of your brainpower, but your excesses can be worn off if we two are able to stay together. You try to play the cheerful, carefree fellow, but you're a solemn enough gentleman at bottom. It would get to you if things should end badly for us. And that's how they'll end if I can't feel differently.

But the unleavened bread of sincerity and truth, I think I understand that. Per, I'm not deceitful, but I haven't been wholly honest either. An episode! that's what you think about my involvement with Hans. Hans! He was not as good as you, but he was seriously real for me. Do you understand that? No, you don't. And it's dishonest of me that I can't bring myself to explain it to you. Thanks! you'd say if I were to try, that's your private affair, I don't care to get into it. For you're so matter-of-fact and modern, as they say, Per, and above all you mean to be a fine fellow. But for that reason we can't get to the bottom of it. I still belong to him, even though I'm faithful enough to you, Per. You've got to take me from him, man! But you can't because you haven't yet become seriously real for me.

I'll have to do it myself, Per. I don't know how, but I must!

Something must happen in me, just as now there is a little person growing in me. The other must grow in me as well: seriousness for you, love for you. It seems so strange, Per, that for it to happen, I'll probably have to reach you through other people! But I'll not learn to love you simply to be your property; I must rather find a true, rich life so that I along with you can mean something for others as well. And maybe I can learn that through

others, through those who suffer, through those whose suffering
I understand. Per, you haven't any suffering I can understand.
Perhaps you don't suffer at all.

Today I've discovered how much I can learn to understand.
There's an older man down there, your colleague. I must try to
help him a little. His mind is like an animal which has sunk its
teeth into its own body and, unable to release them, must go on
biting and biting itself.

And there was another, Per. But how can I tell you about that
man I spoke with on the way to church? Maybe a country teacher's
wife ought not even to stand that way talking to a young man.
And you would probably misunderstand me if I were to say
that I loved him that moment I looked in his eyes. Yes, as I've
never loved you, Per, because I've never seen anything like that,
evil and dark, in your eyes. And it was good to be near him . . .
no, not in just the way you're thinking! It was good because I
sensed that if I were close to him I could help him overcome
something dangerous within himself . . . But I had to hurry on.

The priest in the pulpit is reading from the gospel, about the
women who came to the tomb at sunrise and found it open, the
stone rolled back. They entered, and within there stood one who
said unto them: He is risen!

Risen!

And the priest speaks of the resurrection.

She listens, as if she would seize upon the words even before
they are spoken. She anticipates them, as a newly planted, faint
flower waits for water. But even though they seem to her strong
and beautiful, she by no means understands them all. Many of
these words she remembers from her childhood; they had become, most of them, empty as nutshells. Perhaps she had been
afraid of them and is still somewhat afraid. As yet she dares not
take all the words into herself. Some she does not comprehend
and others seem inconceivably mighty and heavy in her. Resurrection? She dares not fully contemplate what the word means. It
seems to make the very earth tremble beneath her. Mother and
Dad? You too?

No, for the time being she must be satisfied with bits, with
the small crumbs. It must grow calmly and slowly in her. Like you,
little one. You too are a kind of resurrection. For you were not,
then suddenly you began to swell in me!

It was not thinkers or scholars who first discovered it, says the
voice from the pulpit, no, it was three women who could find no
peace of mind, who couldn't sleep during the night because there
was one who lay in need of them. Merely one of the dead who,
they felt, needed them as the dead need gentle hands to beautify
that which in cold fact no longer has any worth. One of the dead,
for whom they meant to perform a last small service, a task which
all of His friends found too insignificant to inconvenience themselves with. Thus were the women privileged to see all. They
came with the light.

She understands this—more intuitively than rationally. Here
perhaps is the narrow way she shall enter upon. Perhaps on
this modest level she will find something, be something. She
need not ponder excessively with her modest intellect, but simply
be something among the modest, in what is nearest. Then it can
happen! Then it will come. And resurrection applies to more than
the dead. It applies as well to the living, she thinks. It happens,
it is real! Then it can happen to me, it can happen to me!

And now she scarcely attends to what is being said. To her it
seems that fresh rain has fallen on faint, hanging leaves. She cannot contain more just now. She is joyful, eased, happy. That
bit which she now understands is real. It is not fantasy and words,
but real like the child she carries. And now she wishes not to
remain here longer, where what she does not understand becomes
beauty and mystery; she will go outside, taking with her that
which is real.

Others are leaving now before communion. The second teacher's
wife whispers to her husband that he mustn't quarrel with the
first teacher today, she'll explain why later. She'll wait for him
outside. And lifting his eyebrows, Per sighs affectedly. This con-
strained task is a plague for him, she knows that, and she'd help

him escape it if she could, even though the lost income would hurt. But what will Per think about this other she is feeling? He'll have to learn to understand it!

She leaves the church just behind an older couple. The woman is stiff in her bearing.

"That wasn't at all a bad sermon," says the man.

"Horsefeathers!" answers the wife.

"Oh, you think so?"

"Horsefeathers!"

"Well . . . hmm."

"We'll stop by to see the old one. We need to talk with him about the Barnholmer!"

"You don't think it would be better another day, do you?"

"It has to be before he kicks off!"

By the church tower the two of them pass a man standing with hands behind his back. The woman nods stiffly and sweeps past him.

"How are you, Johansen?" says the man.

The young wife of the second teacher walks along the path slowly, looking about her. Then deliberately she approaches the solitary man.

"You're the sexton, aren't you?"

"Yes, that's true enough."

"You probably don't know me?"

"Ye-es, you're the new teacher's wife."

"My name is Grethe!"

"I see," mumbles the sexton, turning partially away and rubbing his chin.

"I just felt I wanted to say hello to you. My husband has spoken of you so often. I believe that he—how should I put it?— holds political views similar to yours."

"Yes, but of course he's much better educated . . ."

"My husband is educated and theoretical . . . But you appear to be one who knows a great deal, Herr Johansen."

"Well, I . . . It is fine Easter weather, don't you think?"

The sexton looks into the young woman's eyes for the first time. What does she actually want? But maybe she's just an unusually straightforward person.

"Won't you show me around the churchyard a little?" she says, "I know scarcely anyone here. Maybe it would be nice to start with the dead."

And the sexton walks ahead, pointing here and there without saying much. He is glad she doesn't persist with questions.

At length she feels a little tired and looks about her for a bench.

"I think it's not so healthy for me just now," she says.

"Well, it's more healthy here in the churchyard than it used to be."

"No, I just mean because we're going to have a child, a little child."

The sexton again turns his glance away.

"You're the very first one here to know about it."

"Congratulations," he says.

She bites off something she was about to say. No, it's safe enough with him, she thinks. I'd hurt him if I asked him not to tell anyone. Thinking of the child makes her faint and happy, and without looking at him she says casually: "You must have older children, Johansen."

"Come!" he says.

Hands thrust in his coat pockets, the sexton walks ahead of her, a large, calm, thoughtful man. He leads her to an open, sunlit area between the church and the gate, a spot visible from all the neighboring houses. There he stops, his eyes fixed on a gravestone. It is a handsome little natural stone, and she reads: Erling—Born 19 September 1922—Died 14 March 1931.

The young woman takes the sexton by the hand, though he is scarcely aware of it. "An accident," he says. "Run over. The chauffeur couldn't help it."

"So many beautiful flowers there are," she says.

"Yes, that's his mother's doing," he answers.

"I can understand that."

"We were getting up in years when we got him. And since there aren't any others . . ."

"Don't you have a picture of him I could see?" she asks.

Disengaging his hand from hers, the sexton raises it toward the portals of the church tower. For several moments he stands thus pointing upward before he says: "I was up there while the bells were chiming. Suddenly I saw him standing here."

"Ah, that was nice."

"And I said to myself it must be someone else. Or a shadow. An optical illusion naturally."

"I don't think so."

"Do you mean that it actually . . ."

"Did he look happy?"

"He was playing hopscotch. Exactly as I remember him."

"Then it was him."

"Well, I don't know."

"Yes," she says.

"It's been five years since," he says, "the five years I've been sexton. So I've been able to be here, almost as if . . ."

The actual truth is that the sexton but rarely stands here, rarely even stops here, for the spot lies open to the sight of all, and a man doesn't display his sorrow in the public eye. His grief must observe stern laws.

"Shall we walk on?" he says.

In the parlor Marie busies herself about the old man, whom the book with the forty thousand has kept alive far beyond his time. He is her father, but he has no use for her whatsoever. He can tolerate her husband to some degree, for the time was when he could easily cow Christian, but he reckons him for nothing at all.

"I'm going to fry an egg for you now," says Marie.

"I'll be damned if I'll have egg," he says.

"What kind of nonsense is that?" she says. "Of course you'll have an egg!"

"I'll not touch the damned thing," he says, "there's poison in it."

Nevertheless she goes out into his kitchen to fry an egg for him.

"Well, how are you?" says Christian for the third or fourth time.

"Is it strychnine she has with her this time?" whispers the old man.

"Oh rubbish, Granddad," says Christian, "how are you anyway?"

"You won't be satisfied until I'm in the long box," says the old one.

"Now what kind of talk is that, Granddad?" says Christian. "You know that . . ."

"Yes, I know what I know!" hisses the old man, a piercing look in his corneous eyes. Now he has this fool of a son-in-law where he wants him, this clod who can't conceal anything. There he sits, fidgeting about on his rump, as if on a runaway feather, he knows for certain what's going on out in the kitchen. It's probably blue vitriol this time.

In this way the conversation proceeds, not getting anywhere.

"Christian!" she shouts, summoning him to the kitchen. But Christian doesn't give up; he can't get beyond "how's it going, Granddad," but he keeps trying.

And so she reenters the room.

"Listen, Father, you really ought to let Ingrid have the Barnholmer clock!"

"Ha, think of that!" grins the ancient one. What sort of deception lies behind this?

"No one else wants it, we know that."

"Go ahead and take it, you can have it! After I'm in the box, that is! No one gets a thing until I'm gone!"

"Ingrid's sure to be pleased."

"About that beat-up old box? I can't imagine why. There's something more to it, there's something behind it!"

The old man's eyes glisten; sap is running in the withered trunk. There must be something behind this! He'll figure it out, too. They'll not be able to outfox him. No, they won't get a thing now. His heirs will have it all to fight about afterwards. They'll be able to squabble and bicker to their hearts' content. That thought warms his numbed bowels. If only he could manage to witness the covetous bickering that will follow. But this business! What's behind it?

There is a slight noise outside, something bumps against the wall, a bicycle. Someone is coming through the entry—it's the farm boy from their neighbor's place. Standing there in the doorway, stretching his neck, swallowing, and saying nothing, he seems not to be himself.

"What have you come for?" says Marie.

"I've come to say . . ." he falters, again swallowing hard.

"Who sent you?" she says sharply.

"Nobody," he replies, "it's about Johan. I'm to say . . . he can't live . . ."

Yes, they had lain and talked together there on the horse blanket.

"You could easily get elected to parliament!"

"Yes, if I really wanted to," he answers, stifling a yawn. He lies extended, resting on one elbow with his cheek pressed against his broad, strong hand, staring beyond her at a fissure of light in the shed wall. Her body is curved toward him, her wide hips and her knees inclined gently against his hard thighs. She rests her cheek on her arm, down against the blanket. She loves looking up at him this way; she notices the slightest movements in his face.

"If I want to," he repeats with a yawn. Yawning doesn't make his eyes water. Johan is hard. Probably she'll never see him cry. It might be to her advantage if things were to go badly for him. But she doesn't want that. If he were to break down sometime, perhaps she'd really have him. But he mustn't ever break down. Never!

There is no movement in his face now. He's a little drowsy. His thoughts have been wholly occupied with what he has spoken of; nonetheless during the entire time his blood has watched and waited for her. Hesitatingly, tentatively they lie beside each other. She would gladly meet him now, and the clearest signal of this would be to draw him over her. But she withholds the signal. For she wants it to be perfect for them when it happens. Earlier, back at the house, they had been like wild persons, so wild that that interlude seems never really to have happened. She doesn't know where his thoughts are now, and therefore she hesitates. But she senses that the masculine soul in him wills the same as she, that it should be perfect when it happens. They hesitate with a subtle dissimulation of which they are both aware, two instruments that must be cleanly, perfectly tuned together. But this delicate hesitation is enervating. She too is becoming a little drowsy. If only he would lie down and sleep with his head up against her.

Yet she dares not hope for that now. She scarcely dares hope anything of him. She feels how close the man is to her, yet she knows his mind is not calm and peaceful, the drowsiness notwithstanding. There are thoughts in him which make him uneasy, thoughts she does not know and will not be allowed to know. And though she is proud—well, either proud or humble, she is not sure which—she cannot bring herself to call as a woman in order to tear him from these distant thoughts which make his eyes naked and hard.

In spite of drowsiness she sees clearly that things are not the same for him as for her. This day is not for him the only day. He has told her much—and all of it Johan, Johan. She knows she has egged him on to tell and to keep telling, knows she has sparked his imagination. Ambitious thoughts are not new to him, he has always imagined great things for himself. But she knows that much he has said has first come to his awareness in the moment she drew it forth. She senses now the role she will play and has long played in his plans. She is to be his helper, that much is clear. Nevertheless she feels as if somehow she were not included wholly. She is part of his thoughts in the way of a budgeted amount, a figure, an asset. With herself as she is, loving him, he is not concerned; as such he does not reckon her seriously. And it had not escaped her that he became strangely cold, almost hostile toward her, as increasingly he was caught up in his talk of the future, as if he had already used her up and was now through with her. That's how it was for him. When he reached a certain point in his plan for the future, he'd be through with her, she'd no longer be adequate. That makes her irritating to him even now; doubtless he feels bound and sold already. Even in his mention of the farm there now seems a strange aversion.

Johan, Johan, she thinks, I will not be a burden to you. You mustn't believe that I'll ever stand in your way.

Doubtless there is within him a dream of something more desirable, of another kind of woman. And probably she is more aware of this than he, so subtle are her perceptions just now, so painful are all things for her now. There is an immense radiance above him, and he is like a boy who must reach it. He has a dream of the kind of soul who can meet him in that radiance. Oh Johan, I'm not the one. But I must tell you that no one has ever really known and possessed me. Why didn't you come sooner?

It wouldn't have helped anyway, that she knows. She knows so much about him which he has never consciously realized but which is there nonetheless. And there is something which no living being can give him, she least of all. What she is experiencing as she lies here beside him is not at all what she had hoped for and expected. It is more dreadful and yet better. It requires that she hurt herself. To love someone who loves only himself, and that consumingly, is like lying naked on the ice and loving the ice and willing to change it.

"You ought to sleep a little," she whispers as he yawns again. But his eyes are wide-awake, and he watches her intently. And now she closes her eyes and lies wholly still.

Apparently she sleeps a little. Suddenly she is aware of him springing up; she sees him dash out through the door.

"Johan!"

But her voice is not loud, and she calls but once. Now the blow is falling on her, long before she expected it. No matter, she knew that one day it must come.

As if in a dream she goes outside, where light overwhelms her vision. Then she can see clearly once again, all the small things in the field rise sharply before her eyes. The ground slopes downward toward the barns, and she sees Johan running full tilt down toward the stack yard. Down there between the trees the bull arches its black back. She hears it bellow, then a human cry. Ah, so that's the reason! But still she cannot throw off the heavy dreamlike certainty. The blow has fallen on her. Ah, yes, she thinks, he has done this in order not to be bound. He wants it this way. It's as if he had caused this to happen. She feels certain of it.

By the time she reaches them, Johan has taken the bull by surprise and with a carriage pole has driven the enraged beast into a calf pen. Now he is helping the moaning cattlemaster to his feet. Borge's clothes are ripped and he is scratched up, but he is able to stand. Down at the end of the stable stands the neighbor's pale farm boy. The cow has gotten away from him and bolted down the road.

"Off with you!" cries Johan to him, "fetch a couple of men quickly."

Ingrid smiles at him, touching his arm, but he says: "It won't do just to stand here. Borge, get someone here with a truck, and be quick about it. And Ingrid, you go telephone!"

"Yes!" she replies, smiling, watching the huge animal lunge at the fence posts. Now Borge limps off, and she sees him, out on the road, vomiting.

"Off with you!" says Johan, "it can't be long until he breaks through."

"Then you mustn't stay here either!" she says.

"Go on!" he says, "and watch out. He's mad. He could run out there and crush children on the road—people are starting to come from church. Go on!"

"Yes," she answers and, hesitating momentarily, begins to go. As she reaches the corner of the barn, the bull bursts through the fence. She remains standing there, watches as Johan shatters the carriage pole over the animal's head so that fragments fly. It doesn't deter the charge; Johan is bowled into the grass. But he is not there as the bull storms over the spot.

Now man and beast engage in a deadly game. For a moment it is as if they are lost to her view, she sees only a dark, immense, agitated mass; she hears nothing save only the fury of churning hooves and the rushing of air. And then they separate. She sees him take two long, dancing strides just in front of the bull. And there he stands. Johan!

"My love, my love!" she screams, thrusting her hands forward as if throwing flowers to him. There is no more fear in her, she is unable to feel it now. She sees her lover's deadly, playful struggle with the wild beast, and she understands that he no longer wants her to run to the telephone but rather to remain and watch him.

Now they know each other better, the animal and the man. He stands as if rooted in the earth, but as it charges he slides away, tight up against it. He is daring, his chest grazes the short horns. But the bull learns too, it is treacherous, it lunges out with the horn as Johan glides past, and once it rams him, crashing him to the ground. But he is up before the animal can turn on him. For a moment Johan is corpse-white, but then he grins and dances away.

He means to tire out the mad, bellowing animal or at least keep it preoccupied until help comes. It can't be much longer now. And now she has a closer glimpse of her lover's face; it is almost relaxed, smiling easily, calm as a dancer's, but the half down-turned eyes alertly follow the terrible partner. She realizes that he is happy now.

"Find something for me!" he shouts, making a movement as if he were drawing a cape away before the head of the bull. She understands immediately, she has seen it in films. But what can she get? Suddenly she strips off her red-checked dress, popping buttons, and throws it toward him. Johan snatches it up, and now he contends even more effectively with the bull, retreating a little, suspending the dress before him. If only it were me! she hears herself whisper. The bull charges, and they spin in a mad whirl. For Johan there is purpose in this new game—he is gradually drawing the bull toward the open loading gate. The animal continues to charge wildly, but now and then it comes to a halt, groaning deeply, waiting, slavering.

And now the others come running, the helpers. From around the corner of the barn behind her appears a man, another, three more, with poles and forks. One of them is Borge bearing her father's rifle. And now Johan has the animal inside the loading pen—no, it swings away from him, spins around and moves toward the new antagonists. Trembling violently, Borge raises the weapon, cannot find the sights, then drops the wavering piece as the bull nears him. Now Ingrid too must jump for her life. She glimpses only a shadow launching up alongside the animal, swifter than it, a high leaping man, a picture seared on her memory. Johan, no, Johan!

A violent thrust and shake. Now it is finished, she thinks, and suddenly she is faint, for a moment everything is dark. But she pulls herself together and looks over at them. The bull stands with hanging head, shoulder and head whitened with lime. Several of the men are standing with poles and forks against him. Borge and another are bending over something by the wall, it is Johan lying there. In the wall high above him the stones have been smashed in.

"Johan!" she says. There is blood at the corners of his mouth, but he is smiling.

"It's the chest. It drove him against the wall," says one.

Johan's breath comes in gasps, but his lips open over the white teeth, and the smile broadens. Quietly she bends down over him.

"I'm not going to die," she hears him breathe.

"No, you can't die."

"It could just as easily have been me," says a hoarse voice behind her. "It really ought to have been me," he adds. As Ingrid looks hard into Borge's eyes, he dissolves into tears.

"Spare us that!" she says. Then to the others: "Lay him over here in the grass, and one of you must call the doctor."

"Someone has gone."

"What about the bull, Ingrid?" asks a voice from over there.

"Shoot it," she replies, "at once." She does not turn with the discharge, and she hears the animal collapse.

"I won't die, I can't die," she hears him breathe.

"He can't live," says the country doctor.

And she gazes into his strangely sparkling eyes. She is not in them; he does not see her or anyone else; he sees only himself, a young, wild, ascending bird. But if his eyes were hitherto tender bright buds, they now unfold like flowers. And she closes hers.

They are walking up toward the farm, and today the lime-bordered lane is very long.

"You're hurrying so fast . . . I just can't . . ." she gasps.

"Ordinarily you're the one who sets a stiff pace."

"Well, it's . . . my wind . . ."

Time hasn't been kind to her features, thinks Christian, but this nail-hard woman has always walked briskly. Now she seems to have lead in her shanks. It's because of that Johan. She's had her thoughts and her plans—behind her husband's back. Well, the tables turn, now that's past. It is a darn shame, of course. But it's hard for him to feel much sorrow. Rather it makes him feel younger. Hasn't he just won back his farm and his daughter? Hasn't he now?

"You'd better go on ahead . . . hurry, Christian!"

"It can't do any good."

"There's Ingrid . . . go on now!"

"All right, all right."

And she is alone, an old, worn-out witch standing in the lime-bordered lane. She leans up against a tree. She is plundered and destitute, nothing about this farm means anything now. Her hand gropes aimlessly over the dark, rough bark. And now the deep peace of pain comes over her. Touching the lime tree, a little, yellow-haired being weeps.

It is nearly noon. The long communion is over. Outside the church porch, the communicants are standing here and there in small clusters. They press each other's hands: "Congratulations, God's blessing on you."

The second teacher's young wife has noticed that there are likewise small groups of people standing down along the road. Folks saunter from one to the other. Now and then someone comes walking up toward the churchyard. Is it a beautiful old custom of some kind, an Easter custom? She looks around for her husband, but he has not emerged from the church yet. Nor have the priest and the first teacher. Doubtless they're discussing something or other.

From the slope on which the church stands one can see over several rooftops to cultivated land beyond. And the young wife sees something delicately red moving out there in one of those fields. It must be a young woman in summer dress. A lovely sight. But it's not prudent to go without a coat today, she thinks. And she turns again to listen to the sexton who is saying something about a gravestone, one he doesn't mind standing by for some time.

She had put on the red-checked dress again. In spite of its being torn, she would wear it. Now she walks over the field, out under the trilling larks.

There are their footprints—plainer here where the ground is not yet dry and firm. Those are his footprints, spaced far apart. She walks where she had walked before, and she sees each one of his tracks. Here is the measuring stick where he pushed it into the earth; she pulls it loose and carries it along. By the shed she hesitates a little before entering. Now she lays the horse-blanket and the sacks together, and on the blanket she finds something shiny, something that had fallen from his pocket. A piece of glass.

They had not touched each other here—except that her knee had touched lightly his long, hard leg. And so it is not the other place but this one that she will always think of, though she does not know if she will come here often to be in the shed, or never again.

The piece of glass is the only gift which she, otherwise so spoiled, will ever have from the one she loved. She squeezes the sharp fragment in her hand as she gazes from the low door out over the field, out into the golden Easter sunlight.

Johan, here stands your widow.

"My father lies under that," says the sexton, pointing to a little marble slab mortared into the churchyard wall. "Well, actually

I'm not sure this is entirely the right spot. He didn't find rest here very long, you see; one day we came only to find that they'd broken up the grave. They didn't worry so much about it if it was poor folks. He died of hard work and drink, I was just an eight-year-old serving boy at the time. But now I've set that marker up."

"And so you became what you are?"

"I've had the same convictions since my early youth. And they've been good enough. Those were hard times for folks like my father there. But a lot of things have been changed. He wouldn't believe his own eyes if he could see it."

"Do you believe things will improve and be better for people?"

"Yes," says the sexton.

"It's nice you can believe in that," says the young wife.

"Oh, one has to believe it," says the sexton, leaning up against the wall, again forgetting his handsome serge suit. "It was strange how I came to understand that after it happened—I mean, that with . . . the little fellow. Cases like that we can't do anything about, no matter how well we arrange things, I thought. We can't bring anybody back to life, and just reordering things isn't enough to make a person happy. There's simply nothing you can do in the face of something like that. But that's no excuse to stop trying to improve things. You see, that's what I hoped the boy would want to do—make things better for people. But then . . . Well, it has to be done all the same. I can't explain it any other way . . ."

"I understand just what you mean," she says, "it seems to me I understand a great deal just now. But how is it you never go into the church?"

The sexton straightens up from the wall, and he looks at her, but only for a moment.

"You don't need to answer," she says. "You're on the outside, but God be praised you are here."

At last her husband is coming down the path toward them, waving cheerfully to her. Briefly he stops by some men who stand talking in subdued tones. They are explaining something, at the same time pointing down the road toward the lime-bordered lane.

And now he's coming again! Per nods to her. But what is it with him? There is something in his eyes which she doesn't know—amazement, groping (as if he had lost his balance), loneliness. Only a moment, then he is himself again. But it is an expression she has seen today in another man's eyes. Per, I love you.

Chronology

1909   Born August 20 in Strøby, Denmark, eldest of three children.

1924–26   Period of service on two farms.

1926–30   Student at Haslev (South Zealand) Seminary, history and literature as principal subjects.

1930   Passed teacher examination.

1931–45   Elementary teacher in Copenhagen.

1935   Marriage to Vera Jensen. *Nu Opgiver Han* (*Now He Gives Up*), novel.

1937   *Kolonien* (*The Colony*), novel sequel to *Nu Opgiver Han*.

1941   *Jonatans Rejse* (*Jonathan's Travels*), novel, revised edition 1950.

1945   *Lykkelige Kristoffer* (*Lucky Kristoffer*), novel.

1944–45   Involvement with Danish resistance movement. Extraordinary burst of creativity between September 1944 and March 1945.

1946–50   Extensive participation as essayist and lecturer in postwar cultural debate.

1946   *Tornebusken* (*The Thornbush*), three novellas.

1947   *Agerhønen* (*The Partridge*), short stories.

1948   *Tanker i en Skorsten* (*Thoughts in a Chimney*), essays.

MARTIN A. HANSEN

1948–53 Leading voice in the influential journal *Heretica;* its coeditor along with Ole Wivel, 1950–1952.

1950 *Leviathan,* essays; *Løgneren (The Liar),* novel.

1950 Moved with family from Copenhagen to rural environment in mid-Zealand at Allerslev. Coincident with increasing preoccupation with Denmark's pre-Christian and early Christian cultural past.

1952 *Orm og Tyr (Serpent and Bull),* speculative cultural history.

1953 *Dansk Vejr (Danish Weather),* description; *Paradisæblerne (The Paradise Apples),* short stories.

1954 *Rejse paa Island (Travels in Iceland),* travel description.

1955 Died June 27 of Bright's disease.

Posthumously published works:

1955 *Konkyljen (The Conch Shell),* stories.

1956 *Midsommer Krans (Midsummer Garland),* essays.

1959 *Efterslaet (Aftermath),* stories and essays.